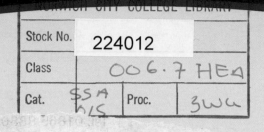

DiDA
DIPLOMA IN DIGITAL APPLICATIONS

D202: Multimedia
using Macromedia Studio MX 2004

F.R. Heathcote

PAYNE-GALLWAY
P U B L I S H E R S

www.payne-gallway.co.uk

Acknowledgements

Published by Payne-Gallway Publishers
Payne-Gallway is an imprint of
Harcourt Education Ltd., Halley Court,
Jordan Hill, Oxford, OX2 8EJ

Copyright© F.R. Heathcote 2006

First published 2006

10 09 08 07 06
10 9 8 7 6 5 4 3 2 1

British Library Cataloguing in Publication Data
is available from the British Library on request

ISBN 1 904467 93 8

ISBN 9 781904467 93 9

Copyright notice

Cover image© Richard Chasemore 2005

Design and Typesetting by Direction Marketing
and Communications Ltd

Printed in Haddington, Scotland by Scotprint

Ordering Information

You can order from:

Payne-Gallway,
FREEPOST (OF1771),
PO Box 381, Oxford OX2 8BR

Tel: 01865 888070
Fax: 01865 314029
E-mail: orders@payne-gallway.co.uk
Web: www.payne-gallway.co.uk

I would like to thank the Headmaster, staff
and pupils of Nyakasura School, Fort Portal,
Uganda for their warm welcome and for
allowing me to take photographs, movies
and sound recordings at the school for the
purpose of this book. Further information
about the school can be found at
http://www.ukfon.org.uk.

We are grateful to the following organisations
for permission to use copyright material:

Acacia Africa (http://www.acacia-africa.com/
acacia_country.htm)

exportinfo.org (http://www.exportinfo.org/
worldfactbook/uganda_WFB.html)

South Axholme Community School (http://
www.southaxholme.doncaster.sch.uk)

Charlie's Sneaker Pages (http://www.sneakers.
pair.com)

Yves Rubin, http://rubinphoto.com

Audacity (http://audacity.sourceforge.net)

Google (http://www.google.co.uk) screenshots
copyright© Google

Every effort has been made to contact
copyright owners of material published in
this book. We would be glad to hear from
unacknowledged sources at the earliest
opportunity.

Contents

Preface

About DiDA

DiDA (Diploma in Digital Applications) was launched by Edexcel in 2005, replacing GNVQ qualifications in ICT.

All assessment is 'paperless': you will submit an electronic portfolio of work via Edexcel Online for on-screen moderation. A Summative Project Brief (SPB), supplied each year by Edexcel via their website, will guide you through a series of tasks to be performed.

About Unit D202

D202 is the Multimedia module. This book will guide you through complete discrete tasks, from putting together a stand-alone movie to creating interactive multimedia products. You will gather components for a sample project, build it and then present the final products along with the development work in an eportfolio. You will also learn to plan your project and to review and evaluate both as an ongoing process throughout development and once it is completed. You will develop skills in many different areas of practical computing:

• The use of hardware such as a digital camera, video camera, sound recorder and scanner

• Image editing

• Video compiling and editing

• Sound editing

• Creating animations using a timeline

• Using website creation software

You will use Macromedia software to develop the sample project; in doing so you will gain all the skills needed to complete your own multimedia project and qualify for the Macromedia Certificate.

To use Windows Movie Maker you will need to be running Microsoft Windows XP or later.

The structure of this book

Section 1 introduces a project brief similar in length, number of tasks and level of difficulty to the one set by Edexcel. It also covers all the preparatory stages of the sample project that must be completed before any work is done on individual tasks.

Section 2 covers the steps needed to complete the major task, the stand-alone movie. This includes researching other movies, planning your own movie and using Flash to implement the movie for the sample project.

Section 3 shows you how to plan and implement an interactive virtual tour for the sample project.

Section 4 demonstrates how to plan and implement a quiz in Flash.

Section 5 teaches you how to put together the eportfolio in Dreamweaver.

Section One
PREPARATION

The project

For this unit you will be given a scenario by Edexcel. You will need to do some research on the topic that has been set, and produce various multimedia components. You will then put all these components into an eportfolio, which will be assessed by the Exam Board; in Chapter 23 and later chapters you will learn more about the eportfolio and how to put it together in Dreamweaver. You will be expected to spend a minimum of 30 hours on the project.

In order to practise the skills required for the set project, in this book you will work through a sample project of a similar nature.

You can view the sample Summative Project Brief (SPB) at
www.payne-gallway.co.uk/didaD202/SPB

and the finished eportfolio, similar to the one you will produce, online at
www.payne-gallway.co.uk/didaD202/eportfolio.

The scenario

Imagine that your school or college has set up an exchange programme with a school in Uganda, and that you have recently completed a term at the school. In order to inform pupils at your school about Nyakasura School, you have been asked to put together a showcase about the pupils, the school and its environment.

The showcase will consist of three multimedia products for young people aged 14–17 years:

- a movie of about 40–50 seconds
- a virtual tour
- an interactive quiz.

Planning your project

For your course assessment, you will be putting the elements of the showcase into an eportfolio together with other items to show how you planned, developed and reviewed your work.

You must produce a detailed plan of how you will complete all the required tasks within the time allowed.

Before you start the plan:

- Read through the project brief.
- Make a list of everything you have to do.
- Decide how long you think each element is going to take.
- Decide on the order in which the tasks need to be done.
- Decide at what points you need to get feedback and to evaluate your work so far.

At regular intervals you must make sure that you are on schedule; if you are not, you must reschedule the remaining tasks into the time you have left to complete the project. **Keep a record of changes made to your schedule**; you will have to include both your initial and final project plan and account for the changes between them in your eportfolio.

The project brief

The Edexcel Summative Project Brief (SPB) is specified on their website and is spread over a number of pages. When the time comes for you to start the SPB, you will have to explore the website and make a list of what you have to do, similar to the list below.

For this sample project, the tasks are given (you don't have to work out for yourself what they are) and each one will be explained in more detail in later chapters in the book.

Here are the tasks which you must complete:

1 Produce a plan listing individual tasks and estimated completion dates.
2 Create an organised directory structure for your project files.
3 Collect primary and secondary components for the 50-second intro movie; this will include photos and video clips you have taken yourself as well as secondary components such as existing photos or school logos.
4 Design and produce the 50-second intro movie.
5 Get feedback and evaluate the intro movie.
6 Collect primary and secondary components for the virtual school tour.
7 Design and produce the virtual school tour.
8 Get feedback and evaluate the virtual school tour.
9 Collect primary and secondary components for the quiz.

10 Design and produce the quiz.

11 Get feedback and evaluate the quiz.

12 Create the eportfolio.

13 Get feedback and evaluate the eportfolio. Make necessary changes.

Creating a project plan

Projects are unlikely to succeed unless they are properly planned. However, before you can start to plan, you have to be absolutely clear about the purpose of the project and what you are required to produce.

You should read the entire project brief first. There are a number of key questions you need to ask, including:

- What do I have to produce?
- What is it for?
- Who is the intended audience?
- When do I have to have it finished?
- What resources can I use?
- How will the success of the project be judged?
- Who will review my work and when?

You could use Word or Excel to produce a plan. This is a skill you will have learnt in D201.

Task Number	Description	Start Date	End Date	Notes
1	Produce a plan listing individual tasks and estimated completion dates.	Sept 20th	Sept 26th	
2	Create an organised directory structure for your project files.	Sept 27th	Sept 27th	
3	Collect components for intro movie.	Sept 28th	Oct 12th	
4	Design and produce movie.	Oct 13th	Nov 9th	
5	etc.			

Figure 1.1: Project plan

Software

We will be using the following software to accomplish this project.

Task	Software	Output
1	Word	Project plan
2	Windows Explorer	Directory structure
4	Flash, Fireworks & Windows Movie Maker	50-second intro movie
6	Flash & Fireworks	Virtual tour
9	Flash	Quiz
12	Dreamweaver	Eportfolio

Figure 1.2: Software to be used

File-naming conventions

It is a good idea to decide on a convention for naming folders and files and then stick to it. For this project all our folders and files will use "camel caps": each word in the file or folder name will start with an uppercase letter but we will not use spaces or underscores in file names.

Creating a directory structure

Components

In this project, it is likely that you will use some components for more than one task. The tasks should be grouped in such a way that you don't store the same set of components twice. For this reason, components will be kept in a separate folder.

IntroMovie

This will hold all the files for the intro movie. There will be two subfolders: **IntroMovieDocumentation** and **IntroMovieFlashFiles**.

In the **IntroMovieDocumentation** folder will be your scanned storyboards of the movie, along with any other paperwork that you created whilst planning and designing the movie. There will also be evidence of development, such as screenshots of the Flash workspace taken at various stages of development. A selection of these files will be added to the eportfolio at the end of the project.

All the Flash files you create while developing your movie will be stored in the **IntroMovieFlashFiles** folder.

VirtualTour and Quiz

These hold similar files and folders to those used in the **IntroMovie** folder.

Eportfolio

This folder will contain HTML files created in Dreamweaver. You will add some subfolders to this folder later when you come to create the eportfolio in Dreamweaver.

ProjectDocumentation

This folder will contain all the Word files used to plan and monitor your project such as your Project Plan, Folder Structure, Review and Evaluation. These documents will be added to the eportfolio at the end of the project.

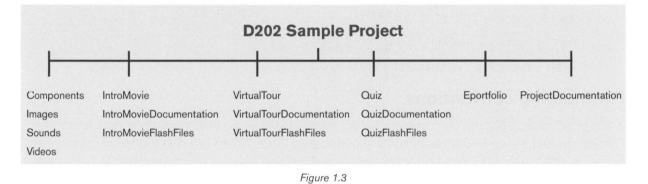

D202 Sample Project

Components	IntroMovie	VirtualTour	Quiz	Eportfolio	ProjectDocumentation
Images	IntroMovieDocumentation	VirtualTourDocumentation	QuizDocumentation		
Sounds	IntroMovieFlashFiles	VirtualTourFlashFiles	QuizFlashFiles		
Videos					

Figure 1.3

 Create a directory structure in Windows Explorer. It should look like the one below:

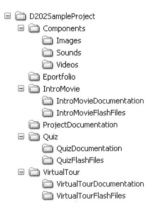

Figure 1.4

Good marks... ✓

You will get good marks if you:

- read the SPB carefully and make a list of everything you need to do;
- use a table, calendar or chart for your plan that includes
    - task numbers
    - a description of each task
    - the date you will start each task
    - the date you will finish each task, and/or time allowed for each task
    - space for any notes relevant to each task
    - a sensible order for the tasks
    - extra time built in to your plan for emergencies or any problems;
- agree your plan with your teacher;
- meet your deadlines by sticking to your plan;
- keep a record of the changes you make to your plan;
- decide on a file-naming convention;
- set up a logical directory structure.

Bad marks... ✗

You will lose marks if you:

- set yourself an unrealistic timetable;
- produce your plan but don't use it;
- produce your plan *after* you have completed your project;
- produce a plan that is the same as everyone else's.

You will use many components to complete all the tasks. Some will be primary components that you create yourself, and some will be secondary. Below are some examples of primary and secondary components:

Primary

photos you have taken

video footage you have taken

sounds you have recorded

music you have composed

graphics you have drawn

text you have written.

Secondary

photos you have found and downloaded from other websites

graphics in clip art

photos on library CDs or those that come with some pieces of software

sounds you download from a website or sound library

school logos you have scanned or copied from a school website.

Obtaining the components for the sample project

All the components you need to work through the sample project are on the Payne-Gallway website **www.payne-gallway.co.uk/didaD202**.

Go to the website and follow the links to download the components for DiDA D202 Multimedia. Save the components in your **Components** folder, in the appropriate subfolder (see Figure 2.1).

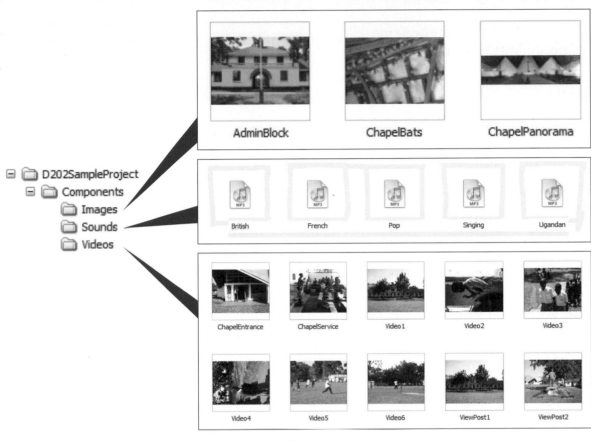

Figure 2.1

⊙ You also need to download the **Storyboard** files and put them in the **IntroMovieDocumentation** folder.

Components table

All the secondary components you use should be entered into a components table. For this sample project you will create a components table, then make entries into that table at various points during the project, as you will when you collect your own components for the Edexcel SPB.

⊙ Create a components table in Word like the one below. You will add the components for the movie in the next chapter. Not all the components are listed, but you will add them as you use them while working through the book.

File Name	Primary or Secondary?	Source	Type

Figure 2.2

9

Save the file in the **Components** folder you have already created. Name the file **ComponentsTable.doc**.

> **For the SPB:** You should create this table in Word before you start collecting anything. The table will help you keep track of where you sourced each component from. You are required to submit your components table in your eportfolio, so keep it up to date! You'll lose marks if you can't state the source of every component you use.
>
> The components table will also help you keep track of how many primary and secondary components you have used, as there are requirements in the SPB about this. As a guide, you should have at least five secondary components that you've collected and edited for use, and at least three primary components that you have created yourself.

Collecting your own primary components

Taking your own photos

The easiest way to do this is with a digital camera. Each digital camera has its own way of working, so you'll have to read the instructions that come with your particular camera.

Which resolution setting?

Some cameras give a choice of image resolutions. Images that you take with a digital camera for printing out on photographic paper are best taken on the highest resolution your camera allows. However, for this project all the photos will be viewed on-screen in the eportfolio. On-screen images are viewed at a resolution of 72 pixels per inch (or DPI, dots per inch). This means that you can get away with using a lower-quality setting. It is always worth using the lowest setting you need to; this prevents wasting space in your camera's memory and also reduces the amount of optimisation you need to do on the photo later on (remember there is a limit on the file size you are allowed for the eportfolio).

- For your project, a 1 Megapixel (or even 640x480 VGA) setting will be fine if you don't plan to enlarge a photo.

- If you are taking a photo that you might want to enlarge significantly, you should use a higher-resolution setting (3M or 5M).

These photos will still have relatively large file sizes and be of a higher quality than needed for web purposes. You will learn to optimise photos and images later using Fireworks.

Viewing your photos in Windows Explorer

After you have downloaded your photos onto a computer, you will need to view them to select which ones you want to use. The easiest way to do this is using Windows Explorer.

▶ Open Windows Explorer and locate the **Components/Images** folder.

Figure 2.3

▶ At the top of the window, click the **Views** icon in the **Shortcuts** bar. Select **Filmstrip** from the menu that appears. Use this to flick through your photos and decide which ones to use.

Views Icon

 Tip:

If there is no **Filmstrip** option shown, this may be because you have some movie files in that folder, so move them to another folder. If you still have no **Filmstrip** option, just double-click each photo to see a larger version of it.

For the SPB: When you come to download your own photos from the camera to a PC, you should give sensible names to any that you think you will use, so that you can easily find them again later. Delete any that you won't use, so you don't end up with far too many photos!

Taking videos

You can take videos on either a video camera or a digital camera with a movie function. The files will be stored as **MPEG** files (**Moving Picture Experts Group** format). You should take the video footage and download it according to the instructions of your particular model of camera. You will learn to edit and optimise the videos using Flash and Windows Movie Maker later in the book.

Recording sounds

Using a digital sound recorder

You can record sounds using a digital sound recorder. This is a small device with a microphone, similar to a dictation recorder. You can record voices, music and sound effects then download them as digital **Wave (WAV)** files.

Using Microsoft Sound Recorder

If you have a microphone, or some other sound source that you can connect to your PC, then you can use Microsoft Sound Recorder. This software records any sound played into your PC's sound card, and then lets you save it to disk.

- To open Sound Recorder, select **Start**, **Programs**, **Accessories**, **Entertainment**, **Sound Recorder**.

- Ensure you have a microphone connected to your PC, and that the volume is set appropriately (you can change this via the **Sounds and Audio Devices** icon in the **Control Panel**).

- Click the **Record** button and start playing the sound you wish to record.

Figure 2.4

- Press the **Stop** button when you have finished.

- Select **File**, **Save** to save the sound, or **File**, **New** to try again.

Collecting secondary components

Copying images from other websites

Good sources

The best way to search for images on a particular subject is to use a search engine. Google is particularly useful because it can search specifically for images.

 Load Internet Explorer then go to the Google homepage **www.google.co.uk** or **www.google.com**

 Type the search criteria then click **Google Search**.

 Now click where it says **Images** at the top of the screen.

Figure 2.5

If you find a suitable image

 click on it to visit the website it originates from

 right-click it, then click **Save Picture As** from the menu that appears

 save the image with a meaningful name in an appropriate place in your **Components** folder

 enter the component filename and origin in your **ComponentsTable.doc** file.

A word about copyright

There is a huge amount of material available on the web and you would be well advised to take advantage of it. A lot of websites are happy for you to download free resources provided they aren't for commercial use; that is, you aren't going to profit financially from using them. If you are using resources for a school or college assignment there is no need to seek permission for each component used. If you decide to publish a book using these components then clearly you must ask permission.

Downloading sounds from other websites

Good sources

There are a lot of websites that will let you download free sounds from a vast library of different types of sound.

Go to **www.wavcentral.com**

> **Tip:**
>
> Another good site that has free sounds and sound effects is **www.findsounds.com**. You will find more sites by searching for **free sounds** in Google.

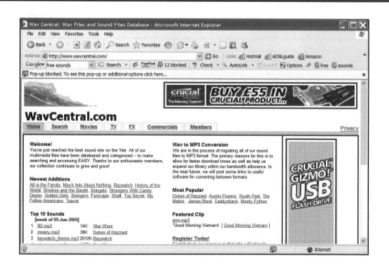

Figure 2.6

Click the **Search** tab at the top of the page, then type which sound you are looking for in the search box. Click the **Search** button.

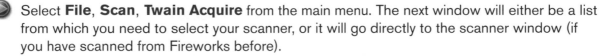

Figure 2.7: Two results found for 'clapping'

 To listen to the sounds, just click them once. Windows Media Player will load and then play the sound clip.

To download a sound, right-click the file name then select **Save Target As** from the menu that appears. Save the file in an appropriate folder with a file name you will remember later.

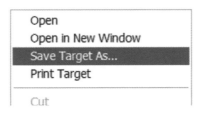

Figure 2.8

Scanning

Scanning is useful when you need an electronic copy of printed media such as a photo or hand-drawn image. For DiDA, you will probably need to scan images and hand-written notes. For example, if you hand-draw a storyboard then you will need to scan it so that it can be included in your eportfolio.

You can scan an image directly from Fireworks if your scanner is TWAIN compliant (Windows); this is very convenient because you can also edit the scanned image using Fireworks to improve image quality and reduce the file size.

Open Fireworks by selecting **All Programs, Macromedia, Macromedia Fireworks MX 2004** from the **Start** menu.

Select **File, Scan, Twain Acquire** from the main menu. The next window will either be a list from which you need to select your scanner, or it will go directly to the scanner window (if you have scanned from Fireworks before).

15

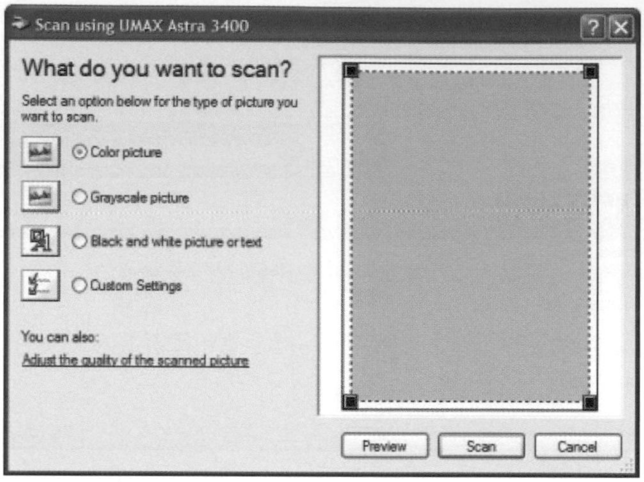

Chapter 2 – Components

Figure 2.9: The scanner window (yours may look different)

Scanned file resolutions

The scanned document will only ever be viewed on-screen (not printed out) so it will be viewed at **72 pixels/inch** (or DPI). It is worth scanning at a higher resolution than this to ensure the document is as clear as possible.

When scanning documents for your eportfolio, use a scanning resolution of about **100 pixels/inch**. Don't be tempted to use a much higher resolution than is needed because it will take longer to scan, be a larger file and will require more optimisation later.

🔘 Set the resolution to **100 DPI**. The technique will depend on your particular scanner.

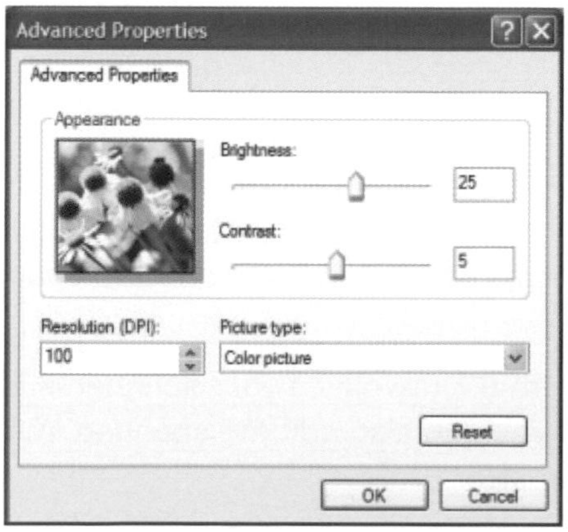

Figure 2.10

🔘 Click the **Preview** button to preview what the scan will look like.

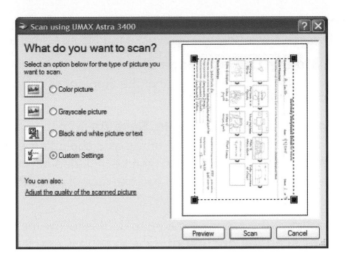

Figure 2.11: Scanner window showing preview (yours may look different)

 If you only want a specific area of the document to be scanned, just click and drag the box in the preview area to be around the part that you want.

 Click **Scan** when you're ready.

The scan will take a minute or so, then the scanned document will appear in the Fireworks workspace.

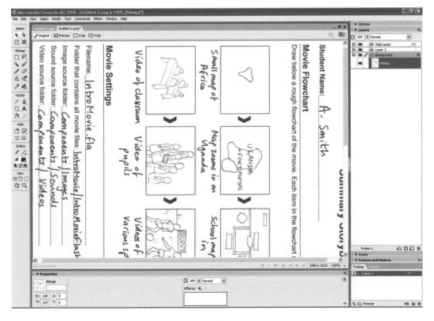

Figure 2.12

 If you need to rotate the image, select **Modify**, **Canvas** from the main menu bar. Select a rotate option to suit.

If the scanned document is a storyboard, you should resize it now so that you don't have to do it when you insert it into Dreamweaver (this will also make the file size smaller).

 Resize by selecting **Modify, Canvas, Image Size** from the main menu bar. Enter the width as **700 pixels**. This should be large enough that the storyboard is legible, while still fitting into the eportfolio. Press **OK**.

Save the scanned document by selecting **File, Save As** from the main menu bar. If you are scanning a storyboard for your movie, you should save it in your **IntroMovieDocumentation** folder so it can then be included in your eportfolio. It will be saved as a **PNG** file by default; this is fine as you can save it as a **JPEG** or **GIF** file when you optimise it.

You might need to optimise the scanned image; to do this follow the steps below to **Optimise a photo or scanned document** – the method is exactly the same.

Editing components

You will need to edit both primary and secondary components for two reasons:

1   To improve the appearance of the component, for example by cropping, altering the brightness or contrast, or editing out parts of a photo.

2   To optimise the file size of the components. It is important that you keep a close eye on the file size of all your components, as your entire project must not exceed the limit specified by the SPB, currently 15 MB.

Optimising a photo or scanned document

You'll learn how to optimise a photo using Fireworks directly from Flash in Chapter 11.

To optimise a photo or scanned image without opening Fireworks from Flash:

Open **Macromedia** Fireworks.

On the main menu bar select **File, Open**. Select the file you want to optimise.

Select **File, Export Wizard** from the main menu bar.

Click the option to **Select an export format**.

Click **Continue**.

Click **The web** in the next window. Click **Continue**.

The **Analysis Results** window will appear with some information about the file format it has selected. Click **Exit**.

The **Export Preview** dialogue will appear. This gives a preview of what the JPEG and GIF files would look like. You can adjust the settings in each to find a good compromise between image size and quality.

 If you can't see anything in the preview windows, it is probably because you are zoomed in on a blank part of the page. Select **50%** in the **Zoom** menu at the bottom of the window (see Figure 2.13). You can click and drag the image in the preview window to move it around.

 When you've finished adjusting both images, click to select the one with the smallest file size (as long as the quality is OK) then click **Export**.

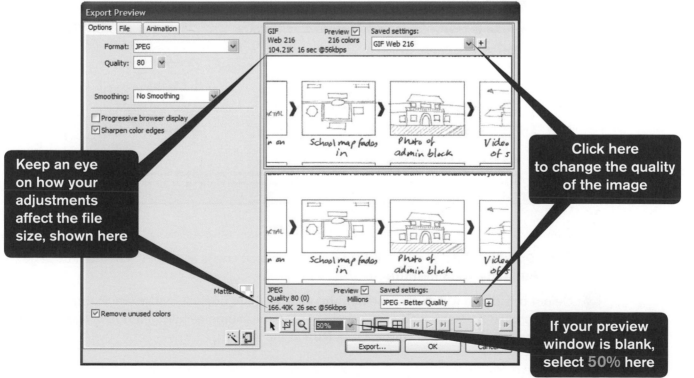

Figure 2.13

19

Save the image under a different file name from the original (unless the original is a PNG file, in which case you can use the same name). If you don't, you will lose the original full quality image; you should always keep the original in case you aren't happy with the optimised image.

Tip:

When optimising an image, always save it using the **Export** option. If you save it using the usual **File, Save** route the file will be saved as a **PNG** file, not a **JPEG**, and you risk overwriting your original file.

Optimising and editing sounds

You can do some sound editing in Flash, but if you want to do a lot Flash is not very convenient. You can download some free software called Audacity that will edit **MP3** and **WAV** files.

 Go to **http://audacity.sourceforge.net/**. You can skip the next two steps if Audacity is already installed on your PC.

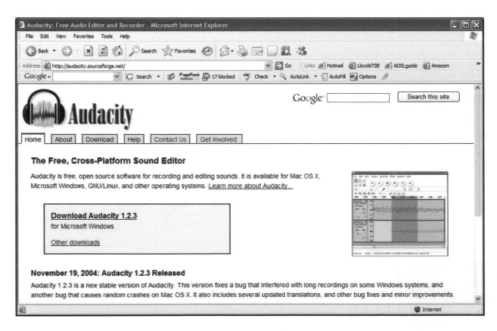

Figure 2.14

 Click **Download Audacity 1.2.3** (or a later version if one is available). On the next page click **Audacity 1.2.3 installer**.

 Select one of the **Mirrors** at the bottom of the page (it doesn't matter which, but a UK mirror should be fastest). The download should start automatically; if it doesn't you should be given a link to click to start it. Click **Run** at the prompt.

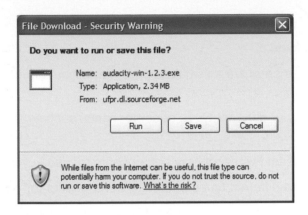

Figure 2.15

Learning how to use Audacity

We won't go into how to use Audacity in this book, but there are online tutorials and documentation on the Audacity website that you should look at.

 Return to the Audacity home page. Select the **Help** tab.

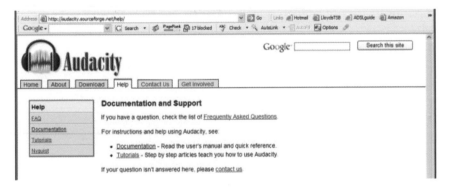

Figure 2.16

 Click on either **Tutorials** or **Documentation** to learn more.

Optimising and editing video footage

We won't go through how to optimise and edit video footage here. Later, when you import videos into Flash, you will be guided through how to optimise them. You will cover how to edit video footage using Windows Movie Maker in Chapter 12.

Good marks... ✓

You will get good marks if you:

- make sure your files sizes are as small as possible without affecting the image quality visibly;

- have a good variety of different types of components, such as video footage, photos, text and sound;

- select and edit at least five secondary components for use in your project;

- create at least three different types of primary components for your project;

- list all components in your components table and acknowledge all sources;

- make sure all your components are fit for purpose (suitable for the intended audience). Don't use irrelevant images, movies or sounds.

Bad marks... ✗

You will lose marks if:

- your components are not of high quality (images are blurred and sound clips cannot be heard);

- file sizes and download times are excessive;

- images are not sized properly (they are too large or too small on screen).

The Intro movie will be a major part of the project. It will be created in Flash and later inserted into the Dreamweaver eportfolio. It will be about 50 seconds long and will play from start to finish with no user input (there will be nothing for the user to click whilst the movie is playing and it will not be interactive in any way).

The movie will be a combination of animation drawn in Flash, text, videos, photos and sound.

Researching other movies

It's important to look at other good examples in order to get a good idea of what can be achieved, what works well and to get lots of ideas for your own project before you begin.

One of the leading schools in the country for creating Flash animations is South Axholme School. Follow the link below to take a look at some of the students' work: **http://www.southaxholme. doncaster.sch.uk**. Select **Subjects**, **Animations** from the main page.

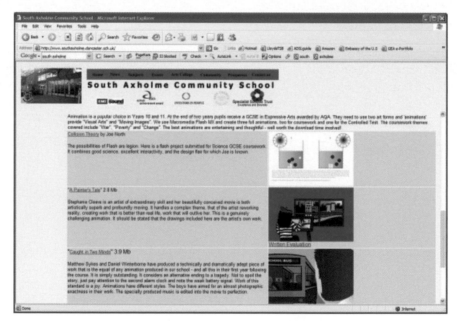

Figure 3.1

The movies on the South Axholme site are quite advanced, and far beyond what is expected for DiDA. They were produced for a performing arts qualification.

These movies are made up purely of animation, with no video, which makes them very time-consuming to produce. Your movie will have some simple animation and some video.

Notice when watching those animations that the same components are used over and over; an object is drawn once then used many times in different ways by moving it across the screen or changing its size. This is a very time-saving and efficient technique used in Flash.

Search on the web to find other animation sites to give you some more ideas for your own movie. You will find that most movies are either all Flash animation or all video, rather than a combination of the two.

Movie storyboard

Before implementing the movie, you have to produce a storyboard that explains exactly what the movie will contain. The storyboard is a set of drawn images with text to explain the different scenes in the movie; it should be a document that could, in theory, be handed to someone else for them to implement with no further explanations from yourself.

For the SPB: You will have to submit your storyboard as part of your eportfolio and will lose marks if you do not submit it or if your finished movie varies significantly from it. You can draw it on paper then scan it in, or, if you'd prefer, draw it straight on the computer.

When you come to do your own project, you can download blank storyboard sheets from the Payne-Gallway website at **www.payne-gallway.co.uk/didaD202**.

This is the storyboard for the sample project:

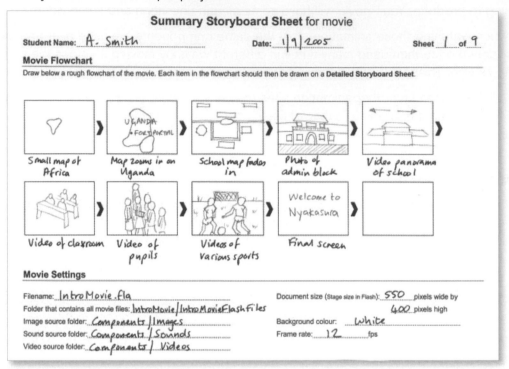

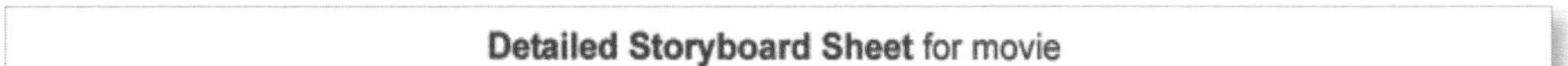

Figure 3.2

Figure 3.3

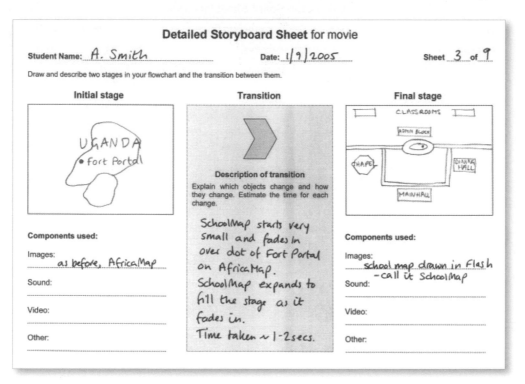

Detailed Storyboard Sheet for movie

Student Name: A. Smith   Date: 1/9/2005   Sheet 3 of 9

Draw and describe two stages in your flowchart and the transition between them.

Initial stage   **Transition**   **Final stage**

UGANDA
• Fort Portal

CLASSROOMS
ADMIN BLOCK
CHAPEL
DINING HALL
MAIN HALL

Description of transition
Explain which objects change and how they change. Estimate the time for each change.

SchoolMap starts very small and fades in over dot of Fort Portal on AfricaMap.
SchoolMap expands to fill the stage as it fades in.
Time taken ~ 1-2secs.

Components used:

Images:
as before, AfricaMap

Sound:

Video:

Other:

Components used:

Images:
school map drawn in Flash – call it SchoolMap

Sound:

Video:

Other:

Figure 3.4

Detailed Storyboard Sheet for movie

Student Name: A. Smith   Date: 1/9/2005   Sheet 4 of 9

Draw and describe two stages in your flowchart and the transition between them.

Initial stage   **Transition**   **Final stage**

CLASSROOMS
ADMIN BLOCK
CHAPEL
DINING HALL
MAIN HALL

Description of transition
Explain which objects change and how they change. Estimate the time for each change.

AdminBlock photo starts small + fades in over admin block in school map.
As photo fades in it spins round and gets larger until it fits the stage –
It comes spinning out of the map!
Estimated time ~ 1-2 secs

Components used:

Images:
as before – SchoolMap

Sound:

Video:

Other:

Components used:

Images:
AdminBlock.jpg

Sound:

Video:

Other:

Figure 3.5

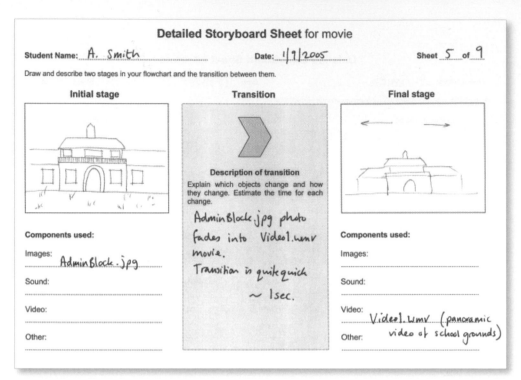

Detailed Storyboard Sheet for movie

Student Name: *A. Smith* Date: *1/9/2005* Sheet *5* of *9*

Draw and describe two stages in your flowchart and the transition between them.

| Initial stage | Transition | Final stage |

Description of transition
Explain which objects change and how they change. Estimate the time for each change.

AdminBlock.jpg photo fades into Video1.wmv movie.

Transition is quite quick

~ 1sec.

Components used:

Images: *AdminBlock.jpg*

Sound:

Video:

Other:

Components used:

Images:

Sound:

Video: *Video1.wmv (panoramic video of school grounds)*

Other:

Figure 3.6

When you come to do your own storyboard, you must follow these steps:

- Scan in your initial storyboard using Fireworks. Save the file(s) in your **IntroMovieDocumentation** folder as a **PNG** file (for example **MovieStoryboard1.png**).

- Optimise the storyboard file(s) using Fireworks (by using **File**, **Export Wizard**). You will most likely save it as a **JPEG** or **GIF** file once optimised. Save the file in your **IntroMovieDocumentation** folder.

- Open a new Word document. In Word, select **Insert**, **Picture**, **From File** from the main menu bar. Find the optimised storyboard file(s) then click **Insert**.

- Add the file name of the scanned image below it.

- Add a title for the storyboard. Under the storyboard, write in some feedback about the storyboard you have received from your peers and teacher, and some of your own observations and suggestions for improvement.

- Redo parts of your storyboard if needed to take into account all the feedback you have received. Repeat the steps above, then insert the revised storyboard into the Word document.

This document will then be used for your eportfolio. The images will be inserted separately into the eportfolio, and you will copy and paste the text you write into the eportfolio from this document.

> **For the SPB:** When you come to do the final project, you will need to gain feedback about your storyboard before you start to implement it in Flash. Marks will be awarded for collecting feedback and altering your storyboard accordingly. In your eportfolio you should include your original storyboard, the feedback you collected and your revised storyboard.

Collecting components for your movie

It is specified in the brief that you must collect all components required for the movie prior to starting work on the movie. You will have already downloaded (in Chapter 2) the components you need for the sample project, but when you come to do your own project you will need to collect your own components then enter them into the components table.

Open the **ComponentsTable.doc** file you created in the last chapter; it should be in the **Components** folder.

Make the following entries into your components table and give it a heading of **IntroMovie components**:

File Name	Primary or Secondary?	Source	Type
AfricaMap.jpg	S	**images.google.com**	Image
AdminBlock.jpg	P	n/a	Photo
Video1.mpg	P	n/a	Video
Video2.mpg	P	n/a	Video
Video3.mpg	P	n/a	Video
Video4.mpg	P	n/a	Video
Video5.mpg	P	n/a	Video
Video6.mpg	P	n/a	Video
Singing.mp3	P	n/a	Sound

Figure 3.7

Save and close the **ComponentsTable**.

For the SPB: Make sure you have collected all the components you need for your movie before your start. Don't forget to enter all the components into your components table. You will need to include the components table in your eportfolio.

Good marks... ✓

You will get good marks for your storyboard if:

- it is clear enough that it could be handed to someone else for them to create the movie in Flash;

- it is clear from the storyboard which components are required for the movie;

- you obtain feedback for the storyboard and make changes where necessary;

- you record the feedback and changes made so they can later be included in the eportfolio.

Bad marks... ✗

You will lose marks if:

- the storyboard isn't detailed enough or is unclear;

- components are not clearly labelled;

- the storyboard isn't included in the eportfolio.

What is Flash?

Flash is known primarily as software used to animate objects and to create multimedia projects. However, although Flash is used for animation, there are actually three distinct areas that Flash is used for:

 Animation    Vector Graphics   Interactivity

Animation

In Flash, each animated document you produce is called a **movie**. You can do **frame-by-frame**, **tweened** and **guided** animations using the **Timeline**.

Vector graphics

Flash is used by many graphic designers simply as a tool for creating vector graphics. The vector graphics capability in Flash was developed because of the need for graphics with small file sizes; vector graphics occupy much less file space than bitmap graphics. For this reason, when you learn Flash, you first need to learn how to create vector shapes. You will do this in Chapter 5.

 Tip:

Vector graphics store information about the shapes that were used to construct an image. The files are small and you can easily edit them later.

Bitmap graphics store an image as a grid of coloured pixels. The files are larger and more difficult to edit, but can be very detailed and are widely supported.

Interactivity

By **interactivity** I mean that the Flash movie changes according to user input. The building blocks of interactivity are **buttons** and **ActionScript**; you place a button in your Flash movie, then attach programming code called **ActionScript** to it, which makes something happen when the button is pressed. You can build a whole website using just Flash, with buttons and a lot of **ActionScript**!

This book covers the basics of **buttons** and **ActionScript**. You will learn how to publish your movie and create an HTML file, how to create a small standalone interactive application, and also how to insert a Flash movie into a Dreamweaver website.

Let's get started!

This chapter will briefly introduce the different parts of the Flash workspace.

🔵 Load Flash. You can do this in one of two ways:

- either double-click on the Flash icon (if there is one) on your Windows desktop

- or click **Start**, **All Programs**, **Macromedia** and then select **Macromedia** Flash **MX 2004**.

🔵 If Flash has never run before on your PC then the **Macromedia Product Activation** window will appear. Follow the on-screen instructions to activate or trial the software, as appropriate.

When Flash opens, you should see the **Start Page**, which has a red bar at the top. If you don't see it this just means that when the software was previously used the **Start Page** was switched off.

Tip:

To show the red **Start Page**, select **Edit**, **Preferences** from the main menu bar. On the **General** tab, set the option **On launch** to **Show Start Page**.

Creating a new document

🔵 On the **Start Page** choose **Flash Document** under **Create New**.

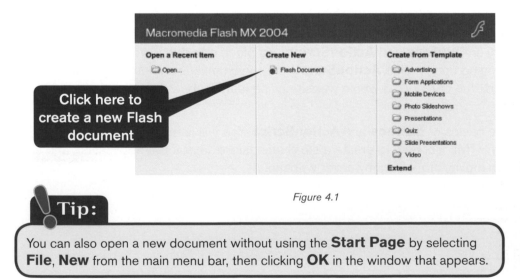

Figure 4.1

Tip:

You can also open a new document without using the **Start Page** by selecting **File**, **New** from the main menu bar, then clicking **OK** in the window that appears.

Your screen will now look something like this. It looks quite complicated!

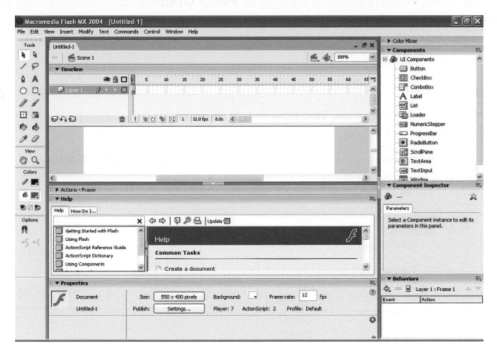

Figure 4.2

Panels

The screen looks complicated because there are lots of open **panels**. Panels are a bit like windows in Microsoft applications, but they can cause confusion if you have not come across them before. If you have used Dreamweaver you will be used to panels.

Panels are not to be feared! They can be opened, closed, maximised and minimised just like windows.

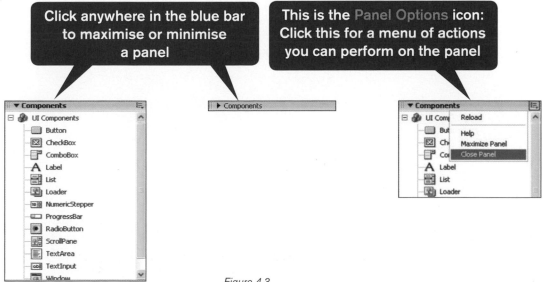

Figure 4.3

Panel Options Icon

 Close the **Components** panel by clicking its **Panel Options** icon then selecting **Close Panel** from the menu that appears.

The panel completely disappears; not even the blue title bar is visible.

Opening a panel

All panels can be opened using the **Window** option on the main menu bar. Some panels are in the main list, and some are in sub-lists.

 Open the **Components** panel by selecting **Window**, **Development Panels**, **Components** from the menu.

Control	Window	Help		
	New Window	Ctrl+Alt+K		
	Toolbars	▶		
	✔ Properties	Ctrl+F3		
	✔ Timeline	Ctrl+Alt+T		
	✔ Tools	Ctrl+F2		
	Library	Ctrl+L		
	Design Panels	▶		
	Development Panels	▶	Actions	F9
	Other Panels	▶	✔ Behaviors	Shift+F3
			Components	Ctrl+F7
	Hide Panels	F4	✔ Component Inspector	Alt+F7
	Panel Sets	▶	Debugger	Shift+F4
	Save Panel Layout...		Output	F2
	Cascade			
	Tile			
	✔ 1 Untitled-1			

Figure 4.4

Minimising panels

Now we'll minimise all the panels to clear up the workspace.

⊙ Start by minimising the **Properties** panel (click the blue bar at the top of the panel).

⊙ Now minimise each of the other panels in turn.

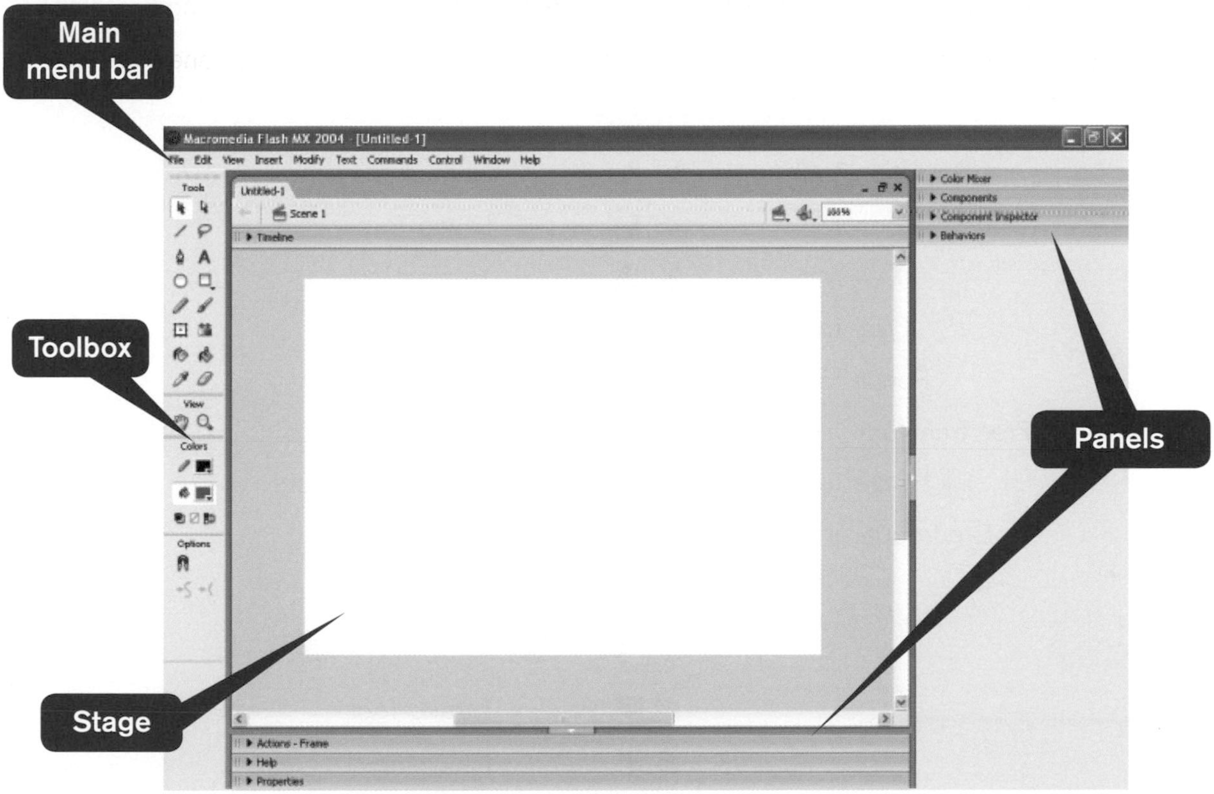

Figure 4.5

The large grey area is the **Work Area**, and the white box is the **Stage**. This is where the content for all your animations and graphics will be drawn or imported to. Notice that the **Work Area** resized to fill the space as you minimised the panels.

⊙ Use the scroll bars to move the white rectangle (the **Stage**) into view.

That looks much better! This is the basic workspace with no panels open. We will open each panel as we need it.

The Toolbox

The **Toolbox** contains all the drawing and text tools, as well as tools for selecting, zooming, and more.

You select a tool by clicking its icon in the **Toolbox**. Some tools have options that control how they work; these are displayed at the bottom of the **Toolbox** and will change according to which tool is currently selected.

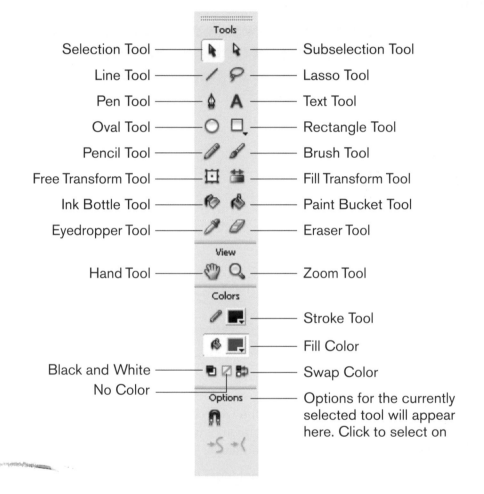

Figure 4.6

> ## Tip:
>
> If you want to know the name of any tool, hover the mouse over its icon and a **tool tip** will appear.

The Properties panel

We'll take a quick look at the properties of the **Stage** using the **Properties** panel (also called the **Property inspector**).

 Maximise the **Properties** panel by clicking anywhere in the blue bar at the top of the panel. (If your **Properties** panel isn't visible, select **Window**, **Properties** from the menu bar.)

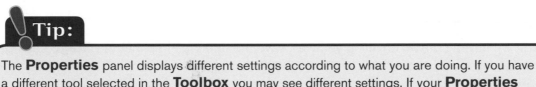

Figure 4.7

Here you can view and change various properties of the **Stage**, such as the size and the background colour. We'll leave these settings as they are for now.

> ### Tip:
>
> The **Properties** panel displays different settings according to what you are doing. If you have a different tool selected in the **Toolbox** you may see different settings. If your **Properties** panel looks different from the one above, just click the **Selection Tool** icon in the **Toolbox** to display the **Stage** settings.

Selection Tool

Zoom options

The Zoom menu

You can choose how large or small to view the **Stage** using the **Zoom** menu, located at the top right corner above the stage. Click the down arrow and select an option from the list, or type in a percentage. **Fit in Window** is a useful option to get the whole **Stage** into view.

Scene 1		100%
		Fit in Window
		Show Frame
		Show All
		25%
		50%
		100%
		200%
		400%
		800%

Figure 4.8

The Zoom tool

If you want to zoom in on a particular part of the **Stage** it's best to use the **Zoom** tool in the **Toolbox**.

Zoom Tool

- Click the **Zoom** tool in the **Toolbox**.
- At the bottom of the **Toolbox**, select the **Enlarge** tool.
- You can either click and drag a rectangle around the area you want to zoom in on, or just click once on the area.

Enlarge Tool

Tip:

You can hold down the **Alt** key to switch quickly between the **Enlarge** and **Reduce** tools.

Selection Tool

- When you are finished with the **Zoom** tool, click the **Selection** tool in the **Toolbox**.

Saving and closing

Even though we haven't drawn anything yet, we'll save the document so that the **Stage** settings will be saved.

- Select **File**, **Save As** from the main menu bar. Find then open the **IntroMovieFlashFiles** folder, which is in the **IntroMovie** folder. Enter **DrawingExercises** as the **File name**. Leave the **File type** as Flash **MX 2004 Document (*.fla)**. Click **Save**.

Figure 4.9

If this is the end of a session, close this document by selecting **File**, **Close** from the main menu bar, and close Flash by selecting **File**, **Exit**.

Chapter 5 – Simple Vector Graphics

One of the things Flash is particularly good at is creating vector graphics. Vector graphics consist of lines and shapes defined mathematically, rather than as a collection of coloured pixels. This makes them very easy to select and transform.

We'll create some drawings as a brief introduction to some of the tools in the **Toolbox**.

Opening a document

Start Flash if it isn't already running. If your **DrawingExercises.fla** file isn't already open, click it on the **Start Page** if you can see it, otherwise click **Open**, find the file, and click **OK**.

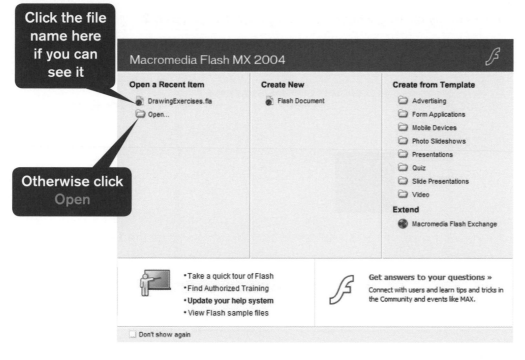

Figure 5.1

The Rectangle tool

Select the **Rectangle** tool in the **Toolbox**.

Now we'll set the tool properties using the **Properties** panel.

Rectangle Tool

Click the colour box next to the pencil icon – this is the outline colour. Click the dropper on **black** in the colour palette that appears (see Figure 5.2).

Pencil Icon

Tip:

When the dropper icon appears, you aren't restricted to choosing a colour in the colour palette – you can click on any colour on the screen. This is very useful when setting a colour to exactly match one you have already used.

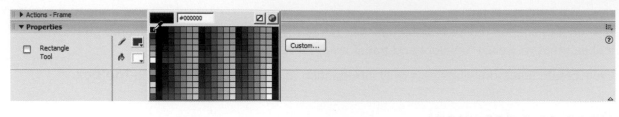

Figure 5.2

Paint Bucket Icon

Now set the fill colour by clicking the colour box next to the **Paint Bucket** icon in the **Properties** panel. Choose a blue colour.

Now set the line width by clicking where it currently says **1** and typing **2**.

Hold down the **Shift** key then click and drag a square on the **Stage**. Holding down **Shift** makes a perfect square.

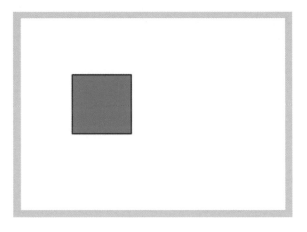

Figure 5.3

Changing the properties of an object

Selection Tool

Click the **Selection** tool in the **Toolbox**. Now click once in the centre of the square to select the fill. Notice that there is a white selection mesh over the fill; this shows it is selected.

Look in the **Properties** panel; the current fill properties are displayed.

Change the fill colour in the **Properties** panel to dark orange.

Figure 5.4

With the **Selection** tool, click and drag the fill away from the outline.

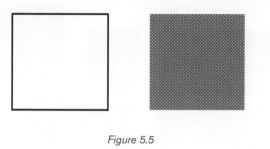

Figure 5.5

Selecting objects

 Now click on the outline of the square to select it; notice that only one side is selected! You can tell this because only the sided you clicked is covered with the white selection mesh.

Flash treats all shapes as a collection of individual objects; the fill is separate from the outline and each line of the outline is its own object, even if it was all drawn at the same time.

 Hold down the **Shift** key then click on the other sides. Holding down **Shift** lets you select multiple objects.

Figure 5.6

 Press **Escape** to deselect everything.

Using a selection box

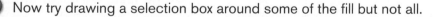 Now click and drag a box around the whole square; everything in the selection box is selected – so the whole outline is selected.

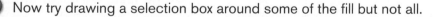 Now try drawing a selection box around some of the fill but not all.

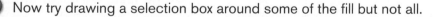 Click and drag the selected portion of the fill (see Figure 5.7).

Figure 5.7

You need to be careful when using a selection box – if you don't select all of the shape, you will break it up.

🔘 Press **Ctrl-Z** to undo (this is the same as selecting **Edit**, **Undo** from the main menu bar). The shape is back together again (if it isn't, press **Ctrl-Z** again).

Overlapping objects

🔘 Press **Escape** to deselect everything.

🔘 Click and drag the fill so that it overlaps a corner of the outline.

🔘 Press **Escape** to deselect the fill. Now click and drag the fill away from the outline.

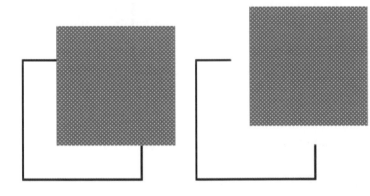

Figure 5.8

The outline has been cut. This is a feature of Flash: all objects at **Stage level** will cut away each other when they overlap (unless they are on different layers – you'll cover layers later).

🔘 Press **Ctrl-Z** until the fill is no longer touching the outline.

Stage level and Overlay level objects

All the objects we have worked with so far have been **Stage level**; all objects (apart from text) start life as **Stage level** objects. At **Stage level**, objects are a collection of individual lines and fills which can be moved independently of each other, and objects get cut away if they overlap. **Overlay** objects behave as single entities and so are more stable; this is good once you have drawn an object and don't want the outline and fill getting separated, or half the object disappearing because another object has overlapped it.

There are two ways to turn a **Stage level** object into an **Overlay level** object.

1   **Group** it, either on its own or with another object (this includes grouping an outline with its fill).

2   Turn the object into a **symbol**.

We'll turn the outline into an **Overlay level** object by grouping it.

 Select the whole outline using a **Selection** box (you should already have moved the fill away by pressing **Ctrl-Z**).

 Select **Modify**, **Group** from the main menu bar.

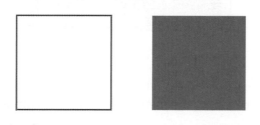

Figure 5.9

The outline gets a blue box around it; all **Overlay level** objects have a blue box around them when they are selected.

 Click and drag the outline to partly overlap the fill. Notice that now the outline is grouped you can select the whole thing with one click.

 Deselect by pressing **Escape**. Now move the outline away again – both objects remain intact! The objects can no longer interact with each other because one is **Stage level** (the fill) and the other is **Overlay level** (the outline).

 Delete the objects on the **Stage** by drawing a selection box around them both then pressing the **Delete** key.

Drawing Play, Pause and Stop buttons

For the virtual tour, you will be creating video clips which the user can play, pause or stop. In this exercise you will create the buttons to be used for this purpose.

⊙ Look at the **Zoom** menu at the top right of the page, above the **Timeline** panel. Set this to **100%**.

We'll draw a **Stop** button first. This will be a simple grey square.

Rectangle Tool

⊙ Select the **Rectangle** tool in the **Toolbox**.

⊙ In the **Properties** panel, set the fill to dark grey and no outline. To get no outline, select the **No Outline** icon at the top of the colour palette.

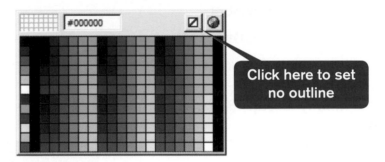

Click here to set no outline

Figure 5.10

Zoom Tool

⊙ Now draw a small square (remember that for a square you need to hold down the **Shift** key). The square should be about the same size as the tool icons in the **Toolbox**.

⊙ Now zoom in on the square by first selecting **Zoom** in the **Toolbox** then drawing a box around the square.

Figure 5.11

The **Pause** shape is similar to the **Stop** shape but has a white gap in the middle.

⊙ Click the **Selection** tool. Now hold down the **Ctrl** key while clicking and dragging the square to the right. This makes a copy of the square.

Selection Tool

Figure 5.12

Press **Escape** to deselect everything. Now use the **Selection** tool to draw a selection box around the middle of the right-hand square. The central strip should now be selected.

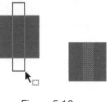

Figure 5.13

 In the **Properties** panel change the fill colour to **white**.

Figure 5.14

You're left with a **Pause** button! Now for the **Play** button shape.

Polystar Tool

 In the **Toolbox**, click and hold the **Rectangle** tool. A menu appears: select the **PolyStar** tool.

 Press **Escape** to deselect everything so that you can see the **PolyStar** tool properties.

 Press the **Options** button in the **Properties** panel. Enter the following settings and click **OK**:

Figure 5.15

 Set the fill to match the pause and stop buttons, and select no outline.

 Draw a triangle on the **Stage**, about the same height as the other buttons. If you don't like the shape press **Ctrl-Z** then try again.

Figure 5.16

Converting objects to symbols

We will now convert these objects to **symbols**. They will automatically become **Overlay level** objects.

The advantage of converting objects to symbols is not that they become **Overlay** level objects (we could just use **Group** if that's all we wanted). It is so that they are added to the **Library**, and many instances of that symbol can then be used throughout your virtual tour, or in other movies. Symbols are a very file-efficient way to store items that you use many times, because the symbol only needs to be stored once; it uses the same file space to include one hundred instances as it does one.

The second advantage is that if you edit the symbol, all instances of that symbol will also be updated, saving a lot of time!

These buttons will be used in your virtual tour to control videos of various parts of the school.

Selection Tool

🔘 Use the **Selection** tool to select the **Stop** shape.

🔘 Select **Modify**, **Convert to Symbol** from the main menu bar.

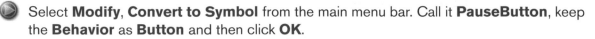

Figure 5.17

Notice that there are three different types of symbol you can choose from:

Movie clip: You would select **Movie clip** if the symbol contained some animation, or a video.

Button: **Buttons** are used when you need to assign actions to a symbol. In our case, we want to attach some code that will tell a video to stop playing, so we will choose this one.

Graphic: **Graphic** symbols are used when the symbol is just a still photo or drawing.

🔘 Copy the settings in Figure 5.17 then click **OK**.

🔘 Now select the **Pause** button shape by drawing a selection box around it.

🔘 Select **Modify**, **Convert to Symbol** from the main menu bar. Call it **PauseButton**, keep the **Behavior** as **Button** and then click **OK**.

🔘 Now do the same for the **Play** button shape, naming it **PlayButton**.

The Library panel

 If you can't see the **Library** panel, select **Window**, **Library** from the main menu bar.

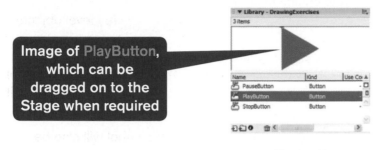

Figure 5.18

All three buttons are now in the **Library**. They are saved here – you can delete them from the **Stage** and they will still remain in the **Library**.

 Select all the buttons on the **Stage** then press **Delete**.

 Now click and drag an instance of each button from the **Library** panel onto the **Stage**, either by dragging its name or the image which appears when the name is selected.

 Delete everything on the **Stage** to leave it blank for the next exercise.

 Save by pressing **Ctrl-S**, or selecting **File**, **Save** from the main menu bar.

Drawing the EyeButton

Next we will draw another button, this time in the shape of an eye. This will be used in the virtual tour for people to click if they want to see more of a particular area.

The Oval tool

 Set the **Zoom** menu to **100%**.

 Select the **Oval** tool in the **Toolbox**.

Oval Tool

Nothing is currently selected so the tool properties should be displayed in the **Properties** panel.

 Copy the following settings to the **Properties** panel.

Figure 5.19

▶ Draw a circle on the **Stage**. Hold down **Shift** to get a perfect circle. Make it quite large – you'll be reducing it later.

▶ With the **Selection** tool, click the circle outline to select it.

▶ Now hold down the **Ctrl** key and click and drag the circle to make a copy.

Figure 5.20

▶ Now move one circle so it overlaps the other. A vertical dotted line should appear to help you align the two shapes horizontally.

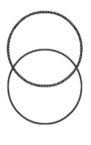

Figure 5.21

▶ Press **Escape** to deselect. Now click to select the top section of the upper circle. Press **Delete**.

▶ Repeat this for the bottom section. You are left with an eye shape!

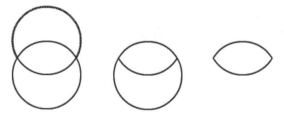

Figure 5.22

We'll group this shape to turn it into an **Overlay level** object; that way it can't be accidentally changed while we draw the rest of the eye.

 Select the eye by drawing a selection box around it. Select **Modify**, **Group** from the main menu bar.

 Using the **Oval** tool, draw another circle next to the eye that is about the same height as the eye.

 With the **Selection** tool, click and drag the circle to the centre of the eye; you will find it wants to stick to the edge of the eye so use the arrow keys to move it to its final position.

Oval Tool

Selection Tool

Figure 5.23

 Now draw another circle to the right of the eye for the pupil. Use the **Selection** tool to move it to the centre of the eye. Click away from the eye to deselect everything.

Figure 5.24

The Paint Bucket tool

We'll use the **Paint Bucket** tool to add some colour to the iris and to make the pupil black.

 Select the **Paint Bucket** tool in the **Toolbox**.

 Make sure nothing is selected, so that you can see the tool properties in the **Properties** panel.

 Select a nice blue fill colour. Click the **Paint Bucket** on the iris to fill it with blue paint.

Paint Bucket Tool

Figure 5.25

Now set the fill colour to black and colour the pupil.

Figure 5.26

 Fill the white of the eye with white, otherwise the eye will be transparent and any coloured background will show through.

The Free Transform tool

The eye is finished, but it needs to be much smaller. We'll resize it using the **Free Transform** tool before converting it to a symbol.

 Select the whole eye by drawing a selection box around it with the **Selection** tool.

Free Transform Tool

 Select the **Free Transform** tool in the **Toolbox**. At the bottom of the **Toolbox** click the **Scale** option. This will ensure that the proportions of the eye are maintained when you resize it.

Scale Option

 Resize the eye to about the size shown in the figure below.

Figure 5.27

 Select the eye using the **Selection** tool. Select **Modify**, **Convert to Symbol** from the main menu bar.

 Copy the settings below.

Figure 5.28

 Click **OK**.

 The **EyeButton** appears in the **Library**.

Button edit mode

- Try selecting bits of the eye with the **Selection** tool. You will find that you can only select the whole eye, rather than any individual circle or fill that it is made of. In order to edit a button, you have to enter **Button edit** mode.

- Look above the **Timeline** panel: it says **Scene 1**.

←	🎬 Scene 1		🎬 🎬 100% ▾

Figure 5.29

- To enter **Button edit** mode, double-click the **EyeButton** symbol on the **Stage**.

- Now look above the **Timeline** panel: it will now say **EyeButton** next to **Scene 1**.

⇦	🎬 Scene 1 🎬 EyeButton		🎬 🎬 100% ▾

Figure 5.30

This is the easiest way to tell if you are in **Button edit** mode, or just in **Normal** mode. Pay attention to this bar because you might accidentally double-click a symbol on the **Stage** and enter this mode without even realising. It isn't made very obvious you have changed modes!

Now we will change the line width of all the lines in the eye from **2** to **1**.

- First of all zoom in on the eye by selecting the **Zoom** tool in the **Toolbox** then drawing a box around the eye.

- Press **Escape** to deselect everything. Now with the **Selection** tool click the outer circle (at the edge of the iris).

- In the **Properties** panel, click where it says **2** then type **1**. Press **Enter** for the change to take effect.

Zoom Tool

Selection Tool

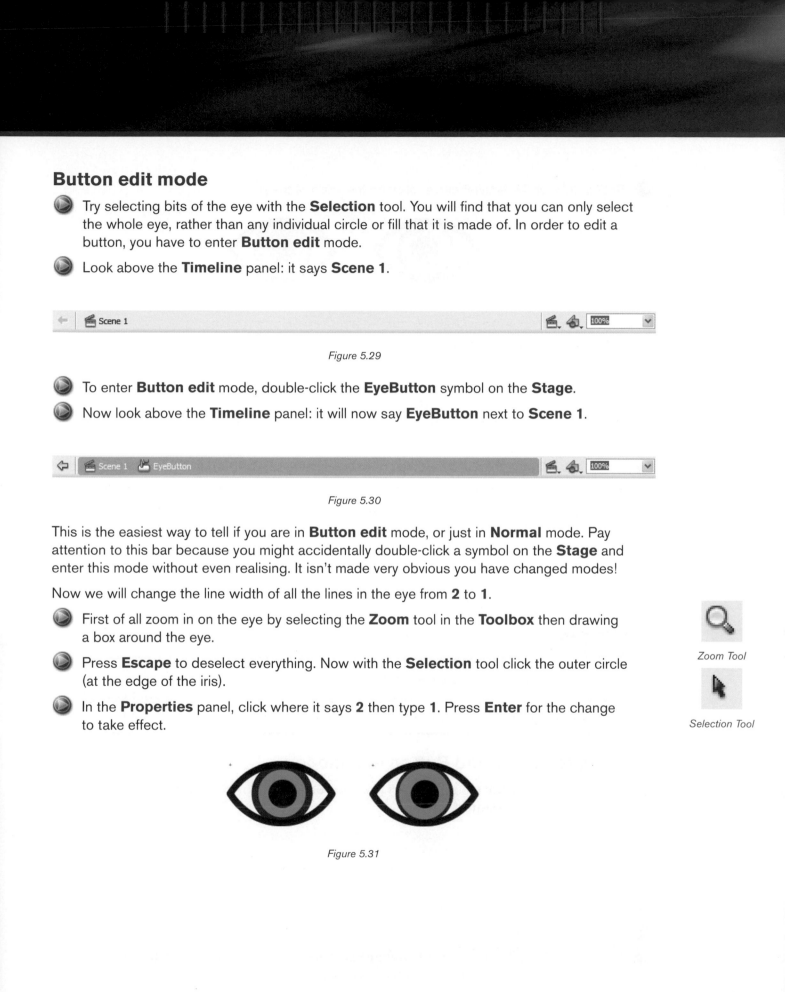

Figure 5.31

Repeat this for the smaller circle (click on the edge of the pupil).

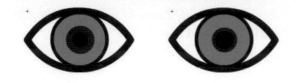

Figure 5.32

We now need to change the outline of the eye. The method for this is slightly different because we grouped the eye outline.

 With the **Selection** tool, click to select the outline. It will have a blue outline around it, and no properties will appear in the **Properties** panel. There is no white selection mesh over it as there was for the other circles; you cannot edit an object unless it has a white selection mesh on it.

 To edit the outline, double-click it. You have now entered **Group edit** mode. Look above the **Timeline** panel.

Figure 5.33

 The eye outline now has the white selection mesh. Change the line weight in the **Properties** panel to **1** then press **Enter**.

> **Tip:**
>
> All the levels of **Button edit** and **Group edit** do seem complicated, but you don't need to keep track of what you have grouped – just remember the simple rule: **to edit an object you need to keep double-clicking it until the white selection mesh appears on it**.

Exiting Group edit and Button edit mode

 To go back to **Normal** mode (where it just says **Scene 1** above the **Timeline** panel), just click where it says **Scene 1**.

Figure 5.34

 Delete the instance of the **EyeButton** from the **Stage** – it is safely stored in the **Library**.

 Set the **Zoom** menu back to **100%**.

 Press **Ctrl-S** to save. Close the **DrawingExercises** file and Flash if this is the end of a session, otherwise leave it open for the next chapter.

Chapter 6 – More Drawing Exercises

In this chapter you will create a **Back** button that will be used in your virtual tour, and also draw the school map that will be used in both the intro movie and the virtual tour. The **Back** button will be another **Button** symbol, and the **SchoolMap** will be a **Graphic** symbol.

 Open the **DrawingExercises.fla** file if it is not already open.

The Line tool

 Select the **Line** tool in the **Toolbox**.

 Set the tool properties in the **Properties** panel to be a **black** line of thickness **1**.

 At the bottom of the **Toolbox** click the magnet to switch on **Snap to Objects**.

 Draw a triangle in the bottom right corner of the **Stage**; draw the vertical and horizontal lines first, and hold down the **Shift** key while you draw to get perfectly vertical and horizontal lines. It doesn't matter if your triangle isn't exactly in the corner.

Line Tool

Snap to Objects

Figure 6.1

 Now draw two more lines to form a second triangle on top of the first.

Figure 6.2

 Click the **Selection** tool. Without first selecting it, click and drag in the centre of one of the lines you have just drawn to bend it.

Selection Tool

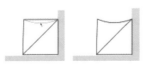

Figure 6.3

53

Insert Layer Icon

Creating a new layer

🔘 At the bottom left of the **Timeline** panel, click the **Insert Layer** icon.

🔘 Rename this layer **Paths**, just like you did the **Grass** layer.

Figure 6.17

🔘 Set the **Rectangle** tool properties to have a beige fill and no outline. (If you can't see the tool properties, make sure nothing is selected, then click once on the **Stage**.)

🔘 Make sure **Frame 1** of the **Paths** layer is selected in the **Timeline** panel. You need to be very careful when you have more than one layer that you are drawing in the right layer!

🔘 Draw the paths as shown in Figure 16.18.

Figure 6.18

Oval Tool

🔘 Now select the **Oval** tool. Set the fill to match the paths and select no outline.

🔘 Draw an oval on a spare bit of grass.

Figure 6.19

Use the **Selection** tool to click and drag the oval onto the path.

Selection Tool

Figure 6.20

Now draw a smaller oval in red on the grass. If you find that the tool properties don't display just click once on the **Stage**. Now move it with the **Selection** tool on to the first oval. Use the arrow keys if it's easier.

Figure 6.21

Press **Escape** to deselect everything. Now click the red oval to select it and press **Delete**. It is deleted, and it has cut away the first oval, leaving the green of the **Grass** layer showing through. It hasn't cut away an oval from the green rectangle because this is in a different layer.

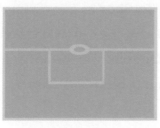

Figure 6.22

61

● Lock the **Paths** layer by clicking under the padlock symbol in the **Timeline** panel.

● Insert a new layer called **Buildings**. If it isn't already the top layer in the **Timeline** panel, click and drag it to the top.

Figure 6.23

Rectangle Tool

● Select the **Rectangle** tool. Press **Esc** to deselect everything. If you can't see the tool properties in the **Properties** panel click once on the **Stage**.

● Set the tool properties to have a dark red fill and black outline, thickness **1**.

● Make sure the **Buildings** layer is selected in the **Timeline** panel. We want to draw the buildings in the **Buildings** layer.

● Draw the buildings as shown in Figure 6.24.

Figure 6.24

PolyStar Tool

● Select the **PolyStar** tool in the **Toolbox** by first clicking and holding the **Rectangle** tool.

● Press **Escape** to show the tool properties (click once on the **Stage** if necessary).

● In the **Properties** panel, click **Options**. Set the number of sides to **8** and press **OK**.

● Set the fill to grey and the outline to black, thickness **1**.

Draw in the chapel as shown in Figure 6.25.

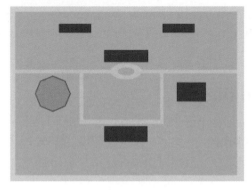

Figure 6.25

Converting to a Graphic symbol

 Unlock all the layers that are currently locked.

 Use the **Selection** tool to draw a selection box around the whole map.

 Select **Modify, Convert to Symbol** from the main menu bar.

 Name the symbol **SchoolMap**. Select the **Graphic** symbol type then click **OK**.

Selection Tool

Figure 6.26

The **SchoolMap** symbol appears in the **Library**.

 Delete the instance of the **SchoolMap** symbol from the **Stage**. Notice that the layers used to create the map are still there, but now they are all empty. When you edit the **SchoolMap** symbol you will find that the symbol has been compressed into one layer. You can delete two of the layers by selecting them then clicking the **Delete** icon at the bottom of the **Timeline** panel, as they are no longer needed.

Delete Icon

 Press **Ctrl-S** to save.

 Close the **DrawingExercises** file. Close Flash if this is the end of a session, otherwise leave it open for the next chapter.

In this chapter we will begin creating the movie step-by-step. We'll be using the storyboard as a reference to see how the animation is supposed to look.

We want the movie to open with a map of Africa. This will then zoom in gradually to Uganda and then Fort Portal, where Nyakasura school is. The first task is to draw a map of Africa and mark on it Uganda and Fort Portal.

Creating a new Flash file

Open Flash if it is not already open. Create a new Flash file by clicking **Create New**, Flash **Document** on the **Start page**, or by selecting **File**, **New**, Flash **Document** from the main menu bar.

Drawing a map of Africa

Don't worry – no artistic talent is required here because we're going to cheat a little by tracing over an existing image.

The first step is to find a map of Africa to trace over.

Open Internet Explorer and go to **www.google.com**. Type in **Africa map** then click **Google Search**.

Now click where it says **Images** at the top of the screen.

Figure 7.1

Choose a nice clear map of Africa that has all the different countries marked; one that is about 50K should be large enough to have the detail you need.

Click on your chosen map then click again to see the full size image.

Right-click on the full size image (not the thumbnail) then select **Copy** from the menu that appears.

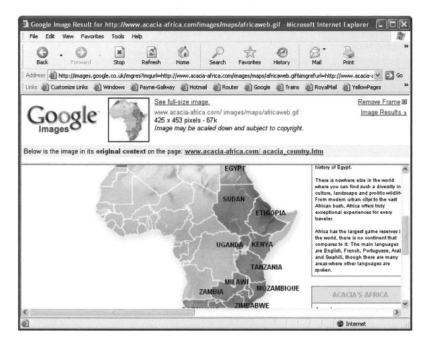

Figure 7.2

Close Internet Explorer and return to the Flash window.

Select **Edit**, **Paste in Center** from the main menu bar.

You will probably find that the map is bigger than the **Stage** and that you cannot see all of it. We'll change the zoom settings then resize it.

In the **Zoom** menu at the top right of the **Stage** (above the **Timeline**), select **Show All**.

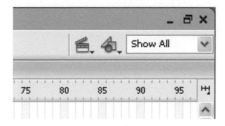

Figure 7.3

Scale Option

Free Transform Tool

⏵ Select the pasted image with the **Selection** tool. Click the **Free Transform** tool in the **Toolbox**, then select **Scale** from the **Options** at the bottom of the **Toolbox**.

⏵ Click and drag a corner of the image until it fits easily onto the **Stage**.

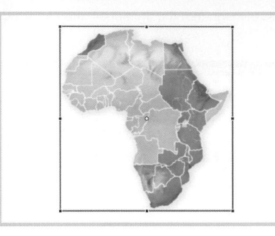

Figure 7.4

⏵ Now click and drag the map to the centre of the **Stage** (you can click anywhere on the map to do this, except the small white dot in the centre).

⏵ On the **Zoom** menu, select **Fit in Window**. You should now be zoomed in on the **Stage**.

Layers

It's a good idea to use a different layer for each object in Flash. We want the pasted map on one layer, and our traced outline on another.

⏵ The **Timeline** panel should be located above the **Stage**. If it is compressed, click it once to expand it so that it looks like the one below. If you can't see it, select **Window, Timeline** from the main menu bar.

Don't worry about all the frames — we don't need these yet. Look at the left of the **Timeline** panel where it says **Layer 1**. By default, you start drawing on **Layer 1**.

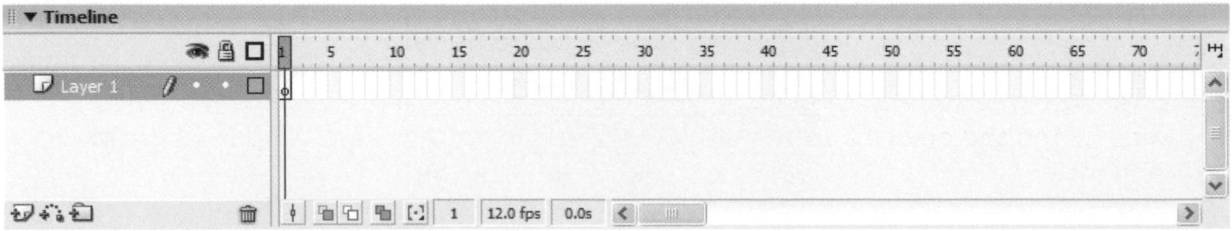

Figure 7.5

Adding a new layer

⊙ Click the **Insert Layer** icon at the bottom left of the **Timeline** panel.

A new layer appears called **Layer 2**.

Insert Layer Icon

Renaming a layer

⊙ Double-click where it says **Layer 2** then type **TracedOutline**. Press **Enter**.

⊙ Rename **Layer 1** as **ImportedMap**.

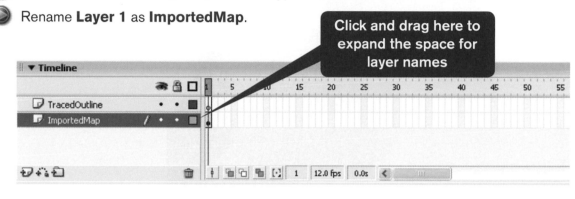

Click and drag here to expand the space for layer names

Figure 7.6

Locking a layer

We'll lock the **ImportedMap** layer so that we don't accidentally edit or move it whilst drawing the outline.

⊙ Click next to where it says **ImportedMap** in the **Timeline** panel under the **Padlock** icon. A **Padlock** icon should appear to show that the layer is locked.

Padlock Icon

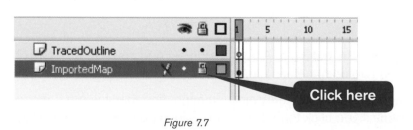

Click here

Figure 7.7

⊙ Save the movie so far by selecting **File**, **Save As** from the main menu bar. In the **Save As** window find and open the **IntroMovieFlashFiles** folder then save the file as **IntroMovie** in this folder.

Tracing over an image with the Pen tool

The **Pen** tool is one that you haven't used yet. It is great for tracing round objects because you can draw point-to-point by clicking round an object, and you can also make it curve the line from one point to the next.

Zoom Tool

🔘 Click the layer name **TracedOutline** in the **Timeline** panel to select that layer.

🔘 Select the **Zoom** tool from the **Toolbox** and click and drag a rectangle to zoom in on a part of Africa.

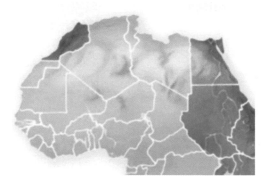

Figure 7.8

Pen Tool

🔘 Select the **Pen** tool from the **Toolbox**.

🔘 In the **Properties** panel, copy the settings below.

▼ Properties
✎ Pen Tool   ✏️ ⬛️   🖍️ ⬛️   2 ∨   Solid ——————— ∨   Custom...

Figure 7.9

🔘 Click a point on the outline of Africa, then a second close to it. A straight line is drawn between the two points. Keep clicking along a short length of coastline.

Sometimes when you click the next point you might find that it is not connected to the previous one. This happens if you click too close to a previous point – Flash assumes that you have clicked on the previous point to finish the line. To correct this just press the **Delete** key to delete the disconnected point then click again.

This might be happening because you have **Snap** switched on, so the **Pen** tool is actually trying to **snap** to the previous point. To switch off **Snap**, select **View**, **Snapping** from the main menu bar. Click any snap options that are ticked to deselect them.

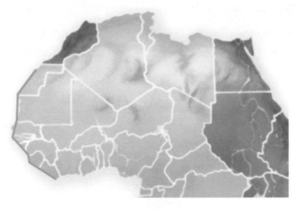

Figure 7.10

That works fine, but it would look better if the lines joining the points were curved.

 Press the **Delete** key. Keep pressing the **Delete** key until you have just two points left.

With the **Pen** tool still selected, click and hold the mouse at the next point. Now, keep holding down the mouse button and experiment with moving the node to create a curve. Release the mouse when you're happy with the shape. Don't worry if you have a few strange looking curves – we'll edit those in a minute! You can always press **Ctrl-Z** to undo your last point.

Figure 7.11

Tip:

I find I get the best curve by keeping the stalk fairly short; stretching it too far makes the subsequent point a bit skewed.

Closing the shape

● Draw the rest of the outline. To join the last point of the outline with the first, you need to click accurately on the first node. When the pen tool is placed over the first node it should have a small circle symbol next to it to indicate it is over an existing node; make sure you can see this before you click.

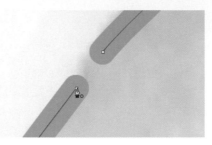

Figure 7.12

When you close the line to form a solid object, it should automatically be given a green fill. If yours isn't, there could be two possible reasons:

● The two ends of the lines don't exactly match up.

● You didn't set the fill property of the **Pen** tool before you started drawing.

Either way, it's easily fixed.

Paint Bucket Tool

● Select the **Paint Bucket** tool from the **Toolbox**. At the bottom of the **Toolbox**, click the left-hand icon under **Options**. Choose **Close Large Gaps** from the list.

*Close Large
Gaps*

● Change the fill colour to match the outline colour (to do this click the colour box in the **Properties** panel then click the dropper on the outline you have drawn).

● Click the **Paint Bucket** tool in the middle of the shape. It should fill with green.

If your outline still doesn't fill, it is probably because there is too large a gap between two of the nodes. Use the **Subselection** tool along with the **Zoom** tool to look for and close any gaps, then try filling the outline using the **Paint Bucket** tool again.

Editing a line using the Subselection tool

The **Subselection** tool is very useful. It lets you edit and delete nodes of an existing line or shape.

Subselection Tool

● Click the **Subselection** tool in the **Toolbox**. Now click on the line you've drawn.

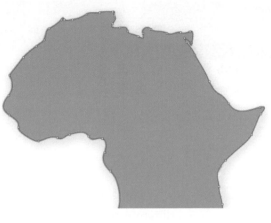

Figure 7.13

The line is selected and each node becomes visible.

Deleting a node

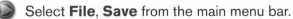 Click on one of the nodes (a point in the line) to select it. This can be a bit fiddly – zoom in to make it easier.

● Delete the node by pressing the **Delete** key. To replace the node, press **Ctrl-Z** to undo.

Editing a node

● Click a node to select it. Try moving the node by clicking and dragging it.

Tip:

You can select more than one node at a time by holding down the **Shift** key while you click each node. This is useful if you want to move a whole section of a line or shape.

● Select **File**, **Save** from the main menu bar.

Drawing Uganda

The next step is to draw Uganda on the map.

● Create a new layer called **UgandaOutline** above all the other layers.

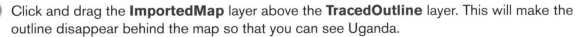 Click and drag the **ImportedMap** layer above the **TracedOutline** layer. This will make the outline disappear behind the map so that you can see Uganda.

● Lock the **TracedOutine** layer, leaving only the **UgandaOutline** layer unlocked.

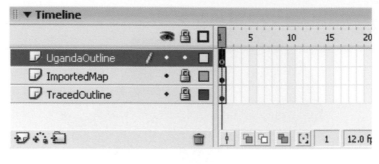

Figure 7.14

Pen Tool

Trace Uganda just like you did for the rest of the map, using the **Pen** tool. The outline and fill should both be light green (choose a different green from the one used for Africa), and the outline should have a thickness of **1**.

Figure 7.15

Grouping Uganda

We'll group the outline with the fill to turn the Uganda map into an **Overlay level** object.

Selection Tool

With the **Selection** tool, draw a selection box around the whole of Uganda. Select **Modify**, **Group** from the menu.

Drawing Lake Victoria

Pen Tool

Now use the **Pen** tool to trace round Lake Victoria. First press **Esc** to deselect everything. Both the outline and fill should be a light blue colour, with outline width **1**. You will notice when you draw the outline that some of it disappears behind the Uganda map – the Uganda map will always sit on top because it is an **Overlay level** object.

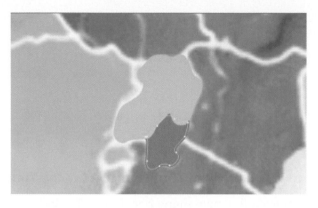

Figure 7.16

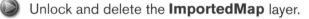 Group the lake in the same way as you did Uganda (draw a selection box around it then select **Modify**, **Group** from the menu). Be careful when you draw the selection box not to start it over the Uganda outline because this will move the map; click and drag from the lower right corner to the upper left corner.

Grouping Uganda with Lake Victoria

With the **Selection** tool, click on the lake, then hold down the **Shift** key and click Uganda. Select **Modify**, **Group** from the menu bar.

Unlock and delete the **ImportedMap** layer.

Figure 7.17

Converting the map to a symbol

Now we'll convert the map into a symbol that will be stored in the **Library**.

Unlock all the layers.

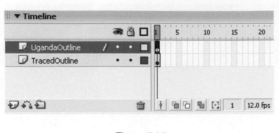

Figure 7.18

 First of all select **Fit in Window** in the **Zoom** menu above the **Timeline**.

 Select **Edit**, **Select All** from the main menu bar. This will select all the objects in all the layers.

 Select **Modify**, **Convert to Symbol** from the main menu bar.

Figure 7.19

 Name the symbol **Africa**. Select the **Graphic** option then click **OK**.

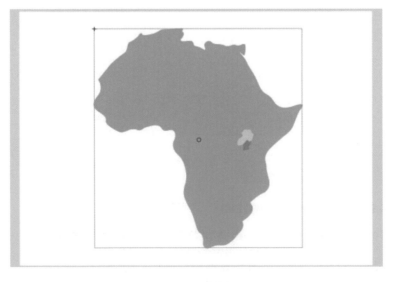

Figure 7.20

The Library panel

All symbols, imported images and tweened images are stored in the **Library**.

 If you can't already see it, select **Window**, **Library** from the main menu bar.

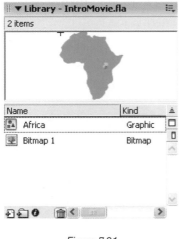

Figure 7.21

The **Library** should have two items in it; the **Africa** symbol you just created and a bitmap file holding the Africa image you imported from the Internet.

 Select the **Bitmap 1** file in the **Library** panel by clicking its name.

Figure 7.22

When you select an item in the **Library**, a preview of that item appears at the top of the **Library** panel. This is the image that you imported into Flash by copying from Google and pasting onto the **Stage**. When you import an image it is automatically added to the **Library**. Once you have saved an image in the **Library**, you can place it on the **Stage** at any time. Try this now.

Click the green **Africa** map on the **Stage** to select it. Now press the **Delete** key.

Don't worry! It isn't gone for good – all you need to do if you want it back is to drag an instance of it from the **Library**.

 Click and drag the **Africa** symbol from the **Library** onto the **Stage**. It doesn't matter whether you select the symbol name, the icon next to the name or the preview of that symbol in the **Library** panel.

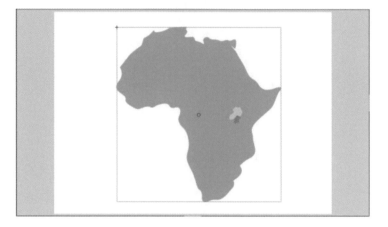

Figure 7.23

Renaming items in the Library

 Double-click where it says **Bitmap 1** then type **ImportedMap**.

Editing a symbol

We are now going to edit the **Africa** symbol to add a dot where the town of Fort Portal is; this is the town where Nyakasura School is located.

There are two ways to edit a symbol. You can either:

 double-click an instance of that symbol on the **Stage**,

 or double-click the symbol in the **Library** panel.

We'll use the first option.

 Double-click the **Africa** symbol instance on the **Stage**.

 Look above the **Timeline** panel, where it says **Scene 1** and **Africa**.

 Scene 1   Africa   131%

Figure 7.24

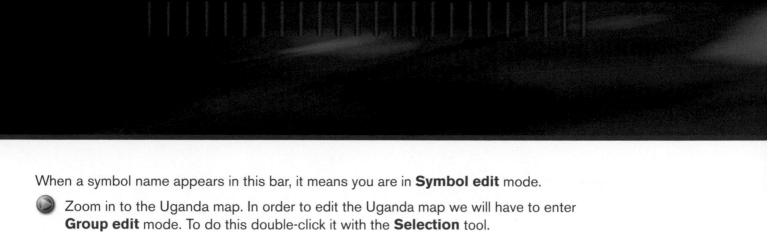

When a symbol name appears in this bar, it means you are in **Symbol edit** mode.

⦿ Zoom in to the Uganda map. In order to edit the Uganda map we will have to enter **Group edit** mode. To do this double-click it with the **Selection** tool.

⦿ Double-click it again to delve into the final layer of grouping. The bar above the Timeline should now look like this:

| ⇐ | 🎬 Scene 1 | 🗺 Africa | 🔲 Group | 🔲 Group | | 🎬 🔷 759% ▾ |

Figure 7.25

Marking Fort Portal on the Uganda map

Look at the map of Uganda below. Look at where Fort Portal is.

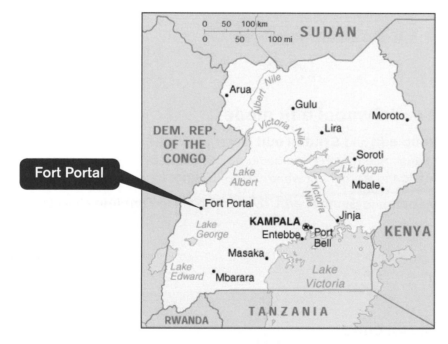

Figure 7.26

⦿ Select the **Oval** tool from the **Toolbox**.

⦿ Press the **Escape** key to make sure nothing is selected, then click once on the **Stage** to bring up the tool properties in the **Properties** panel. Set the fill to white and select the **No outline** option.

Oval Tool

▼ Properties

○ Oval
Tool

Figure 7.27

Holding down the **Shift** key, click and drag a very small circle where Fort Portal is.

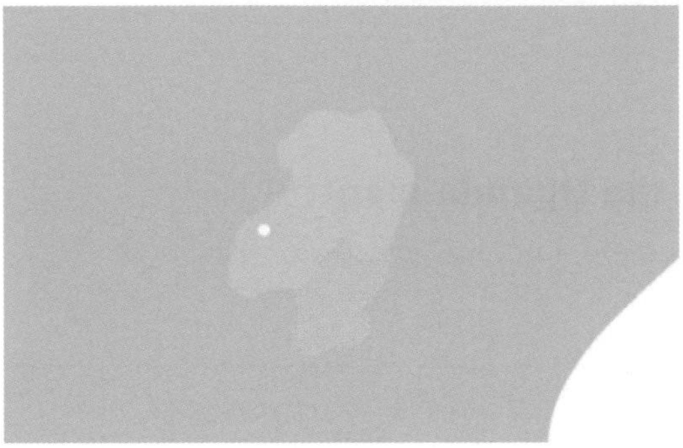

Figure 7.28

Exiting Group edit and Symbol edit mode

To completely exit **Group edit** and **Symbol edit** mode, just click where it says **Scene 1** above the **Timeline** panel. Alternatively, you could go back step by step by clicking where it says **Group**, then **Africa** to the right of where it says **Scene 1**.

When you've exited **Group edit** and **Symbol edit**, the bar above the **Timeline** should look like this:

Figure 7.29

Save your work by pressing **Ctrl-S**.

Adding text

Now we'll add some text labels for Uganda and Fort Portal.

With the **Selection** tool, double-click anywhere on the **Africa** symbol on the stage to enter **Symbol edit** mode.

Selection Tool

Figure 7.30

Select the **Text** tool in the **Toolbox**. In the **Properties** panel, change the text size to **4**, font to **Arial** and the text colour to **black**. Click the **Align Center** icon.

Figure 7.31

Click the **Text** tool once over the Uganda map (we'll reposition the text in a minute).

Type **UGANDA**.

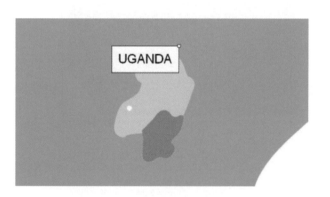

Figure 7.32

Click away from the text. Now, with the **Selection** tool click and drag the text so it is centred over the map. Be careful not to click and drag the map itself; if you do just press **Ctrl-Z** to undo. You might find it easier to first click the text to select it and then use the arrow keys to position it.

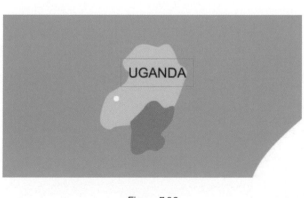

Figure 7.33

Text Tool

- If you want to change the font size, select the **Text** tool in the **Toolbox** then double-click on the word **UGANDA** to select it. Now change the font size in the **Properties** panel. Click outside the text box when you're done.

- Now add a label for **Fort Portal**. You'll probably want a font size of about **1** or **2**.

- Exit **Symbol edit** mode by clicking where it says **Scene 1** above the **Timeline** panel.

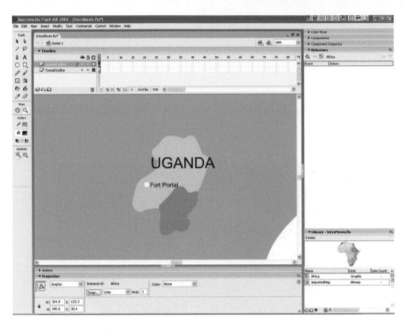

Figure 7.34

- Save the document by pressing **Ctrl-S**, or by selecting **File**, **Save** from the main menu bar.

- Close the **IntroMovie.fla** file and Flash if this is the end of a session, otherwise leave it open for the next chapter.

Chapter 8 – The Timeline and Motion Tweening

In this chapter, we'll use motion tweening to zoom in on the map, to make it look like you're gradually getting closer to Fort Portal.

 Open Flash and the **IntroMovie.fla** file if it is not already open.

 Delete the instance of the **Africa** symbol currently on the **Stage**.

Both the layers on the **Stage** are now empty. These layers were needed in the creation of the **Africa** symbol, which is now safely saved in the **Library**. We need just one blank layer for the next step.

 Delete one of the layers then rename the remaining layer **Layer 1** for now. (See Figure 8.1)

Before we do the tweening, let's take a close look at the **Timeline** panel. You've already used the **Timeline** panel to organise objects with **Layers**; now we'll look at how to use the frames for animation. The **Timeline** panel should already be open above the **Stage**. If you can't see it, select **Window**, **Timeline** from the main menu bar. Expand the panel so that you can see the layers and frames.

The different parts of the **Timeline** are labelled in Figure 8.1.

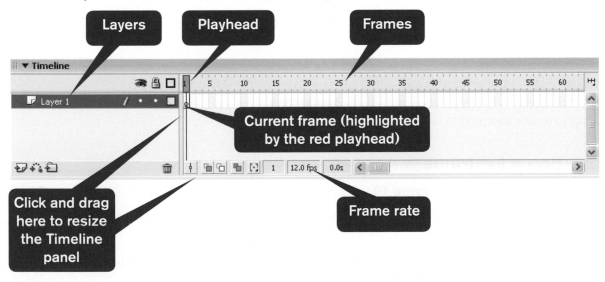

Figure 8.1: The Timeline panel

Frames in Flash are just like frames in a film or cartoon – something different is drawn in each frame and when the frames are put together in a sequence it looks as though the objects are moving. The frames in which you draw are called **keyframes**. It is normal to insert **regular frames** between **keyframes** in order to regulate the timing between the **keyframes**. The contents of a **keyframe** remain in view until the next **keyframe**.

Motion tweening

Tweening is different to frame-by-frame animation. Instead of drawing the contents of each frame, you draw the contents of the first and last frame in the sequence, and Flash will automatically fill in what happens in between.

Frame 1

Look at the **playhead**, highlighted in red. The **playhead** shows which frame you are viewing on the **Stage**. You are currently looking at **Frame 1**. **Frame 1** is a **keyframe** that is automatically inserted by Flash. By default, when you open a new Flash file, you work on **Frame 1**.

- If the **Library** panel is not visible, open it now by selecting **Window, Library** from the main menu bar.

- Click and drag an instance of the **Africa** symbol from the **Library** onto the **Stage**. Change the option in the **Zoom** box to **Fit in Window** if you cannot see all of the map.

- Select the **Free Transform** tool from the **Toolbox** then click the map.

Free Transform Tool

- Select the **Scale** option at the bottom of the **Toolbox**. Click and drag a corner node to make the map much smaller (see Figure 8.2 to see what size to make it).

Scale Option

We will insert another **keyframe** with a larger version of the **Africa** map, and let Flash tween smoothly between the two **keyframes**. This will make it look as though we are zooming in on the map.

Inserting a keyframe

We'll insert a **keyframe** in **Frame 10**.

- In the **Timeline** panel, right-click **Frame 10** then select **Insert Keyframe** from the menu that appears.

You are now looking at **Frame 10** (see Figure 8.2). The contents of **Frame 1** (i.e. the map of Africa) have been copied to **Frame 10**.

Figure 8.2

Free Transform Tool

🔘 With the **Free Transform** tool and the **Scale** option selected, expand the map so that it fills the stage.

🔘 In the **Zoom** menu above the **Timeline**, select **25%**.

Scale Option

Figure 8.3

🔘 Click and drag a corner node to enlarge the map as much as possible. You will be able to drag the corner node right off the workspace out of sight – don't let go of it until the map is as big as it can get.

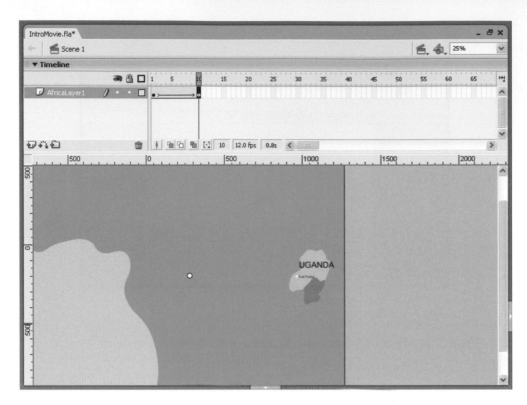

Figure 8.4

Now we can't see the edges of the **Stage**. To mark the edges of the **Stage** we'll temporarily hide the map then add some **guidelines**.

Rulers and Guides

 In the **Timeline** panel, click below the eye symbol to hide **Layer 1**.

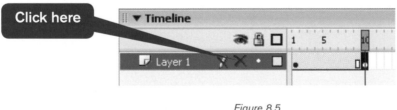

Figure 8.5

 To view the rulers, select **View**, **Rulers** from the main menu bar.

Now click and drag from the top ruler to the edge of the **Stage**. A green guide appears. Repeat this for all four sides of the **Stage**.

If you need to reposition a guide, just click and drag it using the **Selection** tool.

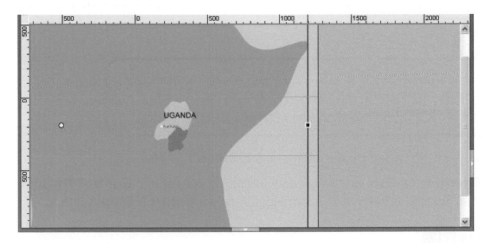

Figure 8.6

 Select **View**, **Guides**, **Lock Guides** from the main menu bar. This will prevent you from accidentally moving one of the guides.

 Unhide **Layer 1** by clicking under the eye symbol again.

 Use the **Selection** tool to reposition the map so that Uganda is in the centre of the **Stage**.

Figure 8.7

 Rename **Layer 1** as **AfricaLayer**.

Scrubbing

There is a technique called **scrubbing** that you can easily use to preview your animation. It simply means dragging the **playhead** through the frames; each of the frames will then be shown on the **Stage** in turn.

 Click and drag the red **playhead** in the **Timeline** panel through all the frames. Be careful to click and drag the top part of the **playhead** – don't click and drag in a frame.

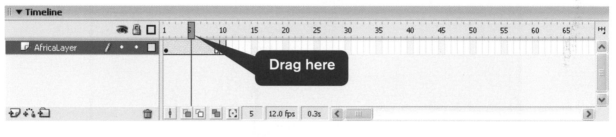

Figure 8.8

At the moment, the map will start small and remain small until **Frame 10**, when it suddenly grows. We want the map to gradually get larger; to do this we need to use **motion tweening**.

Adding a motion tween

 Right-click a frame between **Frames 1** and **10**. Select **Create Motion Tween** from the menu that appears.

Now look at the **Timeline** panel; notice there is now an arrow from **Frame 1** to **Frame 10**.

Tip:

If the arrow has a broken line, this means that Flash couldn't compute the tween. Go back over the previous steps and make sure the contents of **Frame 1** and **Frame 10** are correct, then reapply the tween.

 Now preview the tween by scrubbing over **Frames 1** to **10**.

 Click **Frame 1**. Another way to preview the movie is to select **Control**, **Play** from the main menu bar. Try this. If the movie is looping just select **Control**, **Stop** to stop it.

Tip:

You can select whether or not the movie loops by selecting **Control**, **Loop Playback** from the main menu bar.

 Save the movie by pressing **Ctrl-S**.

Chapter 9 - Publishing

This chapter describes how to view the **IntroMovie** in an Internet browser. At the moment, this file can only be viewed by people with the Flash authoring software. We will save it in a format that anyone with an Internet browser and the free Flash Player can view.

You can skip this chapter for now if you like, and refer back to it when you need to publish your project.

When you save a Flash file in a format that can be viewed outside the Flash authoring environment, this is called **publishing**. You can publish pictures and movies in much the same way.

- Load up Flash and open **IntroMovie.fla**.
- Select **File**, **Publish Settings** from the main menu bar.

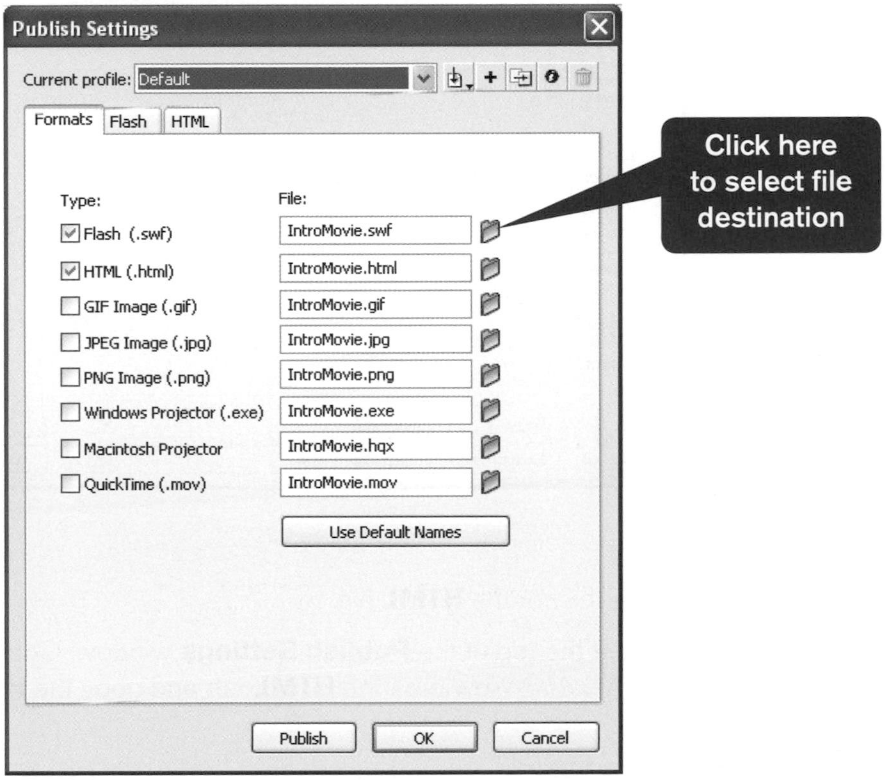

Figure 9.1

There are lots of options here!

- Make sure the Flash and **HTML** options are ticked as shown in Figure 9.1. When you tick **HTML**, **Flash** is automatically ticked too.

These settings mean that two files will be created when you click **Publish** – an **HTML (.html)** file and a Flash **Shockwave (.swf)** file.

Choosing file names and locations

You can give the files different names and specify where they will be saved.

Folder Icon

⊙ Click the folder icon to the right of the top box for the Flash file (see Figure 9.1).

⊙ Make sure the file is saved in the **IntroMovieFlashFiles** folder. Leave the file name as **IntroMovie**.

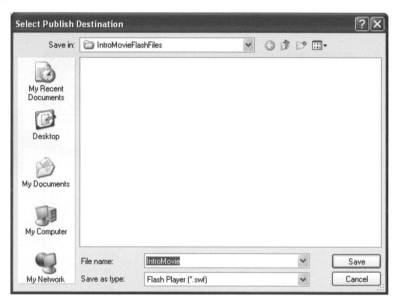

Figure 9.2

⊙ Click **Save**. Repeat this for the **HTML** file.

⊙ Click the Flash tab at the top of the **Publish Settings** window. Copy the Flash settings from Figure 9.3(a). Now click the **HTML** tab and copy the **HTML** settings from Figure 9.3(b).

Tip:

A tab is created in the **Publish Settings** window for each of the file formats you tick on the first page, with the exception of **Projector** files.

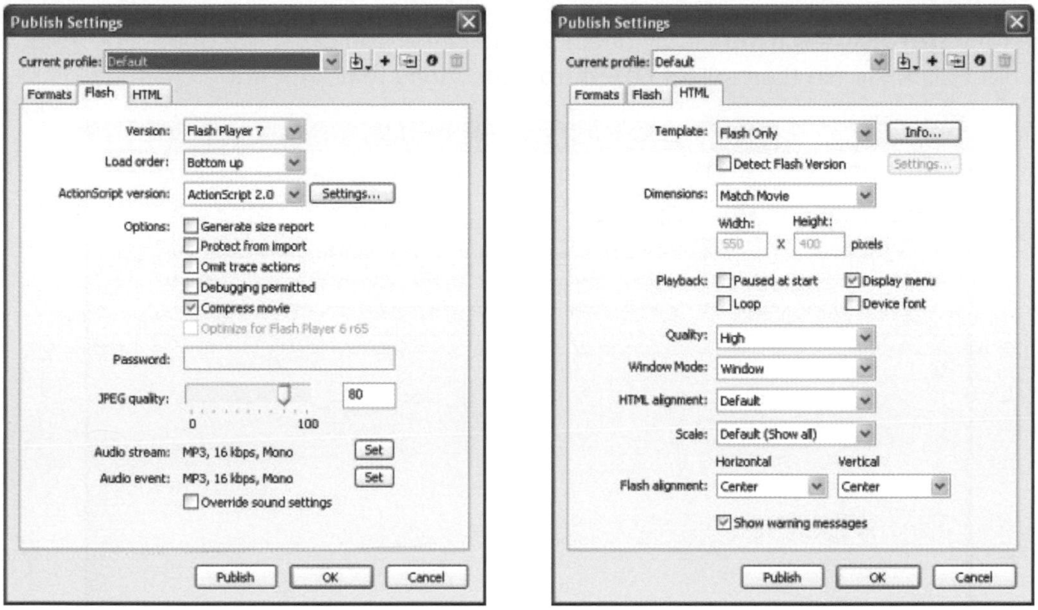

Figure 9.3: (a) Flash settings and (b) HTML settings

◉ Click **Publish**.

A window will pop up briefly to tell you that it is publishing.

◉ Click **OK** to close the **Publish Settings** window.

Viewing the file in an Internet browser

◉ Open up Windows Explorer, or whichever program you use to view the files on your computer.

Tip:

To open **Windows Explorer**, right-click the **Start** menu at the bottom left of the screen then select **Explore** from the menu that appears.

◉ Locate the **IntroMovieFlashFiles** folder and open it. There will be three files in this folder now: the original file **IntroMovie.fla** and the two files you have just created from the **Publish Settings** window.

HTML file just created. To be viewed in an Internet browser like a web page.

Original FLA file you have been working on

SWF file just created. This can be viewed by anyone who has downloaded a free copy of Flash Player.

IntroMovie.fla

IntroMovie.html

IntroMovie.swf

Figure 9.4

Open the **IntroMovie.html** file by double-clicking it. If you don't like double-clicking, you can right-click the file then select **Open** from the menu that appears.

Figure 9.5

You may find that Internet Explorer blocks the movie because it contains active content.

To play the movie, just click the pale yellow bar below all the menus at the top of the Browser window. Select **Allow Blocked Content** from the menu that appears, and **Yes** at the **Security Warning** prompt.

Figure 9.6

The movie should play in the browser. The map does zoom in a bit fast; don't worry about this for now, we'll look at how to speed up and slow down an animation later.

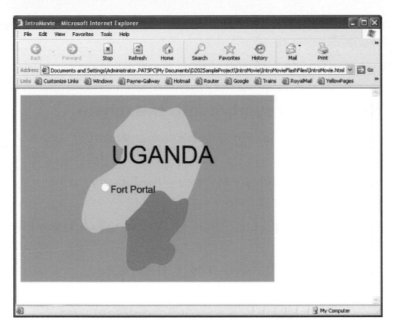

Figure 9.7

Publish Preview

You can preview what the published Flash (**.swf**) file will look like. This is useful because it is very quick and easy; Flash regenerates the published document and opens it.

 Back in Flash, select **File**, **Publish Preview**, **Flash** from the main menu bar. The document is shown on a separate sheet in Flash.

Figure 9.8

 To return to editing the movie, just click the **IntroMovie.fla** sheet tab at the top of the page. You can either leave the other sheet open or right-click its tab and then select **Close** from the menu that appears.

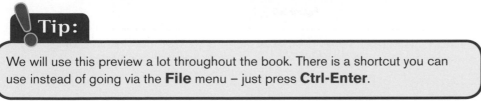

Tip:

We will use this preview a lot throughout the book. There is a shortcut you can use instead of going via the **File** menu – just press **Ctrl-Enter**.

 Save the **IntroMovie.fla** document by pressing **Ctrl-S** on the keyboard, then close it if this is the end of a session.

After zooming in to Uganda, we want to zoom in on a map of the school. The map we use for this is the one you created in Chapter 6.

 Open the **IntroMovie.fla** file if it is not already open.

Inserting the SchoolMap symbol into the movie

 Make sure the **Library** panel is visible. If it isn't, select **Window, Library** from the main menu bar.

 Open the **DrawingExercises.fla** file. Make sure the **Library** panel for this file is visible; select **Window, Library** from the main menu bar if it isn't.

 Click and drag the **SchoolMap** symbol from the **DrawingExercises Library** to the **IntroMovie Library**.

 Close the **DrawingExercises** file. Click **Yes** if you are asked whether you want to save changes.

 Create a new layer in **IntroMovie** and name it **SchoolMapLayer**.

 Right-click **Frame 10** of the **SchoolMapLayer** then select **Insert Keyframe** from the menu that appears.

 Click and drag the **SchoolMap** symbol from the **Library** onto the **Stage**. Use the arrow keys to position it centrally over the **Stage**.

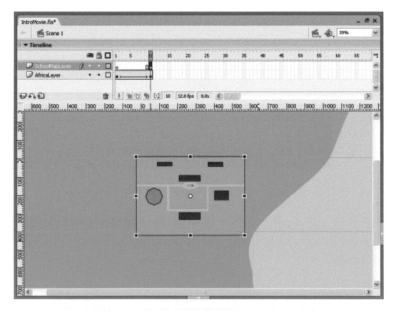

Figure 10.1

Editing the SchoolMap symbol

We will add some text to the **SchoolMap** symbol.

 In the **Library** panel, double-click the **SchoolMap** symbol to enter **Symbol edit** mode.

Tip:

There are two different ways to edit a symbol. Double-clicking an instance of a symbol on the **Stage** means that you can edit the symbol in place. Double-clicking a symbol in the **Library** edits the symbol on a blank **Stage**.

 Insert another layer named **Text**.

 Use the **Text** tool to add the labels shown below. You'll need to use a text size of about **12**.

Text Tool

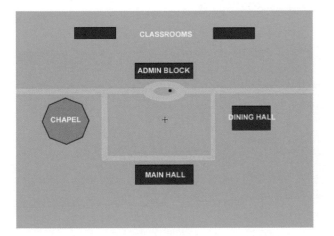

Figure 10.2

 Exit **Symbol edit** mode. The instance of the **SchoolMap** symbol on the **Stage** has been updated.

Fading in the school map

We'll use the **Alpha** value in the **Properties** panel to make the map change from transparent to opaque, to fade it in gradually.

 Insert another **keyframe** in the **SchoolMapLayer** in **Frame 15**. Insert a motion tween between **Frames 10** and **15**.

 Select **Frame 10** of **SchoolMapLayer** by clicking it in the **Timeline** panel. With the **Selection** tool, click once on the **SchoolMap** symbol on the **Stage** to select it.

 In the **Properties** panel, select **Alpha** from the **Color** menu.

Outline Icon

⊙ Type **0** into the **Alpha** value box (where it currently says **100%**).

⊙ Preview the fade by scrubbing the **playhead** over **Frames 10** to **15**.

We need the Uganda map to remain in the background whilst the school map is fading in.

⊙ In **AfricaLayer**, insert a **keyframe** in **Frame 15**.

⊙ In the **Timeline** panel, click the **Outline** icon next to **SchoolMapLayer**. This shows an outline of the contents of the layer and is useful for showing a layer when the contents have a low alpha value (i.e. are transparent).

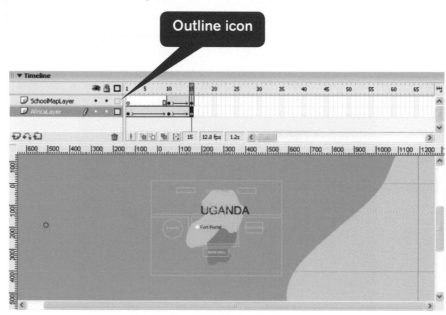

Figure 10.3

Free Transform Tool

⊙ In **Frame 10** of **SchoolMapLayer**, use the **Free Transform** tool (hold down the **Shift** key to retain the proportions) to shrink the map to just larger than the size of the white dot representing **Fort Portal**. (Use the **Zoom** tool to make this easier.)

⊙ Use the **Selection** tool to reposition the map over the white dot as shown in Figure 10.4.

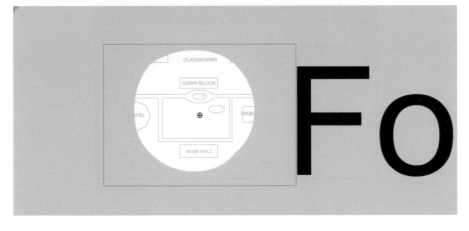

Figure 10.4

 Preview the map by pressing **Ctrl-Enter**. It goes too quickly so now we will slow down the animation.

Tip:

If you want the edges of the **SchoolMap** symbol to be less obvious when it is being tweened, go back and edit the **SchoolMap** symbol in **Symbol edit** mode and change the grass colour to match the green of the **Africa** symbol. Alternatively, you could delete the **Grass** layer in the **SchoolMap** symbol then add a **GreenRectangle** layer below the **SchoolMapLayer**; in this new layer you could add a green rectangle that fades in at the same time as the **SchoolMap** symbol.

 Press **Ctrl-S** to save the movie.

Slowing down an animation

The animation is a bit fast. There are two ways in which we can slow it down:

1   Edit the frame rate. However, this is not recommended. The frame rate should be left at the default of **12 fps** (frames per second), which is considered best for the Web and can be played on most computers.

2   Insert some **regular frames** between **keyframes**. This is a better way of slowing down a movie.

We will experiment first with changing the **frame rate**.

 Select **Modify**, **Document** from the main menu bar.

 Change the **Frame rate** to **8 fps**, as shown in Figure 10.5. Click **OK**.

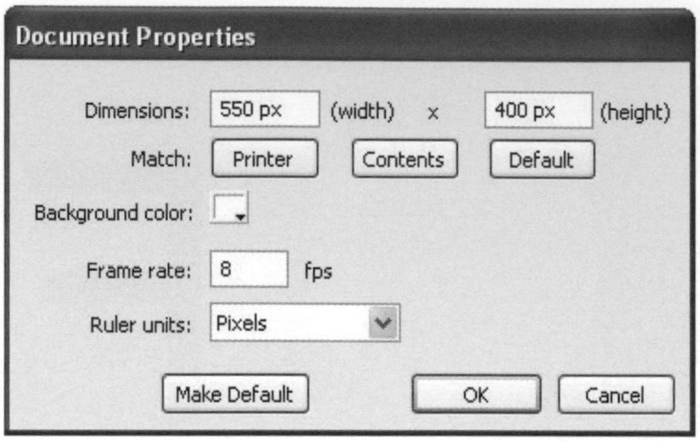
Document Properties
Dimensions: 550 px (width) x 400 px (height)
Match: Printer Contents Default
Background color:
Frame rate: 8 fps
Ruler units: Pixels
Make Default OK Cancel

Figure 10.5

- Zoom out if necessary and then play the movie again by selecting **Control**, **Play** from the main menu bar; it should be a bit slower now.
- Change the frame rate back to **12 fps**.

We'll now use the second method to slow down the movie, by inserting some **regular frames** between **keyframes**.

- Click where the red **playhead** sits above the **Timeline**, at **Frame 5**. Make sure that you click above the **Timeline**, not in an actual frame.

> **Tip:**
>
> If you have one frame selected (by clicking in a frame, not above the **Timeline**) when you press **F5** you will add a regular frame to the selected layer only. By clicking above the **Timeline** you will be adding frames to all the layers, which is what we want.

- Press **F5** (this is the shortcut to insert a regular frame).
- Press **F5** four more times so that you have inserted **five** regular frames in total.
- Repeat this between the other two keyframes in **Frame 15** and **Frame 20**, by first clicking above the **Timeline** in about **Frame 17**, and then adding five more regular frames.

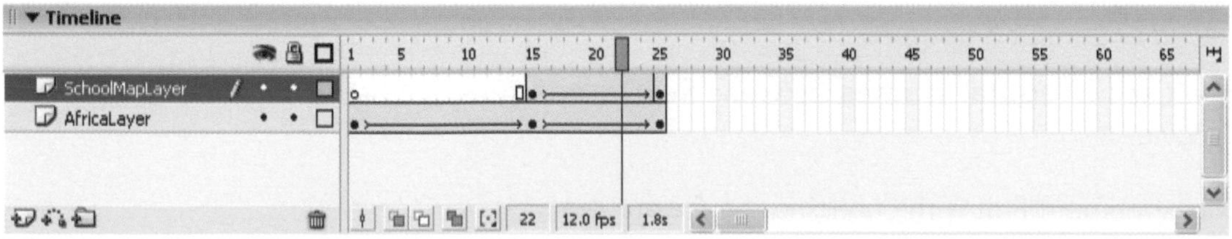
Timeline
SchoolMapLayer
AfricaLayer
22
12.0 fps
1.8s

Figure 10.6

Your movie should now be **25** frames long.

- Preview the movie by pressing **Ctrl-Enter**. Close the preview when you have finished watching it.

Taking screenshots for the eportfolio

Remember that you should be taking screenshots of the Flash workspace as you develop the project. These will be included in your eportfolio as evidence of development.

 Take a screenshot now of the Flash window (press **Alt-PrintScrn**). Paste it into a Word document then save it in the **IntroMovieDocumentation** folder as **Screenshots**.

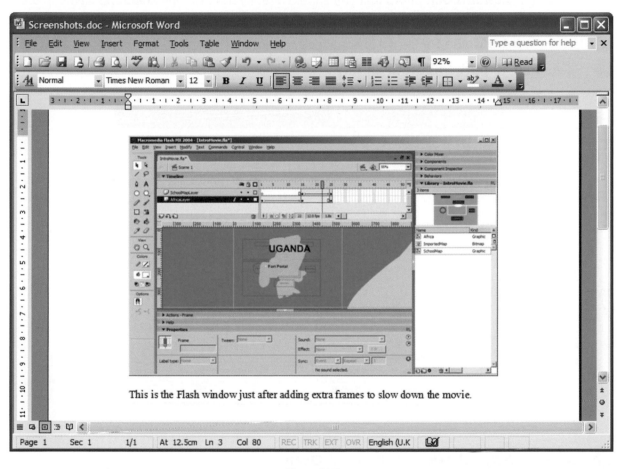

Figure 10.7

For the SPB: When you come to do your own project you should add some commentary to each screenshot to say when it was taken and to explain what you are doing in the screenshot. Collect some feedback at each stage and record the feedback with the screenshot. You will then be able to include the feedback and changes made to the eportfolio later.

 Save the movie then close it if this is the end of a session.

Chapter 11

– Importing, Optimising and Tweening Photographs

In this chapter we will insert a photograph of the front of the Admin block. The photo will be tweened so that it looks as though it comes spinning out of the Admin block rectangle on the school map.

Importing a photo

We'll import the **AdminBlock** photo that you should already have downloaded and saved in the **Components/Images** folder.

⦿ Open the **IntroMovie.fla** file if it is not already open.

⦿ Select **File**, **Import**, **Import to Library** from the main menu bar.

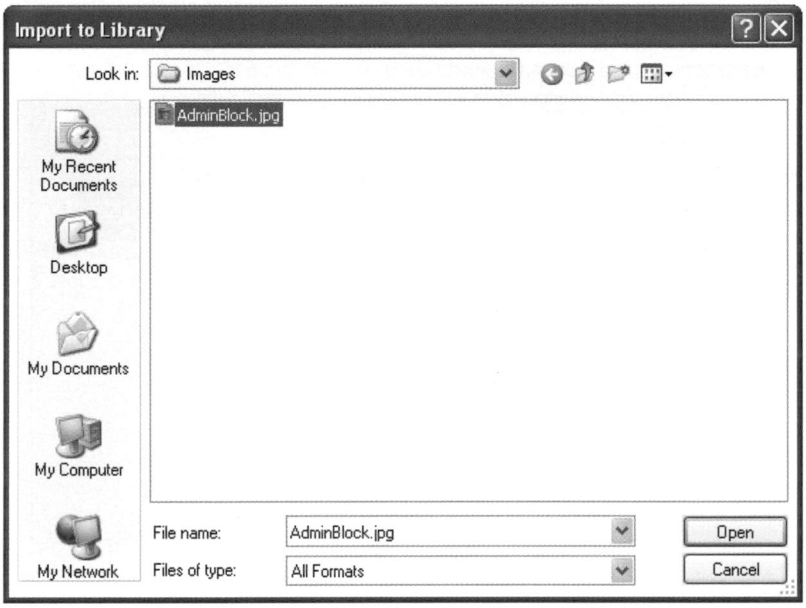

Figure 11.1

⦿ Locate the **AdminBlock** photo then click **Open**.

The photo appears in the **Library**.

Figure 11.2

 Lock the **SchoolMapLayer** in the **Timeline** panel.

 Create a new layer in the **Timeline** panel. Rename it **AdminBlockLayer** by double-clicking it then typing the new name. Make sure that the new layer is at the top of the list (click and drag it if necessary).

Editing photos with Fireworks

We will resize and optimise this photo using Fireworks.

 Right-click the **AdminBlock** photo in the **Library** and select **Edit with** Fireworks from the menu that appears. If you don't get this menu option, select **Edit with** then find the **Macromedia** folder in the **Program Files** folder. In the **Macromedia** folder double-click the Fireworks **MX 2004** folder then the **Fireworks.exe** file.

We will edit the file directly, as this file does not come from a **PNG** file.

Figure 11.3

 Click **Use This File**.

Figure 11.4

Crop Tool

If you can't see the whole photo, select **View**, **Zoom Out**. Repeat this until the whole photo is in view.

Click the **Crop** tool in the **Toolbox**.

Drag out a rectangle as shown in Figure 11.5. You can edit the crop by clicking and dragging the sides of the crop box.

Figure 11.5

 Press **Enter** to complete the crop.

Resizing a photo using Fireworks

The photo is too big. We will resize the photo to be just larger than the **Stage**. We could resize the photo using the **Free Transform** tool in Flash; however, this would be reducing the size of the image without benefiting from a reduction in file size.

First we'll look at how large the **Stage** is.

 Return to the Flash window. Click the **Selection** tool. Click in the **Stage** then press the **Escape** key to make sure nothing is selected. Look in the **Properties** panel.

Selection Tool

Figure 11.6

The **Stage** is **550** pixels wide by **400** pixels tall. We'll resize the photo to be **450** pixels tall, and however wide it needs to be to maintain its proportions.

 Return to Fireworks.

 Select **Modify**, **Canvas**, **Image Size** from the main menu bar in Fireworks.

- Make sure the **Constrain proportions** and **Resample image** boxes are ticked at the bottom of the **Image Size** window.

- Enter **450** in the second box, as shown in Figure 11.7, then click **OK**.

Image Size		

Pixel dimensions

↔ 665 Pixels

↕ 450| Pixels

Print size

↔ 9.235 Inches

↕ 6.25 Inches

Resolution: 72 Pixels/Inch

☑ Constrain proportions
☑ Resample image   Bicubic

OK   Cancel

Figure 11.7

Optimising a photo using the Export Wizard

You will need to use this same method to optimise your own photos and scanned images when you come to do your own project.

The **Export Wizard** guides you through optimising an image.

- Select **File**, **Export Wizard** from the main menu bar.

- Click the option to **Select an export format**. Click **Continue**.

- Select **The web** in the next window. Click **Continue**.

- The **Analysis Results** window will appear with some information about the file format it has selected. Click **Exit**.

 Tip:

The most common file format used for images on the web are **JPEG** and **GIF**. **JPEGs** are generally better for photos, and **GIFs** are good for images with continuous blocks of colour.

- The **Export Preview** dialogue will appear.

- The preview of the **JPEG** image is in the top window. Try changing the option from **JPEG – Better Quality** to **JPEG – Smaller File**.

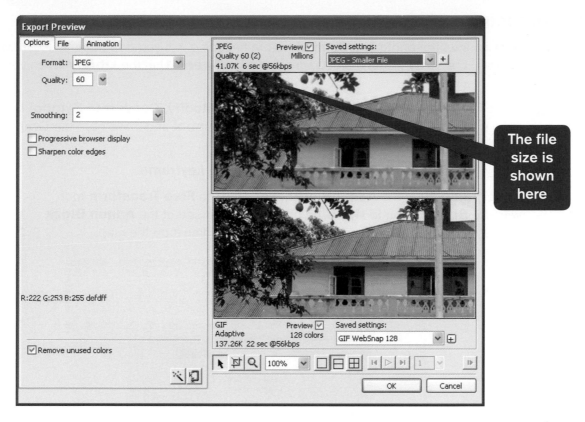

Figure 11.8

🔘 This still looks fine, and is half the file size of the **Better Quality** image. When you're happy with the optimised image, click **OK**.

Returning to Flash

🔘 Click where it says **Done** at the top of the screen.

| Done | 🔘 **Editing from Flash** |

Figure 11.9

You are returned to Flash.

🔘 Make **Frame 40** of the **SchoolMapLayer** a **keyframe**. This will ensure it remains in the background while the **AdminBlock** photo is tweened.

🔘 Make **Frame 30** of the **AdminBlockLayer** a **keyframe**. Click and drag the **AdminBlock** photo from the **Library** onto the **Stage**.

Tweening a photo

We'll first convert the photo to a **Symbol** before tweening it. If you don't do this Flash will automatically create a symbol (named something like **Tween 1**) in the **Library** when you insert the tween.

 Select the photo with the **Selection** tool. Select **Modify**, **Convert to Symbol** from the main menu bar. Name the symbol **AdminBlockSymbol** and make sure the **Graphic** symbol type is selected. Click **OK**.

 Now make **Frame 40** of the **AdminBlockLayer** a **keyframe**.

Free Transform Tool

 Click **Frame 30** of the **AdminBlockLayer**. Use the **Free Transform** tool with the **Scale** option to shrink the photo to be the size of the **Admin Block** on the school map. Use the **Selection** tool to position it on the map.

Scale Option

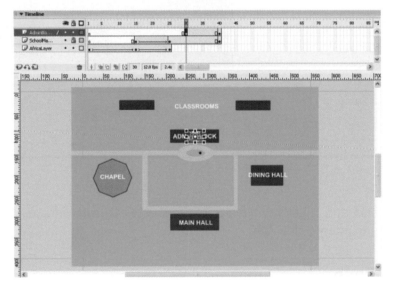

Figure 11.10

 Add a motion tween between **Frames 30** and **40** in the **AdminBlockLayer**.

> **Tip:**
>
> If your tween isn't working, just check some of the tween properties. Click a frame in the tween between the two **keyframes**. In the **Properties** panel, make sure that the **Scale** box is ticked.

We will now create the effect of the **AdminBlock** photo spinning out of the admin block on the **SchoolMap** symbol.

 In the **AdminBlockLayer** select a regular frame in the tween (between **Frames 30** and **40**). In the **Properties** panel select **CW** from the **Rotate** list (see Figure 11.11). Preview the rotation by scrubbing the **playhead**.

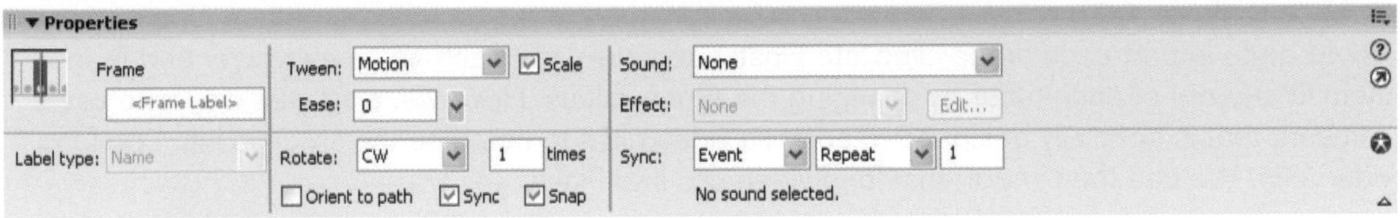

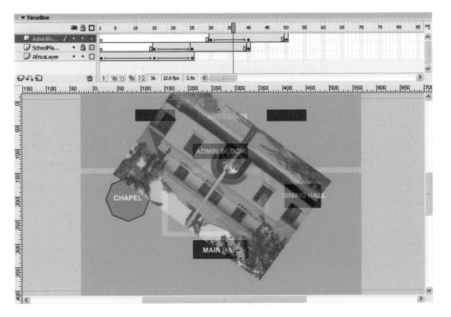

Figure 11.11

Tip:

You can make the photo rotate any number of times by changing the number in the **times** box next to the **Rotate** option in the **Properties** panel.

Now we'll fade in the photo at the same time as it rotates.

- Select **Frame 30** of the **AdminBlockLayer**, then click the **AdminBlock** photo on the **Stage** using the **Selection** tool. In the **Properties** panel, change the **Alpha** value to **0%**.

Selection Tool

- Add another **keyframe** in the **AdminBlock** layer in **Frame 50** so that the **AdminBlock** photo stays for a few seconds.

- Save and preview the movie so far. The **AdminBlock** photo should rotate and fade in.

Figure 11.12

- Close the **IntroMovie** if this is the end of a session, or leave it open for the next chapter.

In the IntroMovie there are six short video clips that need to be compiled together. One option would be to import each of the clips into Flash separately, put each on its own layer and fade them in and out of each other by changing the Alpha values. However, a simpler way is to use software that is specially designed to compile video clips to combine the six clips into one long video clip. We can then import that long video clip into Flash.

The software we will use for this is free software called Windows Movie Maker that comes with Windows XP.

Do you already have Windows Movie Maker?

You need to check if you have Windows Movie Maker, and also if you have the most up-to-date version.

 Click the **Start** button at the bottom left of your screen. Click **All Programs**. Windows Movie Maker should be listed in this menu. If you can't see it in the main list it may be under **Accessories**, **Entertainment**.

Figure 12.1

 Click it to open it.

In Windows Movie Maker, select **Help**, **About Windows Movie Maker** from the main menu bar.

Figure 12.2

 Look where it lists the **Version** number on the fourth line (not the second) – you want it to start with a **2**. If it doesn't, just follow the instructions below to download the latest version. Click **OK** to close the window.

Updating Windows Movie Maker

 Select **Help, Windows Movie Maker on the Web** from the main menu bar.

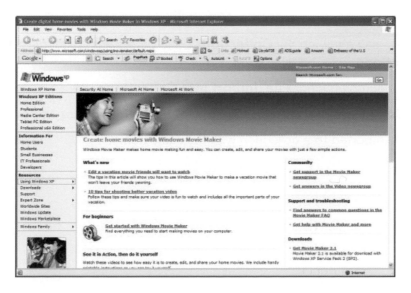

Figure 12.3

 Click where it says **Get Movie Maker 2.1** on the right of the screen.

⊙ You will need to download it as part of **Windows Service Pack 2**; it was developed and tested as part of Service Pack 2 so it is not possible to download it without **SP2**. Follow the instructions on-screen to download **SP2** with Windows Movie Maker **2.1**.

⊙ Open up Windows Movie Maker once it is installed.

Importing the video clips

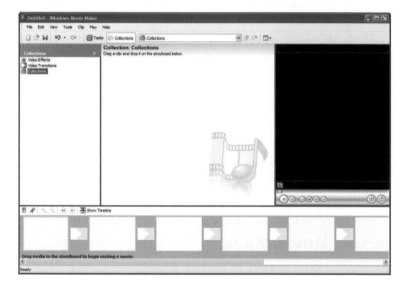

Figure 12.4

⊙ If your window isn't showing the **Collections** pane on the left (see Figure 12.4) then select **View**, **Collections** from the main menu bar.

⊙ On the main menu bar select **File**, **Import into Collections**.

⊙ Locate the **Components/Videos** folder. Select **Video1** then click **Import**.

The **Video1** clip is imported to a collection with the same name.

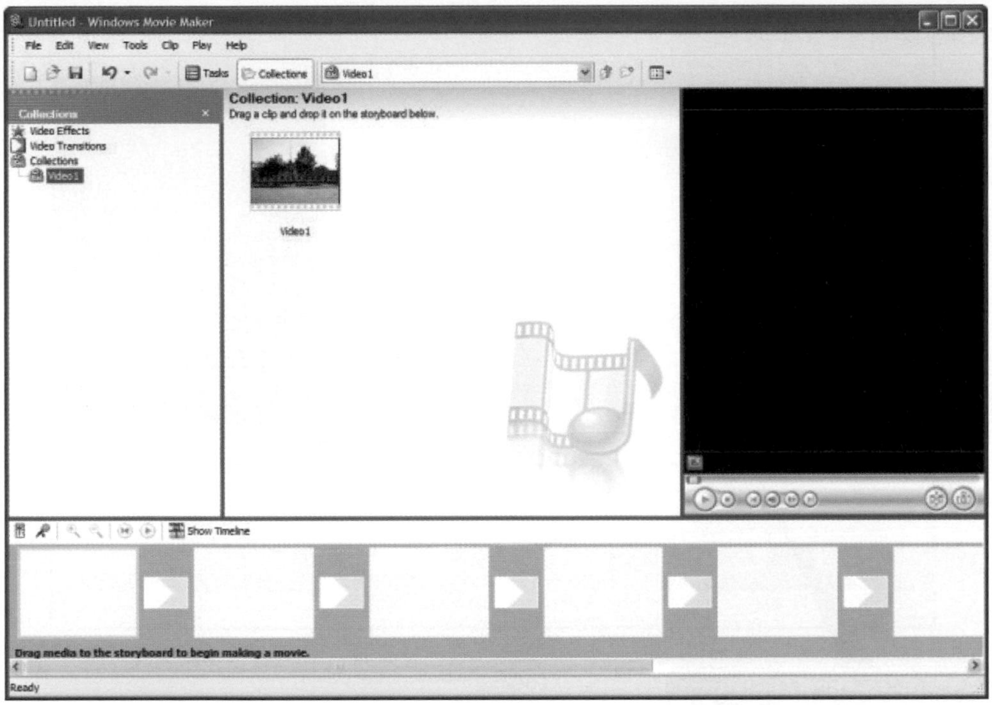

Figure 12.5

Click the thumbnail to preview the movie in the right-hand window. You can play the movie here by using the controls at the bottom of the right-hand window.

Importing the other video clips

Repeat this to import the other five video clips (select **File**, **Import into Collections** from the main menu bar – you can hold down the **Ctrl** key to select more than one file to import at once).

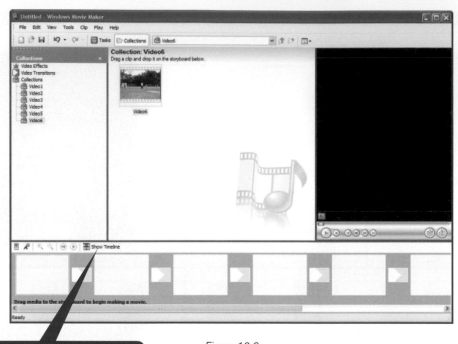

Figure 12.6

If you don't currently have the Storyboard displayed there will be an option here to Show Storyboard. Click this.

Compiling the video clips

We'll start by compiling the clips into one long movie, and then apply transitions between the clips. We will also do some editing of individual clips to shorten them and rotate them.

🔘 Make sure you have the movie storyboard visible at the bottom of the window (your screen should look like Figure 12.6). If you don't, click where it says **Show Storyboard**.

🔘 In the left-hand window, where the **Collections** are listed, click **Video1**.

🔘 Now click and drag the **Video1** thumbnail and drop it in the first white box in the **Storyboard** at the bottom of the screen.

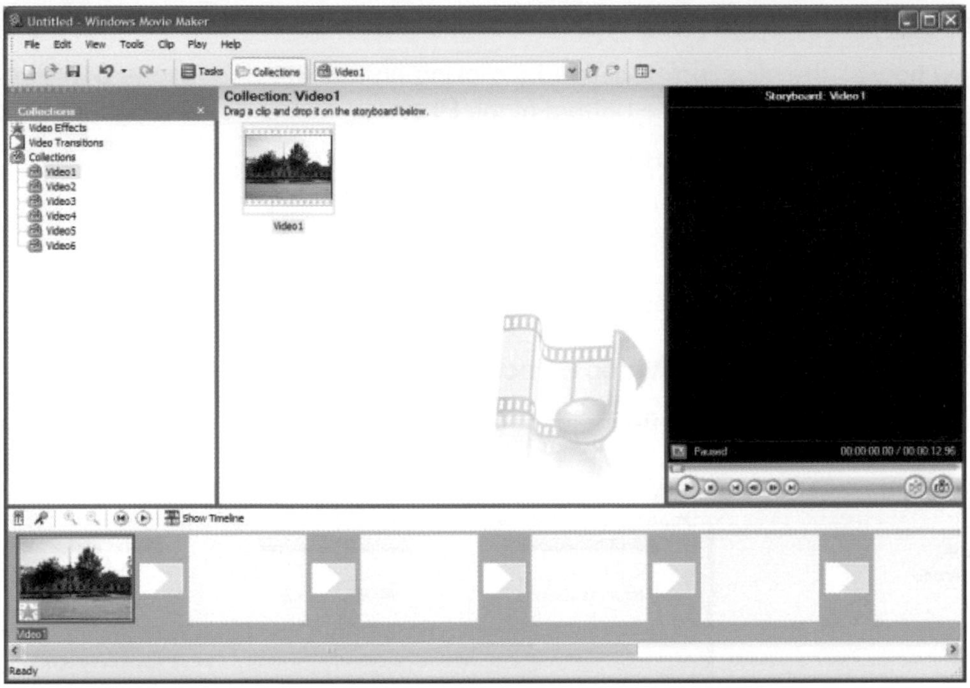

Figure 12.7

The thumbnail of **Video1** is now shown in the **Storyboard**.

- Repeat this for **Video2**, dragging and dropping the thumbnail onto the second box in the **Storyboard**.

- Add the remaining videos in order.

Figure 12.8

- Save the file by selecting **File**, **Save Project** from the main menu bar. Save the file in the **Components/Videos** folder as **VideoCompilation**.

Previewing the compilation

Play Button

 Preview how all the clips look together by clicking on the first video in the **Storyboard**, then pressing the **Play** button at the bottom of the **Preview** window on the right of the screen.

There is a lot that still needs to be done!

Rotating video clips

The second clip needs to be rotated 90 degrees.

 In the left-hand window, click **Video Effects**.

 Find the effect called **Rotate 90**.

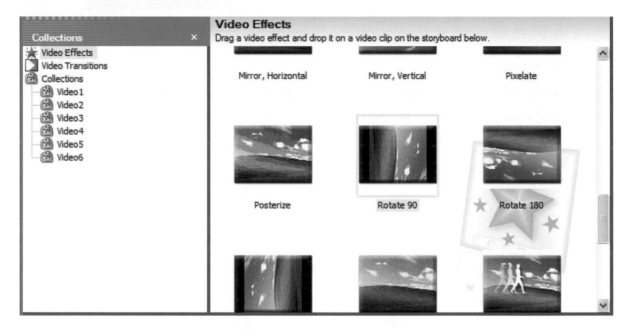

Figure 12.9

 Click and drag this effect onto the **Video2** thumbnail in the **Storyboard**. The thumbnail in the **Storyboard** won't show the rotation but you will see it is rotated in the **Preview** window. The star icon will turn blue to show that a video effect has been applied.

 Repeat this for **Video4**.

 Tip:

Notice that the rotated clips now have black space on each side; there is no way to prevent this. It is a good idea when you come to take your own video footage that you stick to only landscape movies. Landscape movies are much better because they match the proportions of the Flash movie they will be inserted into.

Editing clips using the Timeline

Windows Movie Maker has a **Timeline** similar to Flash. It is slightly simpler to use as you've only got to worry about one layer and it is very easy to see what is happening in each frame.

⦿ To view the **Timeline**, click where it says **Show Timeline** above the **Storyboard**.

The **Storyboard** is now replaced with the **Timeline**.

Figure 12.10

⦿ To expand the **Timeline** to make the shorter clips easier to see, click the **Zoom Timeline In** icon above the **Timeline** twice.

Zoom Timeline In Icon

Figure 12.11

We only really want less than half of **Video1**; we'll edit it now.

⦿ If you can't see **Video1**, use the scroll bar at the bottom of the **Timeline** panel to scroll left. Click to select **Video1**.

⦿ Click and drag the end of **Video1** to the left as shown in Figure 12.12.

Figure 12.12

In the sports videos, you want to make sure you are capturing the action and deleting the parts where nothing is happening. You can use scrubbing just like you did in Flash; just click and drag the blue **playhead** to preview the video frame by frame. It's a good idea to do this before you edit a clip.

- Go through the other clips and edit them by dragging and dropping the start or end of each clip. Remember to first select a clip before you click and drag the edges.

- If you cut a clip more than you mean to, just click and drag to expand the clip again.

- Your finished video should be no longer than about 30 seconds. You can see the length of your video by looking at the bottom of the **Preview** window.

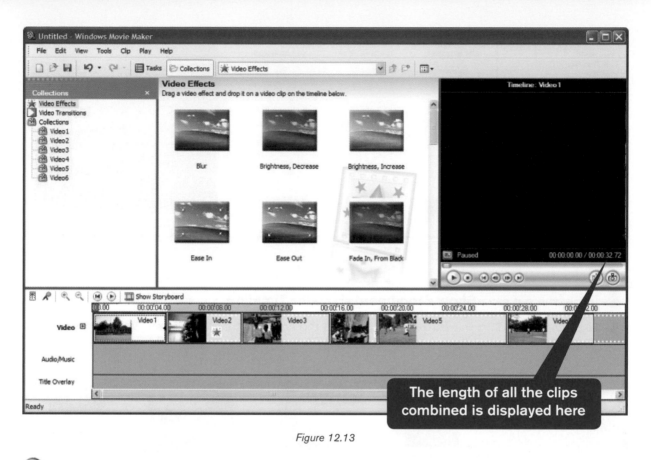

Figure 12.13

⦿ Save the file by selecting **File**, **Save Project** from the main menu bar. Alternatively you can just press **Ctrl-S**.

⦿ Preview the movie on a full screen by first clicking the first clip in the **Timeline** then selecting **View**, **Full Screen** from the main menu bar. To return to Movie Maker just click the mouse on the screen. The video will look a bit pixellated because it is being shown on too large a screen; don't worry about this as it will be much smaller when it is imported into the **IntroMovie**.

Adding transitions

This is the fun bit. At the moment, each clip is played one after the other with no fading or special effects when the scene changes from one clip to another. We'll add some more interesting transitions now.

⦿ In the left-hand window, click **Video Transitions**. There's a lot to choose from here!

⦿ Find the **Fade** transition.

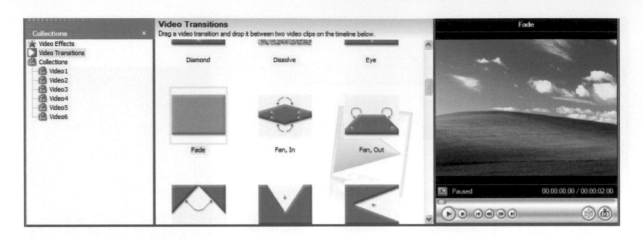

Figure 12.14

⊙ Click where it says **Show Storyboard** above the **Timeline**.

⊙ Now click and drag the **Fade** transition onto the small rectangle between **Video1** and **Video2**.

Figure 12.15

⊙ The icon for the **Fade** transition is now displayed in that rectangle.

⊙ Select a different transition then drag and drop it to the transition area between **Video2** and **Video3**.

⊙ Add a transition between all the remaining clips. Don't get too carried away though; sometimes the best effect is achieved by just using the simplest **Fade** transition.

Fading out the compilation

⊙ Fade out **Video6** by right-clicking it in the **Storyboard** then selecting **Fade Out** from the menu that appears.

⊙ Preview the compilation. If you want to change any of the transitions just click and drag a different transition into the rectangle between two clips.

⊙ Press **Ctrl-S** to save.

Exporting the movie as a WMV file

As it stands, the movie is a Movie Maker file, which is a file format that you cannot import into Flash. We'll export the movie as a **WMV** file, which Flash does support.

 Select **File**, **Save Movie File** from the main menu bar.

 Leave the first option (**My computer**) selected then click **Next**.

 Leave the file name as **VideoCompilation**. Click the **Browse** button to select the **Components/Videos** folder and click **OK**. Click **Next**.

 In the next window select the option **Best quality for playback on my computer**.

> **! Tip:**
>
> You could compress the video here by clicking **More Options**. Because you will be importing the video into Flash, you should keep the file as the best quality file you can and then let Flash do all the work compressing the movie when it is imported.

Save Movie Wizard ☒

Movie Setting
Select the setting you want to use to save your movie. The setting you select determines the quality and file size of your saved movie.

⊙ Best quality for playback on my computer (recommended)
Show more choices...

Setting details

File type: Windows Media Video (WMV)
Bit rate: 2.1 Mbps
Display size: 640 x 480 pixels
Aspect ratio: 4:3
Frames per second: 25

Movie file size

Estimated space required:
6.97 MB

Estimated disk space available on drive C:
52.86 GB

[< Back] [Next >] [Cancel]

Figure 12.16

 Click **Next**. The movie will take a minute or two to save.

 Leave the option **Play movie when I click Finish** selected then click **Finish**.

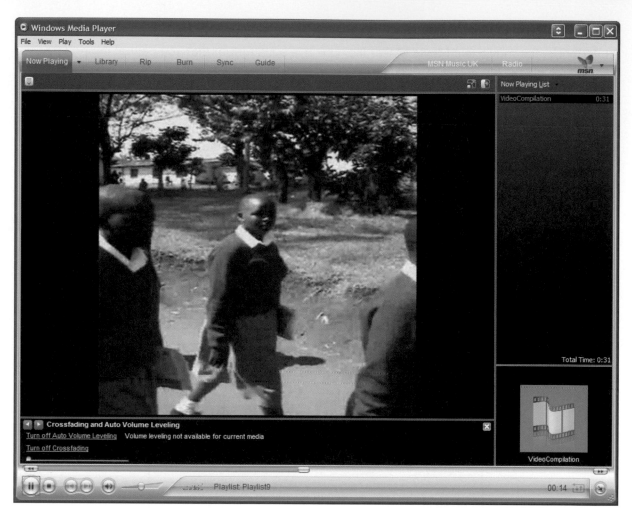

Figure 12.17

Close Icon

Return to Movie Maker. Select **File**, **Save Project** from the main menu bar.

Close Windows Movie Maker either by selecting **File**, **Exit** from the main menu bar or by selecting the red **Close** icon in the top right of the window.

Chapter 13 – Inserting a Movie Clip and Adding Sound

Importing the movie clip to the Library

The next step is to import the compiled movie clip that you created in Windows Movie Maker.

- ⊙ Open Flash and the **IntroMovie** file.
- ⊙ Create a new layer called **VideoLayer**. Position this above the other layers.
- ⊙ Make **Frame 50** of the **VideoLayer** layer a **keyframe**.
- ⊙ Select **File**, **Import**, **Import to Library** from the main menu bar.
- ⊙ Find the file **VideoCompilation**; it should be in the **Components/Videos** folder.

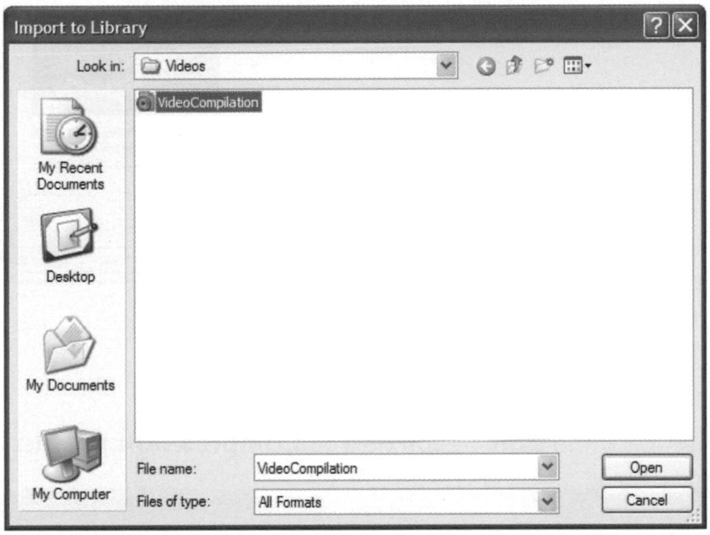

Figure 13.1

- ⊙ Select the file and click **Open**.

The **Video Import** wizard appears.

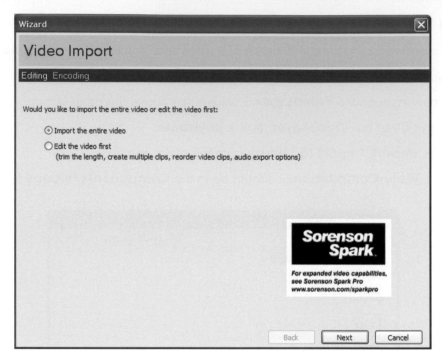

Figure 13.2

🔘 Make sure the first option is selected then click **Next**.

🔘 In the next window, click the **Edit** button next to **Compression profile**.

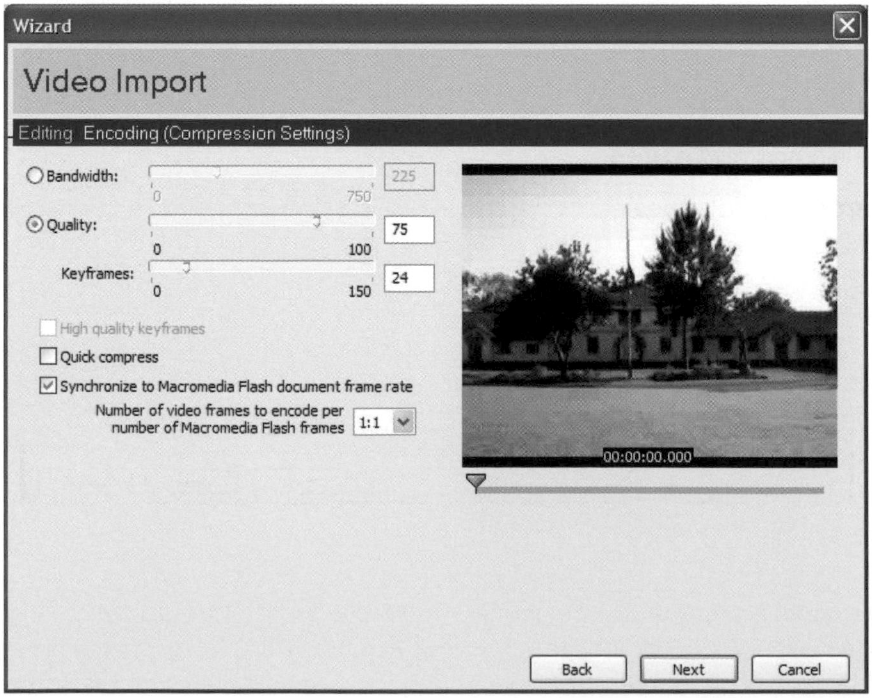

Figure 13.3

Click the **Quality** option and drag the slider next to it; look at the image on the right of the window to see how it degrades when the quality is low. You need to set the quality as low as possible before the image on the right looks unacceptably degraded. A quality of **75** is probably about right.

> **Tip:**
>
> The lower the **Quality** setting, the smaller the Flash file size will be when you import the video. The smaller the file size, the shorter the download times – and the less chance you'll exceed the file size allowance for your eportfolio!

Change the other settings in this window to look like Figure 13.3. Click **Next**.

Click **Next** again.

Now under **Advanced Settings** select **Create New Profile** from the drop-down list.

Click the arrow next to **Scale**. Click and drag the **Scale** slider until the size of the movie is just larger than the size of the **Stage** (which is width **550** and height **400**).

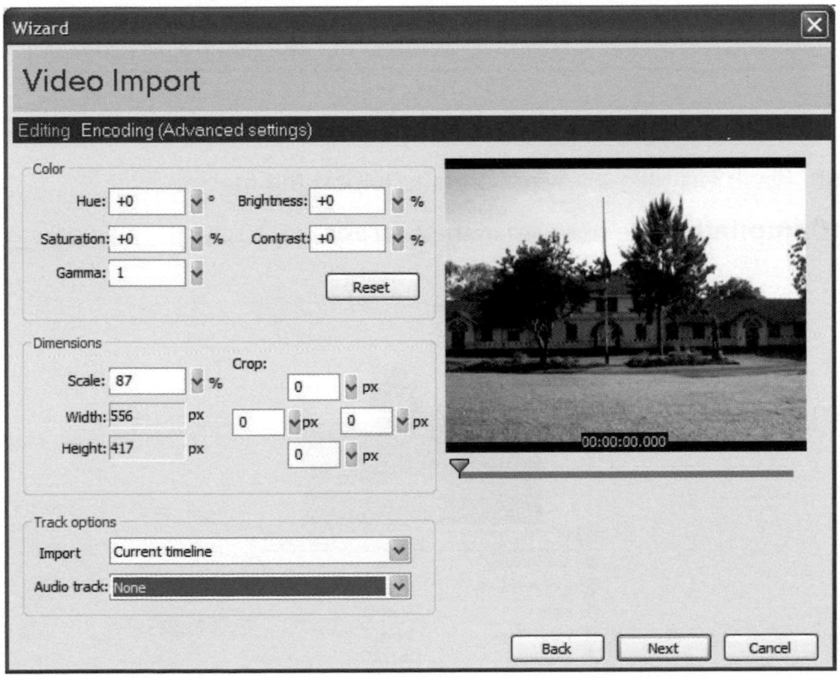

Figure 13.4

You should select **None** under **Audio track** at the bottom of the window. This is because we will add one sound track of pupils singing over the whole **IntroMovie** later. If you leave the audio track of the video it will interfere with the sound track when we come to add it.

Make sure the other settings match those in Figure 13.4, then click **Next**.

 Enter **Video** as the profile name in the next window, then click **Next**.

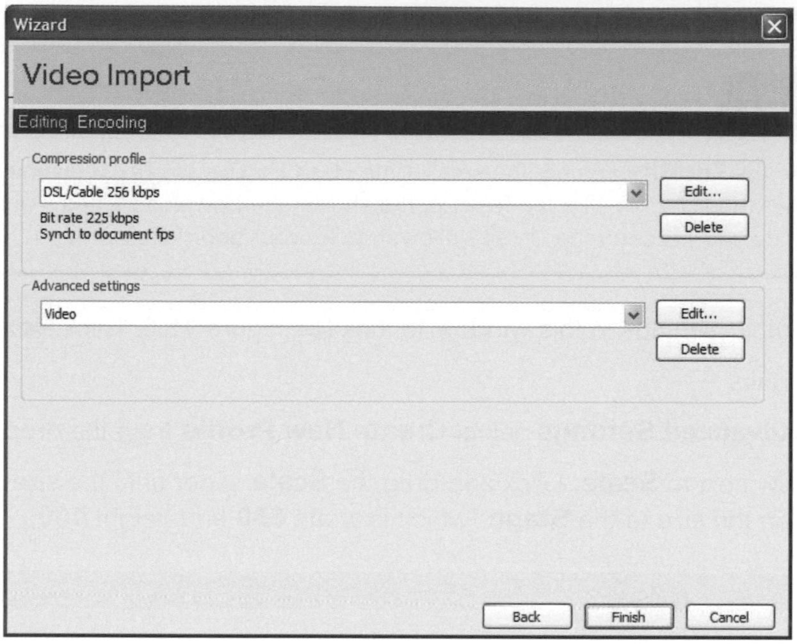

Wizard	☒

Video Import

Editing Encoding

Compression profile

DSL/Cable 256 kbps ⌄   Edit...

Bit rate 225 kbps
Synch to document fps   Delete

Advanced settings

Video ⌄   Edit...

Delete

Back   Finish   Cancel

Figure 13.5

 Click **Finish**. Flash will take a few seconds to import the movie.

 The **VideoCompilation** file appears in the **Library**.

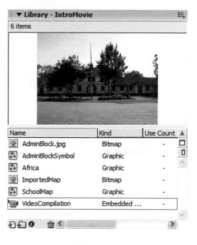

Figure 13.6

Inserting the video

 Select **Frame 50** of the **VideoLayer**. Click and drag the **VideoCompilation** from the **Library** onto the **Stage**.

Figure 13.7

 You will be asked if you want frames automatically inserted into the timeline. Click **Yes**.

Figure 13.8

 Use the arrow keys to centre the video on the **Stage**. Save then preview the movie by pressing **Ctrl-Enter**.

 Tip:

If you're not happy with the quality of the video you should delete the **VideoCompilation** currently in the **Library** then re-import the video with a higher **Quality** setting. You'll need to run through the steps above to insert the movie on to the **Stage** again.

Fading in the movie

At the moment, the movie starts quite abruptly. We'll fade in the movie by moving the **AdminBlockLayer** above the **VideoLayer** then fading out the **AdminBlock** photo, leaving the video behind.

Tip:

It isn't possible to change the **Alpha** value of an embedded video. If you want to change the **Alpha** value of a video you must first make it a **Movie clip** symbol. You will learn how to do this when you create your virtual tour.

- Close the preview by right-clicking the **IntroMovie.swf** page tab at the top of the screen then clicking **Close** from the menu that appears.

- Click and drag the **AdminBlockLayer** above the **VideoLayer** in the **Timeline** panel.

- Insert a **keyframe** in **Frame 55** of the **AdminBlockLayer**.

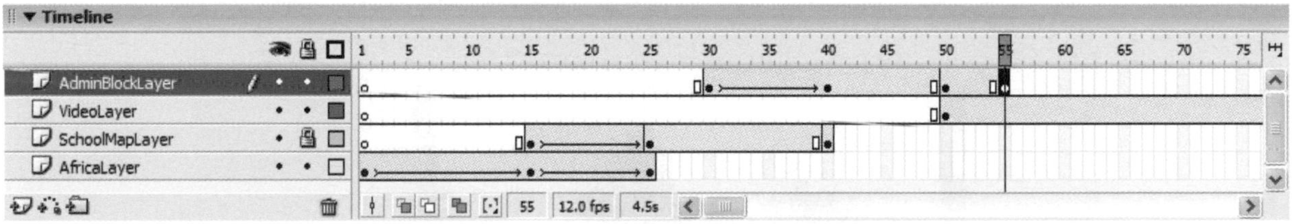

Figure 13.9

- With **Frame 55** of the **AdminBlockLayer** still selected, click to select the **AdminBlockPhoto** on the **Stage**.

- Change the **Alpha** value in the **Properties** panel to be **0%** (you'll need to first select **Alpha** from the **Color** menu in the **Properties** panel).

- Insert a **Motion Tween** between **Frame 50** and **Frame 55** in the **AdminBlockLayer**.

- Save then preview the movie.

The **AdminBlockPhoto** fades out a little too quickly. We can extend the time it takes to fade by simply moving the last **keyframe** in the **AdminBlockLayer** from **Frame 55** to **Frame 60**.

In the **Timeline** panel, click to select **Frame 55** of the **AdminBlockLayer**. Now click and drag the frame along to **Frame 60**.

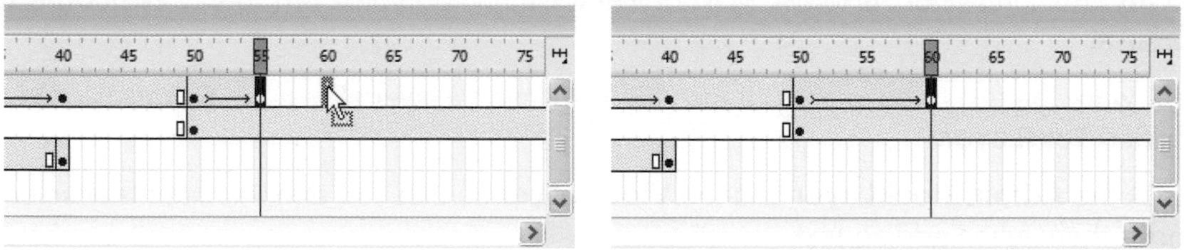

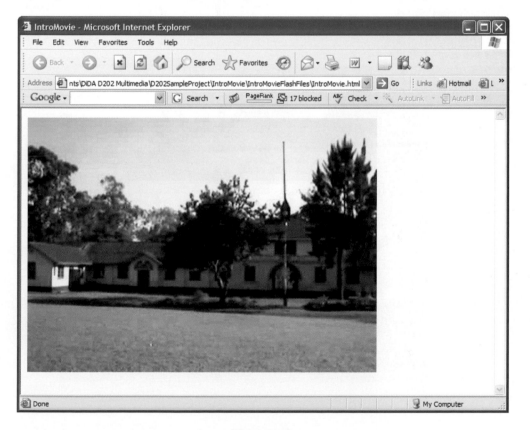

Figure 13.10

Save the movie.

Publish the movie by selecting **File**, **Publish** from the main menu bar.

This time preview the **HTML** file by finding it in Windows Explorer (it should be in your **IntroMovieFlashFiles** folder) then double-clicking it. You might need to click at the top of Internet Explorer to **Allow Blocked Content**.

Figure 13.11

Finishing off the movie

The video will fade out at the end of the compilation (if it doesn't it's because you didn't add the **Fade Out** effect in Windows Movie Maker). We will then add some text to say **Welcome to Nyakasura**.

 We want the text to be in front of the video, so insert a layer above the **AdminBlockLayer** named **TextLayer**.

 Lock the **AdminBlockLayer** and the **VideoLayer** so that you don't accidentally select or move them when adding text.

🔘 In the **TextLayer** insert a **keyframe** in the tenth frame from the end.

🔘 In the **keyframe**, write **Welcome to Nyakasura** in the centre of the **Stage** using the **Text** tool. Match the text colour to the green of the grass in the video. You can use the **Bold style** button in the **Properties** panel to make the name **Nyakasura** stand out.

Text Tool

B

Bold Style

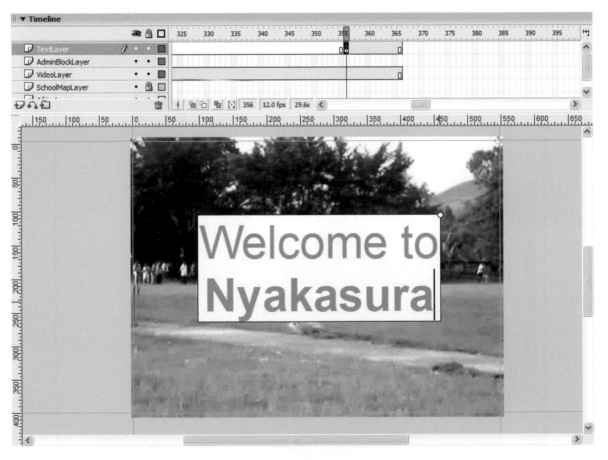

Figure 13.12

Fading in the text

In order to fade in the text, you need to first make the text a symbol.

 Select the text on the **Stage** with the **Selection** tool.

 Select **Modify**, **Convert to Symbol** from the main menu bar. Enter **FinalText** as the symbol name and make it a **Graphic** symbol. Click **OK**.

Selection Tool

Figure 13.13

 Insert a **keyframe** in the final frame of the **TextLayer**.

 Change the **Alpha** value of the text in the **keyframe** in the tenth frame from the end to **0%**. Add a motion tween so that the text fades in smoothly.

 Save and publish the movie.

 Preview the HTML file in Internet Explorer.

Figure 13.14

Stopping the movie looping

The movie previews fine, but it loops continuously if Flash Player's **Loop** option is set. We need to add a **Stop** command to stop this.

 Insert a new layer and name it **Actions**.

 Select the last frame in the **Actions** layer (the last frame in the movie). Make this frame a **keyframe**.

 Expand the **Actions** panel (it should be above the **Properties** panel); if you can't see it then select **Window**, **Development Panels**, **Actions** from the main menu bar.

 Type **stop()** into the **Actions** panel.

Figure 13.15

Further editing

If you like, you can edit the movie further. The start of the movie could be slowed down a little more by adding some more **regular frames** between **keyframes**. You could even pause the initial tween once Africa is the size of the **Stage** (to do this, add two **keyframes** in the middle of the tween then insert regular frames between them).

There are lots of other things you could change or add to the movie if you have time. Just play around and if you don't like the results, select **File**, **Revert** from the main menu bar to revert to the last saved version.

Adding a sound track

At the moment, there is no sound in the movie. We will add a sound track of some pupils singing, which lasts the length of the **IntroMovie**.

 Select **File**, **Import**, **Import to Library** from the main menu bar.

 Find and select the **Singing.mp3** file in the **Components/Sounds** folder, then click **Open**.

The **Singing** file appears in the **Library**. Click to select the file in the **Library**. Notice that the sound is shown as a sound wave in the preview window in the **Library**.

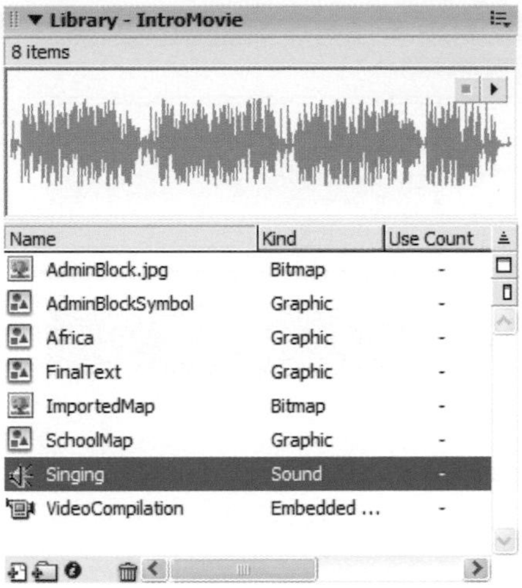

Figure 13.16

● Play the sound by clicking the **Play** button in the preview window in the **Library** panel. Stop it by clicking the **Stop** button.

● Create a new layer called **SoundTrack** in the **Timeline** panel.

● Select **Frame 1** of the new layer. Click and drag the **Singing** file from the **Library** then drop it anywhere on the **Stage**.

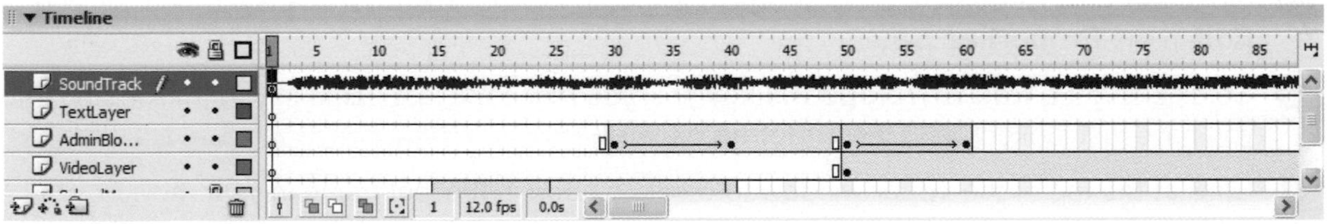

Play Button

Stop Button

Figure 13.17

● Click to select **Frame 1** of the **SoundTrack** layer, if it is not already selected, then click the **Edit** button in the **Properties** panel.

The **Edit Envelope** window appears, as shown in Figure 13.18. The two windows represent the right and left channels; we will edit both channels equally so that the volume will be the same through each speaker.

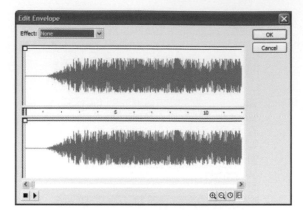

Figure 13.18

Frames Icon

 At the moment, the axis is showing seconds; it would be more helpful to view it as **Frames**. Click the **Frames** icon at the bottom right of the window.

Fading out a sound

We will edit the sound so that it fades out as the **IntroMovie** ends.

 First we'll look at how many frames long your movie is. First click **OK** to close the **Edit Envelope** window. Look in the **Timeline** panel and remember the number of the last frame.

 Open the **Edit Envelope** window again by clicking in the **SoundTrack** layer then clicking **Edit** in the **Properties** panel.

 Scroll along the **Edit Envelope** window until you reach the last frame in your movie (the one you have just looked up in the **Timeline** panel).

 Click at the top of the upper window to create a node in the last frame in your movie.

 Click twice on the **Zoom Out** icon at the bottom of the window.

Zoom Out Icon

 Now click to make a second node at **twenty five** frames from the end of your movie.

 Click and drag the last node to the baseline; repeat for the lower window.

 Tip:

To make the fade happen over a longer time you would click the left-hand node and drag it to the left.

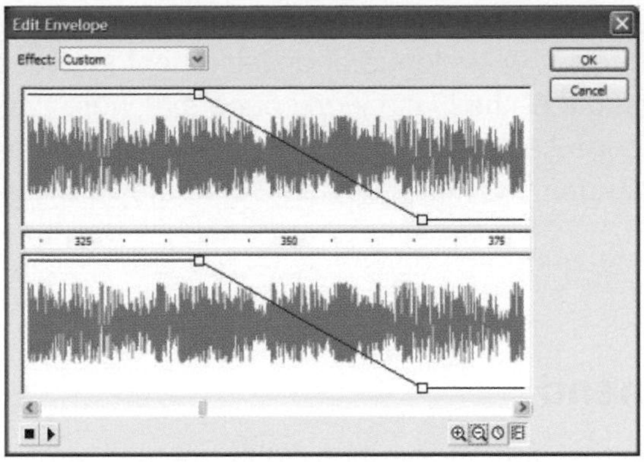

Figure 13.19

▶ Click **OK**.

▶ To listen to the sound you need to preview the movie. Press **Ctrl-Enter** to preview the **IntroMovie** with sound.

▶ If you want to edit the sound further, just click a frame in the **SoundTrack** layer then click **Edit** in the **Properties** panel to open the **Edit Envelope** window.

▶ Save the **IntroMovie**.

Tip:

If you edit the movie to make it longer, you will need to extend the **SoundTrack** layer. To do this, click to select the last frame in the **SoundTrack** layer in the **Timeline** panel. Now click and drag the frame to be level with the last frame in the movie. You will also need to edit the sound using the **Edit Envelope** window as shown above.

Further sound editing

▶ You will notice that the singing doesn't end in a natural place. Play around with the nodes in the **Edit Envelope** window to make the sound end in a better place. This will probably mean there is some silence at the end of the movie; you could add your own sound here.

▶ It would be quite effective to start the sound at the start of the movie but not the animation, so that you hear the sound for a couple of seconds before you see the Africa map. Do this by inserting some regular frames on every layer except the **SoundTrack** layer and the **AfricaLayer** at the start of the movie. For the **AfricaLayer**, make sure none of the frames in that layer is selected. Click and drag from the first to the last frame in the layer to select both tweens. Now click and drag the selection to the right until it lines up with the other layers as it did before you inserted the regular frames. Insert another layer with just a black background that fades leaving the Africa map.

131

For the SPB: You need to show evidence of development in your eportfolio. This means including screenshots of the Flash workspace that were saved at varying stages of development in the eportfolio. You should also get feedback at each stage and record the feedback and the changes you made as a result so they can later be added to the eportfolio.

Test, review and amend

It is really important that you test your movie thoroughly yourself, and also get feedback from others.

Good marks... ✓

You will get good marks if you:

- create a detailed storyboard that sets out exactly what will be in the movie;
- use different types of multimedia components in the movie;
- test out different designs and seek feedback as you go along, and record the feedback for the eportfolio;
- use the feedback to make positive changes to your movie, and record the changes you make for the eportfolio;
- collect evidence of development by taking screenshots as you create the movie.

Bad marks... ✗

You will lose marks if:

- your movie varies significantly from your plan;
- you do not use your storyboard when creating the movie, or your movie varies significantly from it;
- you do not get feedback, or do not use the feedback to make changes to your movie;
- the different scenes of the movie don't go well together or the transitions between them are clumsy.

For the SPB: You should update your plan as you go along. It is likely you will need to move things around or change some of the timescales. Make sure you keep a copy of the original plan as well as subsequent versions to include in the eportfolio.

Section Three
THE VIRTUAL TOUR

The virtual tour will be an interactive map of the school. Users will click on an area of the school they are interested in and they will be taken to another page which explains that area in more detail. We'll create the virtual tour in Flash.

Researching other virtual tours

It's important to look at other good examples in order to get a good idea of what can be achieved, what works well and to get lots of ideas for your own tour before you begin.

Take a look at the following websites to give you some ideas:

http://www.sydneyoperahouse.com/sections/tours/virtual_tour/

http://www.chem.ox.ac.uk/oxfordtour/lmh/

http://www.chem.ox.ac.uk/oxfordtour/citymap.html

http://www.thefull360.co.uk/demo.htm

http://www.bbc.co.uk/history/multimedia_zone/virtual_tours/

http://www.whitehouse.gov/history/whtour/

There are many more examples on the web: try searching for more tours using Google.

Think about the techniques used in each of the websites above. Ask yourself the following questions:

- Which tour do you like best? Why?
- How easy is the tour to use?
- Does it give a clear impression of the area?
- Which types of components are used in each tour – text, photos, animation, video, sound?
- How easy would the tour be to navigate if it was in a different language? How reliant is the tour on text?
- Which techniques would you like to use in your tour?

Before implementing the virtual tour you have to produce a storyboard of all the screens and a structure chart of how they are linked together.

For the SPB: You will have to submit your structure chart and storyboard as part of your eportfolio, and will lose marks if you do not submit them or if your finished virtual tour varies significantly from the planned structure. You can draw them on paper then scan them in, or, if you'd prefer, draw them straight on the computer. You can download blank sheets for the structure chart and storyboard from **www.payne-gallway.co.uk/didaD202**.

Here is the structure chart and three storyboard sheets for the sample project:

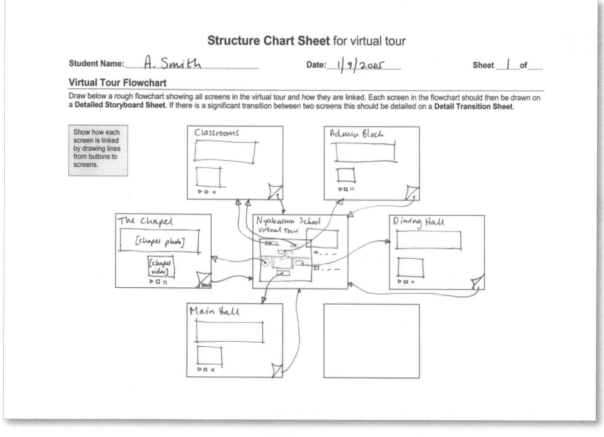

Figure 14.1

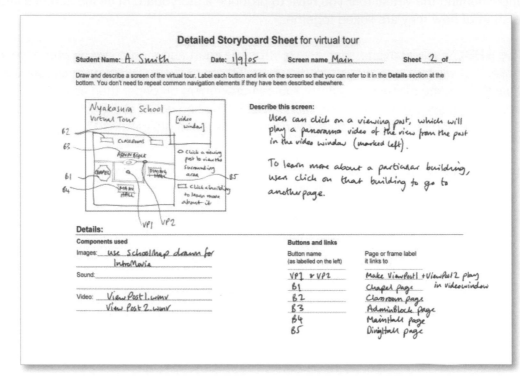

Figure 14.2

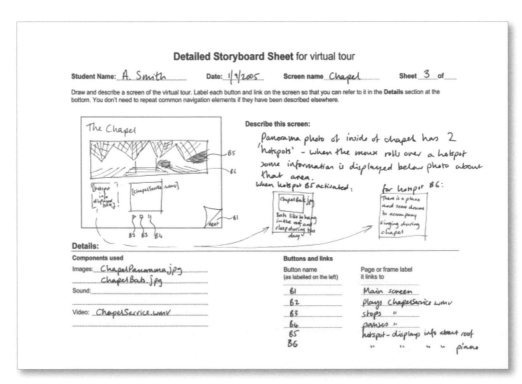

Figure 14.3

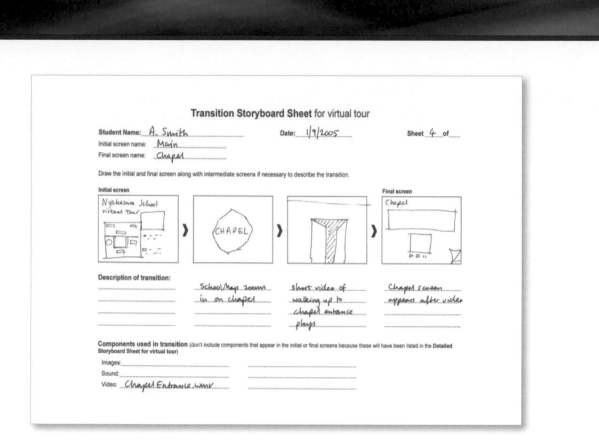

Figure 14.4

> **For the SPB:** When you come to do the final project, you will need to gain feedback on your structure chart and storyboard before you start to implement the tour. Marks will be awarded for collecting feedback and altering the storyboard accordingly. In your eportfolio you should include your original structure chart and storyboard, the feedback you collected and the final versions.

Collecting components for your virtual tour

It is specified in the brief that you must collect all components required for the virtual tour prior to starting work on the tour. You will have already downloaded, in Chapter 2, the components you need for the virtual tour.

> **For the SPB:** Make sure you have collected all the components you need for your virtual tour before you start. Don't forget to enter all the components into your components table. You will need to include the components table in your eportfolio.

Open the **ComponentsTable** document that you saved in the **Components** folder. Make a second table within the **ComponentsTable** document for all the components in the virtual tour. Add the entries from Figure 14.5 into your components table and give it the heading **VirtualTour components**.

File Name	Primary or Secondary?	Source	Type
ViewPost1.wmv	P	n/a	Video
ViewPost2.wmv	P	n/a	Video
ChapelPanorama.jpg	P	n/a	Photo
ChapelBats.jpg	P	n/a	Photo
ChapelService.wmv	P	n/a	Video
Pop.mp3	S	**www.wavcentral.com**	Sound
ChapelEntrance.wmv	P	n/a	Video

Figure 14.5

Good marks... ✓

You will get good marks if:

- you produce a structure chart to show how the tour is put together;
- you produce a storyboard to show what each screen will look like;
- the storyboard and structure chart are clear enough that they could be handed to someone else for them to create the tour in Flash;
- it is clear from the storyboard which components are required for the tour;
- you gain feedback for the storyboard and structure chart and make necessary changes;
- you record the feedback and changes made so they can later be included in the eportfolio.

Bad marks... ✗

You will lose marks if:

- the storyboard or structure chart isn't detailed enough or is unclear;
- components are not clearly labelled;
- the storyboard and structure chart aren't included in the eportfolio.

Virtual Tour in Flash

Creating the school map

The virtual tour will be an interactive map of the school. When a user clicks on an area of the school map they are taken to a more detailed page about that area. In this book we will develop the main school map and one of the detailed areas. If you have time you can go on to develop pages for the other areas.

You will create the virtual tour entirely in Flash. In Chapter 28 you will learn how to add Flash files, such as the intro movie and the virtual tour, to your eportfolio using Dreamweaver.

 Open Flash and create a new Flash document. Save the document as **VirtualTour** in the **VirtualTourFlashFiles** folder, which is in the **VirtualTour** folder.

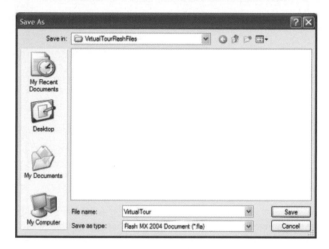

Figure 15.1

We will use the school map you used in the **IntroMovie** file as the basis for the school map in the virtual tour. We'll copy it across now.

 First make sure you can see the **Library** for the **VirtualTour**. If not, select **Window, Library** from the main menu bar.

 Open the **IntroMovie.fla** file by selecting **File, Open** from the main menu bar; the **IntroMovie.fla** file should be in the **IntroMovie/IntroMovieFlashFiles** folder.

 Make sure you can see the **Library** for the **IntroMovie** file.

You are now going to copy the **SchoolMap** symbol from the **IntroMovie** library to the **VirtualTour** library.

Click the **SchoolMap** symbol in the **IntroMovie** library. A small preview of the **SchoolMap** symbol is shown in the **Library** panel. Click and drag the **SchoolMap** in the preview window then drop it on the main part of the **VirtualTour** library (where the names of the symbols would be listed).

The **SchoolMap** symbol is now copied to the **VirtualTour** library.

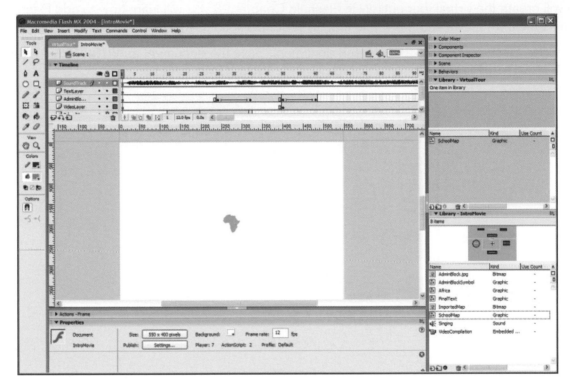

Figure 15.2

 Now close the **IntroMovie** file.

First we'll create the main page of the virtual tour, which will contain the school map.

*Free Transform
Tool*

 Drag an instance of the **SchoolMap** symbol onto the **Stage**. Use the **Free Transform** tool with the **Scale** option to size it as shown in Figure 15.3.

Scale Option

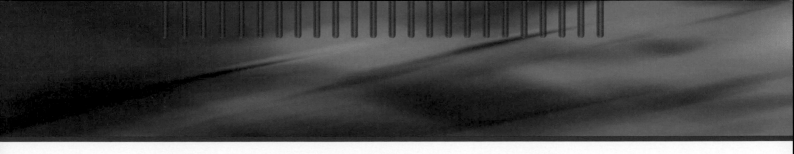

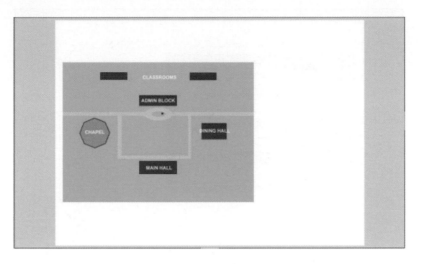

Figure 15.3

 Rename **Layer 1** as **SchoolMapLayer**.

Resizing the Stage

In this book we will create the virtual tour using the default **Stage** size of **550 x 400 pixels**. However, if you feel that this is a bit small, you can make the **Stage** larger. Don't make it wider than about **650** pixels though because then it will be a bit wide for the eportfolio.

To change the size of the **Stage**:

 Click the **Selection** tool in the **Toolbox**. Click on the **Stage** and then press **Escape** to make sure nothing is selected.

Selection Tool

 In the **Properties** panel, click where it says **550 x 400 pixels**.

 Enter a different size then click **OK**.

Resizing the text

The text is a bit small. We'll enlarge the text in **Symbol edit** mode.

 Double-click the map on the **Stage** to enter **Symbol edit** mode.

 Click the **Text** layer in the **Timeline** panel. Now click the **Selection** tool in the **Toolbox**. All the text on the **Text** layer should now be selected.

Selection Tool

 If the text properties aren't showing in the **Properties** panel, click once on one of the text labels on the map.

 In the **Properties** panel, change the size of the text until it is easily readable.

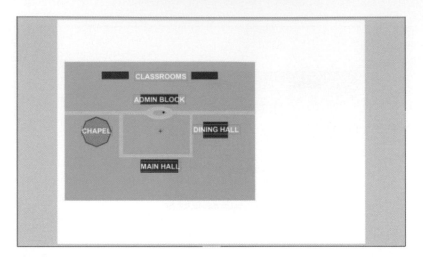

Figure 15.4

 You might also choose to move some of the text once it has been resized. Press **Escape** to clear the selection and then click the text label you wish to move. Use the arrow keys or the mouse to move the text label (if using the mouse, you should first turn off any ticked options under **View**, **Snapping**).

 Click where it says **Scene 1** above the **Timeline** to exit **Symbol edit** mode.

 Press **Ctrl-S** to save.

Inserting viewing posts

Now we'll add two viewing posts to the map. The user will click on a viewing post, then a panoramic movie of what someone would see if they were standing by the viewing post and turning around will play on the right of the screen. The movie will be added later in this chapter.

 Make sure the **Library** panel is visible.

 Open the **DrawingExercises.fla** file, which is in the **IntroMovieFlashFiles** folder. Make sure the **Library** panel is open for this file too.

 Click and drag the **EyeButton** from the **DrawingExercises** library to the **VirtualTour** library. Now close the **DrawingExercises** file.

 Click and drag two instances of the **EyeButton** symbol onto the **Stage** as shown in Figure 15.5.

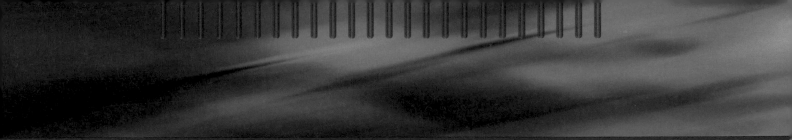

Figure 15.5

● Group the viewing posts with the **SchoolMap** symbol by drawing a selection box around everything, then selecting **Modify**, **Group** from the main menu bar; this will ensure that if you resize or move the map, the viewing posts won't be left behind.

● Save the file.

Importing the viewing post movies

● Select **File**, **Import**, **Import to Library** from the main menu bar. Find and click the **ViewPost1.wmv** video in the **Components/Videos** folder. Click **Open**.

● Select **Import the entire video**. Click **Next**.

● Click **Edit** next to **Compression profile**. Enter the following settings:

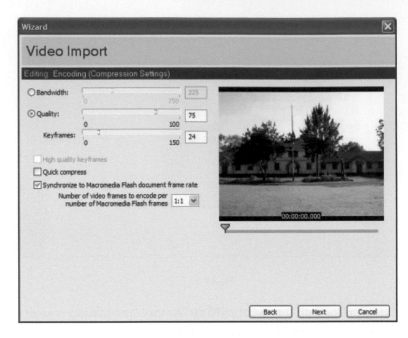

Figure 15.6

 Click **Next** twice.

 Under **Advanced settings** select **Create New Profile**.

 Enter these settings:

Figure 15.7

 Click **Next**. Enter **ViewPost** as the name of the profile then click **Next** again.

 Click **Finish** to import the video. Click **Yes** to the message about frames.

Importing the second viewing post video

 Select **File**, **Import**, **Import to Library** from the main menu bar. Find the **ViewPost2** video then click **Open**.

 Click **Next** to import the entire video.

 Under **Advanced settings** select **ViewPost** from the list; this is the profile that you set up when you imported the **ViewPost1** video. Click **Finish**.

 Click **Yes** to the prompt about **Frames**.

The two **ViewPost** videos are now in the **Library**, both as **embedded video** and as **movie clip** symbols.

Putting all clips into one movie clip symbol

We will create a movie clip symbol, then insert the first clip in **Frame 5** and the second in **Frame 10**. If you had more clips you could continue to add them at different points along the movie clip timeline. Each clip corresponds to a viewing post.

The second step will be to attach **ActionScript** to each viewing post button that tells the new movie clip to start playing at either **Frame 5** or **Frame 10**.

 In the **Library** panel, click the **Create New Symbol** icon.

 Enter the details shown in Figure 15.8 then click **OK**. You are now in **Symbol edit** mode.

*Create New
Symbol Icon*

Figure 15.8

 Select **Frame 5** then make it a **keyframe**. Click and drag an instance of the **ViewPost1** movie clip symbol (not the embedded video) on to the workspace.

● Rename **Layer 1** as **ViewPost1**. Insert another layer, called **ViewPost2**, underneath.

● Insert a third layer, above the others, called **Border**.

Figure 15.9

● Make sure **Frame 5** of the **Border** layer is selected in the **Timeline** panel (it is not a **keyframe** so whatever we draw here will actually be put in **Frame 1**).

Rectangle Tool

● Select the **Rectangle** tool (you might have to click and hold the **PolyStar** tool to display the **Rectangle** tool). Make sure the **Snap** icon is selected at the bottom of the **Toolbox**.

Snap Icon

● Press **Escape** to make sure nothing is selected. You should now see the **Rectangle** tool properties in the **Properties** panel; if not, click once on the **Stage**.

● Use the border thickness of **1** and no fill to draw a border round the clip. Use the **Free Transform** tool if necessary to adjust the border so that it fits exactly.

Figure 15.10

● Select **Frame 10** of the **ViewPost2** layer then press **F6** to convert it to a **keyframe**.

● With **Frame 10** still selected, drag out an instance of the **ViewPost2** clip on to the **Stage**.

Add a **keyframe** to the **Border** layer to coincide with the last frame of the **ViewPost2** layer. This will ensure that the border remains visible throughout the duration of the clip.

 Use the arrow keys to align the video perfectly within the border.

Figure 15.11

 Save by pressing **Ctrl-S**.

Adding Stop commands

We need to add some **stop** commands to initially pause the **ViewPostWindow** on **Frame 1**, and to stop the timeline at **Frame 5** and **Frame 10** while the videos play. Without these commands, the **ViewPostWindow** would just play flashes of the first frame of both videos.

 Add a new layer called **Actions** above all the others.

The Actions panel

 Make sure you can see the **Actions** panel (it should be above the **Properties** panel). If you can't, select **Window**, **Development Panels**, **Actions** from the main menu bar.

 Select **Frame 1** of the **Actions** layer. In the **Actions** panel, type **stop()**.

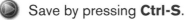

Figure 15.12

▶ Select **Frame 5** of the **Actions** layer. Press **F6** to make it a **keyframe** then type **stop()** in the **Actions** panel.

▶ Repeat this for **Frame 10**.

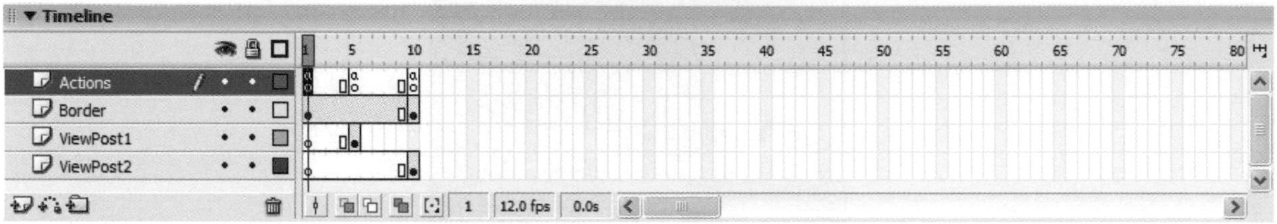

Figure 15.13

Stopping the video clips looping

At the moment, when each **ViewPost** clip is played, it will continuously loop until a different viewing post is clicked. We'll add a **stop** command in the last frame of both of the **ViewPost** clips.

▶ Select **Frame 5** of the **ViewPost1** layer. Double-click the clip to enter another level of **Symbol edit** mode.

Figure 15.14

▶ Insert another layer called **Actions**. Make the last frame of the **Actions** layer a **keyframe**. In the **Actions** panel type **stop().**

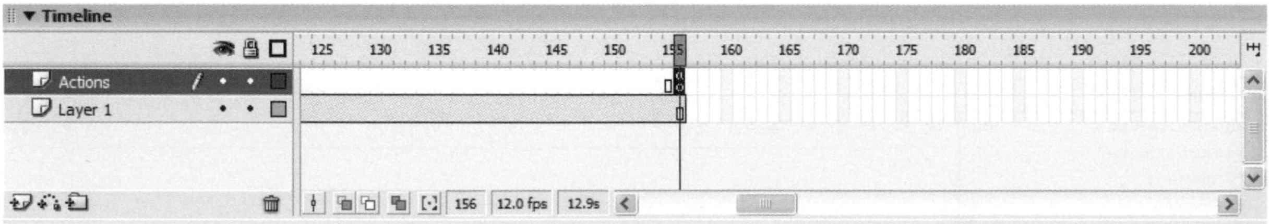

Figure 15.15

▶ Click where it says **ViewPostWindow** above the **Timeline** panel to return to editing the **ViewPostWindow** symbol rather than the **ViewPost1** symbol.

▶ Repeat the previous three steps for the **ViewPost2** clip (select **Frame 10** in the **ViewPost2** layer this time).

Naming frames

It is good practice to name frames which you need to refer to from the code. That way, if you add or remove frames and the frame numbers change, a reference to a particular frame won't be affected.

We need to name some frames so that we can easily refer to them in the code for the buttons.

 Insert a new layer above the **Actions** layer called **FrameLabels**.

 Select **Frame 5** of the **FrameLabels** layer; this is the start of the **ViewPost1** clip.

 Make it a **keyframe**. In the **Properties** panel, click where it says **<Frame Label>** then type **Post1**.

A small flag appears with the label **Post1** in the **Timeline** panel to show that this frame has a label.

 Repeat this for **Frame 10**, this time naming the frame **Post2** (don't forget to make it a **keyframe**). Make **Frame 15** a **keyframe** in the **FrameLabels** layer just so that you can read the second frame label more easily.

Figure 15.16

 Exit **Symbol edit** mode by clicking where it says **Scene 1** above the **Stage**.

 Save the movie.

Inserting the ViewPostWindow symbol

You have just created the **ViewPostWindow** symbol, which contains the two **ViewPost** clips. The symbol was created in **Symbol edit** mode so at the moment it only exists in the **Library**; it hasn't yet been added to the **VirtualTour**. We'll do this now by dragging it onto the **Stage**.

 Insert a new layer and name it **ViewPostWindow**.

 Select **Frame 1** of the new layer.

Click and drag an instance of the **ViewPostWindow** symbol that we have just created from the **Library** onto the **Stage**. You might need to resize or move the **SchoolMap** symbol to fit the **ViewPostWindow** beside it.

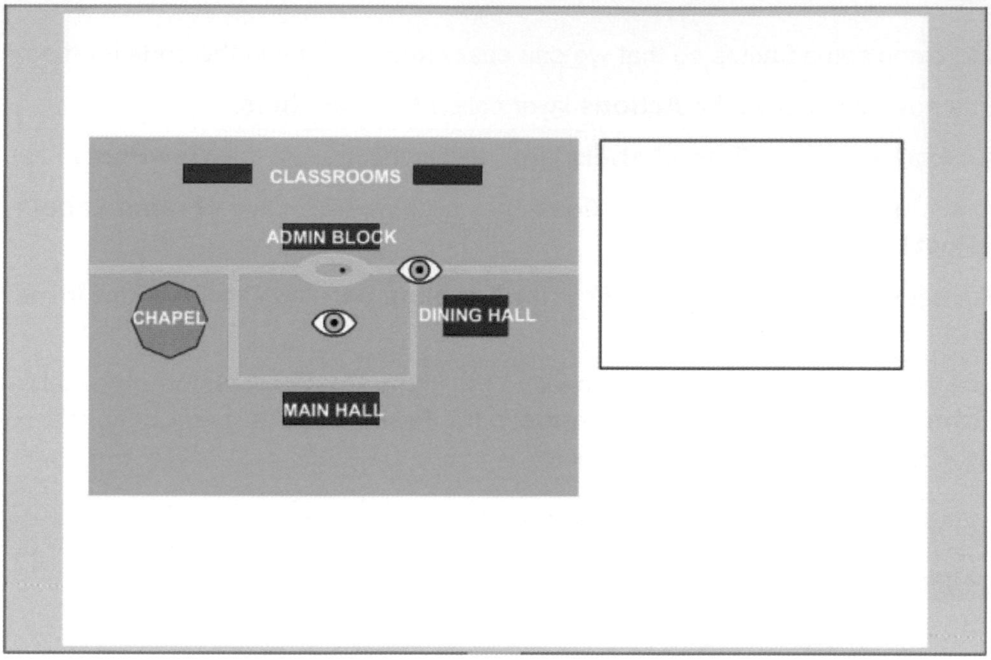

Figure 15.17

The clip will be just a blank box because it will be showing the contents of **Frame 1**, which is blank as the first clip starts in **Frame 5**.

Naming a symbol instance

Although the **ViewPostWindow** symbol already has a name, we need to actually name the instance of it on the **Stage** so that we can refer to it using **ActionScript**.

With the **Selection** tool, select the **ViewPostWindow** symbol on the **Stage**. In the **Properties** panel, type **ViewPostWindow** where it says **<Instance Name>**.

Adding ActionScript to the buttons

Double-click the map to enter a level of grouping. It should now say **Group** above the **Timeline** panel.

Select just the viewing post in the centre of the map. In the **Actions** panel, type the following code. Make sure you use capital letters where specified and also that you use the right shape of bracket – there are two different types used.

```
on(release) {
    tellTarget ("ViewPostWindow") {
        gotoAndPlay ("Post1");
    }
}
```

Figure 15.18

 Press the **Check Syntax** icon at the top of the **Actions** panel, just to check you haven't missed a bracket or something. If it says the script contains errors go back and check that the code you typed in exactly matches that in Figure 15.18.

Check Syntax Icon

Select the code then press **Ctrl-C** to copy it (this will save you some typing in a moment).

This code is basically telling the **ViewPostWindow** instance (of the **ViewPostWindow** symbol) to start playing at the frame label **Post1**.

Now select the other viewing post on the **Stage**. Click the cursor in the **Actions** panel then press **Ctrl-V**; this should paste in the code you copied.

Change where it says **Post1** to **Post2**.

Save the movie then preview it by pressing **Ctrl-Enter**. Test both the viewing post buttons. If your movie doesn't work as expected, go back over the last few steps and double-check.

Try rearranging the window to overlap the map slightly. (First click on **Scene 1** to exit **Group edit** mode.) This arrangement looks more interesting and less crowded.

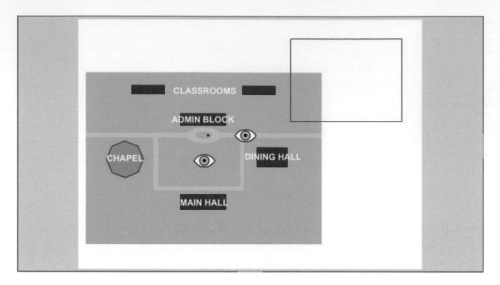

Figure 15.19

 Save the document.

Adding text

 Now add a title and some details about the viewing posts.

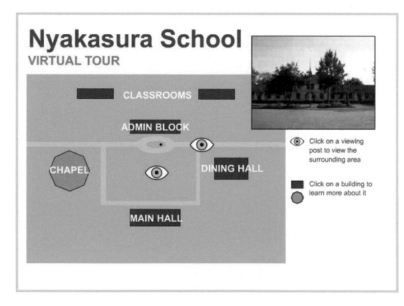

Figure 15.20

 Save and then publish the tour. View the HTML file in Internet Explorer.

 Close Flash if this is the end of a session, otherwise leave it open for the next chapter.

In this chapter we will create the screen that users will be directed to when they click on the chapel on the school map.

In Flash, you don't actually create pages in the same way as you do in Dreamweaver. In Flash, each page the user sees is actually a different frame. For example, **Frame 1** might contain one page, and **Frame 5** will contain another. Each frame will have a **stop** command on it so that it displays for more than a fraction of a second. You will use ActionScript to add actions to make the movie skip from **Frame 1** to **Frame 5** and back again when the user clicks certain buttons.

Don't worry if this seems complicated – we'll work through it now.

Scenes

To help organise the different pages, we will use **scenes**. You can create different parts of a movie in different scenes. When the movie is played, all the scenes are played one after another. We will use one scene for the **Main** page with the school map, and a second for the **Chapel** page.

 If you can't see the **Scene** panel, select **Window**, **Design Panels**, **Scene** from the main menu bar.

Figure 16.1

At the moment there's just one scene, called **Scene 1**.

 Double-click the scene name then type **Main**.

Creating a new scene

 At the bottom of the **Scene** panel, click the **Add scene** icon.

 Rename the new scene **Chapel**. With the **Text** tool just write **The Chapel** in **Frame 1** of the **Chapel** scene.

Add Scene Icon

Text Tool

The Chapel

▼ Scene

🎬 Main
🎬 Chapel

Figure 16.2

Adding Stop actions

 Play the movie by pressing **Ctrl-Enter**.

Oops! At the moment, when the movie plays it is running through all the frames in the movie then looping. We need to insert a **stop** command in **Frame 1** of both scenes.

 Close the preview by right-clicking the page tab and then selecting **Close** from the menu that appears.

 In the **Main** scene, insert a new layer, called **Actions**, above both of the others.

 Select **Frame 1** of the **Actions** layer.

The Actions panel

▼ Actions - Frame

Global Functions
Global Properties
Statements
Operators
Built-in Classes

```
stop()
```

Current Selection
  Actions : Frame 1

Actions : 1
Line 1 of 1, Col 7

Figure 16.3

 Now try running the movie again. The school map remains on the page.

 Insert an **Actions** layer in the **Chapel** scene and insert a **stop** command in **Frame 1**, just as you did for the **Main** scene. You won't be able to test this **stop** command until we've added a button to take us from the **Main** scene to the **Chapel** scene.

Adding buttons

We need to add some buttons for each of the buildings to the main page. The buttons will be the same shape as the buildings and sit in a layer on top of the map, but will be made transparent so users will think they are clicking on the building rather than a button.

 In the **Main** scene insert another layer above the others and name it **Buttons**.

▼ Timeline																		
	👁 🔒 □		5	10	15	20	25	30	35	40	45	50	55	60	65	70	75	Hϫ
Buttons	/ • • □																	
Actions	• • □																	
ViewPostWindow	• • ■																	
SchoolMapLayer	• • □																	

Figure 16.4

 With the **Selection** tool, double-click the map on the **Stage**. You should now be in **Group edit** mode – it should say **Group** in the bar above the Timeline panel. This is the group containing the **EyeButton** symbols and the **SchoolMap** symbol. Double-click again to enter **Symbol edit** mode.

Selection Tool

▼ Timeline																		
	👁 🔒 □		5	10	15	20	25	30	35	40	45	50	55	60	65	70	75	Hϫ
Text	✕ • ■																	
Buildings	/ • • □																	
Paths	✕ • □																	
Grass	✕ • ■																	

Figure 16.5

 Right-click the **Buildings** layer in the **Timeline** panel, then select **Hide Others** from the menu that appears.

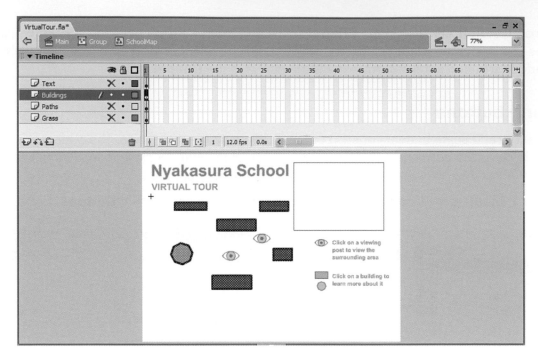

Figure 16.6

○ Press **Esc** to deselect everything. With the **Selection** tool, click the fill of the chapel to select it. Now press **Ctrl-C** (this is the same as selecting **Edit**, **Copy** from the main menu bar).

○ Exit **Symbol edit** mode by clicking where it says **Main** above the **Timeline** panel (this used to say **Scene 1** until you renamed **Scene 1** as **Main**).

○ Click **Frame 1** of the **Buttons** layer. Select **Edit**, **Paste in Center** from the main menu bar.

○ Use the **Free Transform** tool to position the pasted shape over the chapel.

Free Transform Tool

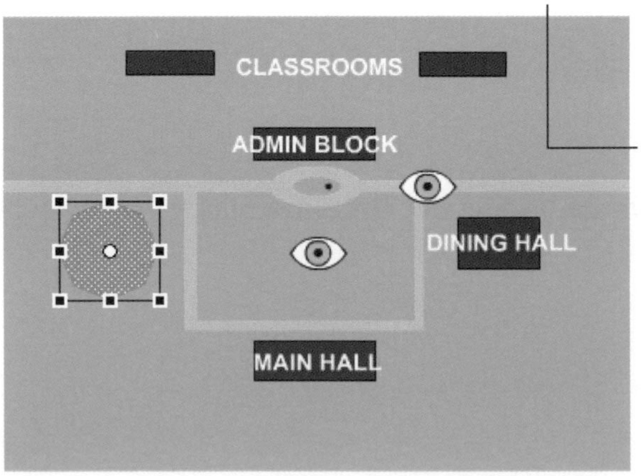

Figure 16.7

- With the fill still selected, select **Modify**, **Convert to Symbol** from the main menu bar.
- Name the symbol **ChapelButton** and select the **Button** option. Click **OK**.

Convert to Symbol	
Name: ChapelButton	OK
Behavior: ○ Movie clip Registration:	Cancel
● Button	
○ Graphic	Advanced

Figure 16.8

Naming frames

It is good practice to name frames which you need to refer to in code. That way, if you add or remove frames and the frame numbers change, a reference to a particular frame won't be affected.

- Click the **Chapel** scene in the **Scene** panel to go to that scene.
- Insert a new layer called **FrameLabels**. Click **Frame 1** of the **FrameLabels** layer.
- In the **Properties** panel, enter **ChapelStart** where it says **<Frame Label>** then press **Enter**.

▼ Properties				
Frame	Tween: None	Sound: None		
ChapelStart		Effect: None Edit...		
Label type: Name		Sync: Event Repeat 1		
		No sound selected.		

Figure 16.9

A small flag will appear in the **Timeline** panel. You can't read the frame label in the **Timeline** panel because there aren't enough regular frames after the label to display the label.

The Behaviors panel

We'll use the **Behaviors** panel to add actions to the **ChapelButton** in the **Main** scene.

- Return to the **Main** scene then select the **ChapelButton** on the **Stage**.

In the **Behaviors** panel, click the small **+** symbol in the top left. Select **Movieclip**, **Goto and Play at frame or label** from the menu that appears.

We want the button to make the movie go to the **ChapelStart** frame, which is at the start of the **Chapel** scene.

 Fill in the **Goto and Play** window as shown in Figure 16.10 (it is case sensitive, so include the capital letters). Click **OK**.

Figure 16.10

> **! Tip:**
>
> A **Goto and Stop** behavior would work for now, but **Goto and Play** is used because of the **ChapelIntro** scene you will be adding later.

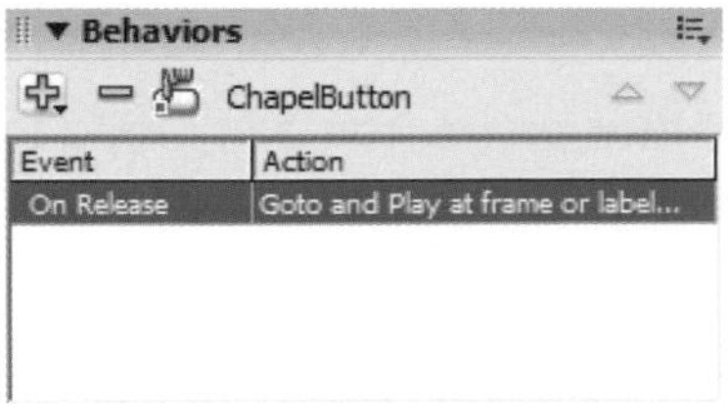

Figure 16.11

The Actions panel

The **Actions** panel is where all the code for any object can be viewed.

 Expand the **Actions** panel. Select the **ChapelButton** on the **Stage** if it's not already selected.

```
| ▼ Actions - Button                                                    ≡

  ↗ Global Functions      ^    ⊹ ⊘ ⟇ ⊕ ✔ ☰ ⊡              ⊘ ℗ ⊡

  ↗ Global Properties
                               on (release) {
  ↗ Statements

  ↗ Operators                      //Movieclip GotoAndPlay Behavior

  ↗ Built-in Classes               this.gotoAndPlay("ChapelStart");

  ↗ Constants                      //End Behavior

  ↗ Compiler Directives  ∨

  ⊟ ↗ Current Selection   ^    }

      ⋰⊞ ChapelButton

  ⊟ 🎞 Main                    <

      ⬚ Actions : Frame 1       🎬 ChapelButton ┤⊟

      ⋰⊞ ChapelButton    ∨    Line 8 of 8, Col 2
```

Figure 16.12

 This is the **ActionScript** code that the **Behaviors** panel has written for you. When you become more familiar with **ActionScript** you can just type in the code to the **Actions** panel instead of using the **Behaviors** panel.

 Save the movie.

Testing the buttons

 Press **Ctrl-Enter** to preview the movie.

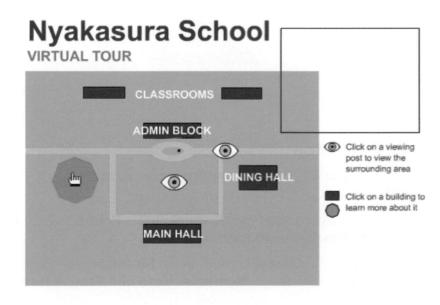

Figure 16.13

 Click the button. It should take you to the **ChapelStart** frame (**Frame 1** of the **Chapel** scene).

The only problem is that you're now stuck on the **Chapel** page! We'll add a button to return to the main page in a moment.

Hiding the button

The button is hiding the **Chapel** text on the **SchoolMap** symbol; we'll make it an invisible button.

Selection Tool

- Select the button with the **Selection** tool. In the **Properties** panel click the arrow in the **Color** box and change the **Alpha** value to **0%**.

Adding a Back button to the Chapel page

We'll insert the **BackButton** that you created in the **DrawingExercises** file.

- Make sure the **Library** panel is visible.

- Open the **DrawingExercises** file in the **IntroMovieFlashFiles** folder. Open the **Library** for this file if it isn't visible.

- Click and drag the **BackButton** from the **DrawingExercises** library to the **VirtualTour** library. Close the **DrawingExercises** file.

- Insert a layer called **Buttons** to the **Chapel** scene.

- Click and drag the **BackButton** onto the **Stage** and position it as shown below.

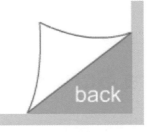

Figure 16.14

Adding code to the button

We'll do this in the same way as we did the **ChapelButton** in the **Main** scene. First we'll name the first frame in the **Main** scene.

- In the **Main** scene add a layer called **FrameLabels**. Select **Frame 1** of the **FrameLabels** layer then name it **MainStart** in the **Properties** panel.

+ Icon

- Select the **BackButton** in the **Chapel** scene with the **Selection** tool. Click the **+** icon at the top of the **Behaviors** panel. Select **Movieclip**, **Goto and Stop at frame or label** from the menu that appears.

160

 Enter **MainStart** in the **Goto and Stop** window. Click **OK**.

Figure 16.15

 Save and preview the movie.

That should work – try moving between the **School Map** and the **Chapel** page. If something doesn't work, go over the previous steps and check the following things:

 the frame labels **MainStart** and **ChapelStart** are in the first frame of each scene

 the code attached to the **ChapelButton** and the **BackButton** is correct and points to the labels **ChapelStart** and **MainStart**

 the **stop()** code is in the first frame of each scene.

In the next chapter we will add the contents of the **Chapel** page.

Chapter 17 – Inserting a Photo with Hotspots

We will insert a photo of the chapel. When the user moves the mouse over certain parts of the photo, some text will appear to explain more about the contents of the photo.

This will be done using a similar method to that used in the **Main** scene to display the panoramic videos. You will create a movie clip that has the information about each hotspot in a different frame. You will then add some code to the hotspots (which are actually buttons) to make the movie clip display the information in the relevant frame. Don't worry, we'll go through it step by step.

Inserting a photo into the Chapel page

- Click on the **Chapel** scene.
- Insert a new layer above **Layer 1** called **Photo**. Rename **Layer 1** as **Title**.

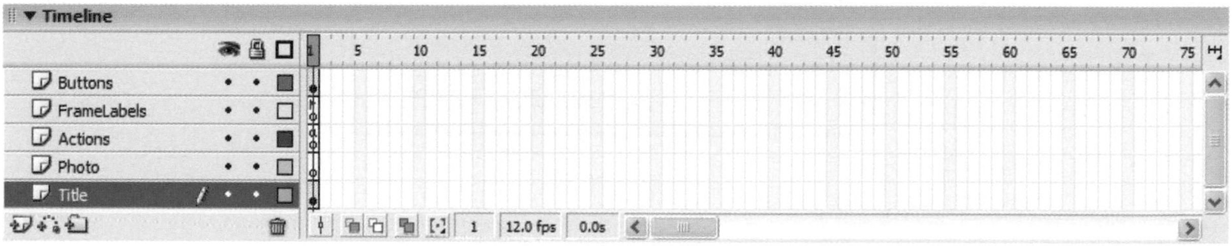

Figure 17.1

- Select **File**, **Import**, **Import to Library** from the main menu bar. Locate **ChapelPanorama.jpg** in the **Components/Images** folder then click **Open**.

Resizing the photo in Fireworks

- Right-click the **ChapelPanorama** in the **Library** and select **Edit with** Fireworks from the menu that appears.
- Select **Use This File** from the dialogue box in Fireworks.
- Select **Modify**, **Canvas**, **Image Size** from the main menu bar in Fireworks.
- Change the units from **Inches** to **Centimeters**. Enter the settings from Figure 17.2 then click **OK**.

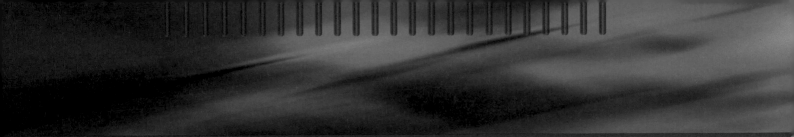

Image Size

Pixel dimensions

↔ 500 Pixels ▼

↕ 146 Pixels ▼

Print size

↔ 17.639 Centimeters ▼

↕ 5.151 Centimeters ▼

Resolution: 72 Pixels/Inch ▼

☑ Constrain proportions

☑ Resample image Bicubic ▼

OK   Cancel

Figure 17.2

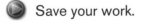 Return to Flash by clicking where it says **Done** at the top of the workspace. Close Fireworks by selecting **File**, **Exit** from the main menu bar in Fireworks.

Make sure **Frame 1** of the **Photo** layer is selected in the **Chapel** scene.

Click and drag an instance of the **ChapelPanorama** from the **Library** onto the **Stage**.

Figure 17.3

Save your work.

Tip:

This panorama was created from three different photos using a special feature in **Adobe Photoshop Elements**. For more information on how to create panoramic images for your own project go to **www.payne-gallway.co.uk/didaD202**.

Drawing the hotspots

Brush Tool

We'll use the **Brush** tool to draw irregular shaped buttons over various parts of the photo.

◉ Select the **Brush** tool and set it to have a red fill.

◉ Insert a new layer, called **Hotspots**, above the **Photo** layer.

◉ Select **Frame 1** of the **Hotspots** layer in the **Timeline** panel.

◉ Colour in a lump over the various parts of the photo, as shown below; make sure none of the patches touch each other. You might need to change the size of the brush. If you make a mistake, press **Ctrl-Z** to undo.

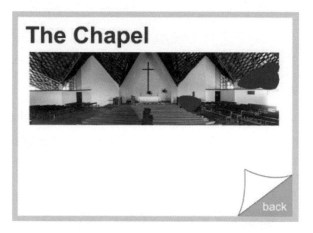

Figure 17.4

Turning the hotspots into buttons

Selection Tool

◉ With the **Selection** tool, click the left-most hotspot. Select **Modify**, **Convert to Symbol** from the main menu bar.

◉ Copy the settings below then click **OK**.

Figure 17.5

◉ Now click the other hotspot and do the same, calling it **RoofHotspot**.

Creating the movie clip

Now we'll create the movie clip symbol that contains the information about each hotspot.

 Select the **Text** tool and write the following text below the photo:

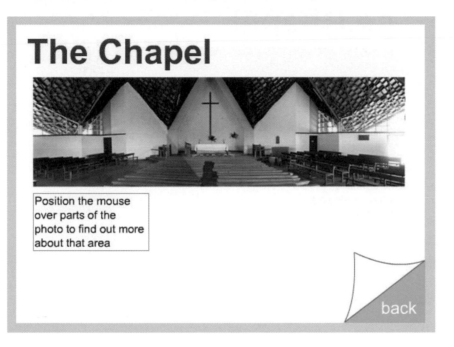

Figure 17.6

Select the text with the **Selection** tool.

Select **Modify, Convert to Symbol** from the main menu bar. Name the symbol **HotspotWindow** and make it a **Movie clip** symbol. Click **OK**.

Selection Tool

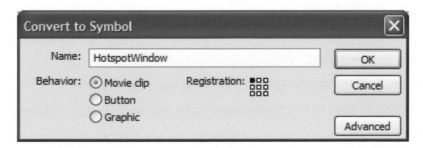

Figure 17.7

Double-click the text to enter **Symbol edit** mode.

Insert a **keyframe** in **Frame 10**.

Text Tool

The text from **Frame 1** has been copied to **Frame 10**; we'll edit it now.

 In **Frame 10**, use the **Text** tool to edit the text so it looks like Figure 17.8.

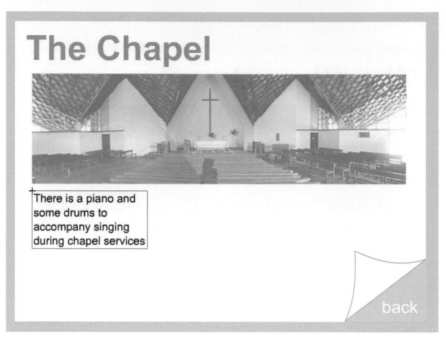

Figure 17.8

 Now create a **keyframe** in **Frame 20**.

The text from **Frame 10** has been copied to **Frame 20**, we'll delete it now.

 Press **Escape** to deselect everything. Now with the **Selection** tool click the text then press **Delete**.

Selection Tool

Adding a close-up photo

In **Frame 20** we will insert a close-up photo of the roof, which will appear when someone puts the cursor over the **RoofHotspot**. We'll import the photo first.

 Select **File**, **Import**, **Import to Library** from the main menu bar.

 Find the file **ChapelBats** in the **Components/Images** folder. Click **Open**.

 Drag the **ChapelBats** photo from the **Library** onto the **Stage**. Add some text so that it looks like Figure 17.9.

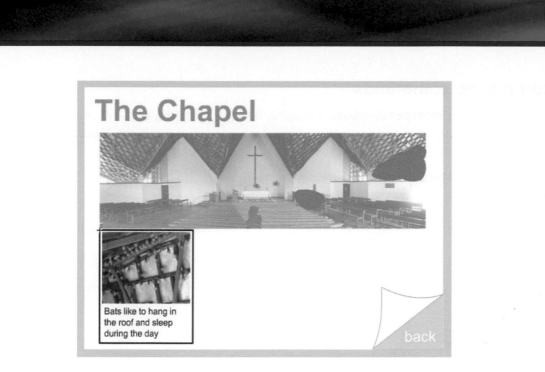

Figure 17.9

If you had other hotspots, you could carry on entering information in **Frame 30**, then **40** and so on.

Naming frames

🔘 Rename **Layer 1** as **Details** and add a new layer called **FrameLabels**.

🔘 Enter **HotspotStart** as the frame label for **Frame 1** of the **FrameLabels** layer.

🔘 Make **Frame 10** a **keyframe**, then in the **Properties** panel enter **PianoHotspot** as the frame label.

🔘 Repeat this for **Frame 20**, naming the frame **RoofHotspot**. Add another **keyframe** in **Frame 30** so that you can read the frame label in the **Timeline** panel.

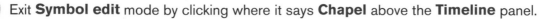

Figure 17.10

🔘 Exit **Symbol edit** mode by clicking where it says **Chapel** above the **Timeline** panel.

🔘 Save then preview the tour.

Adding Stop commands

At the moment, the **HotspotWindow** is looping through all the frames. We need to add some **stop** commands. We also need to add code to the hotspots to make the **HotspotWindow** display the relevant frame when the mouse is over the hotspot.

 To edit the **HotspotWindow** symbol double-click it in the **Library**.

Insert a new layer called **Actions**.

Select **Frame 1** of the **Actions** layer and in the **Actions** panel type **stop()**.

Figure 17.11

Repeat this for **Frame 10** and **Frame 20**, making each of them a **keyframe** first.

Exit **Symbol edit** mode.

Naming a symbol instance

Selection Tool

You need to name the instance of the **HotspotWindow** symbol so that you can refer to it in code.

With the **Selection** tool select the **HotspotWindow** symbol by clicking the text below the photo.

In the **Properties** panel, name the instance **HotspotWindow**.

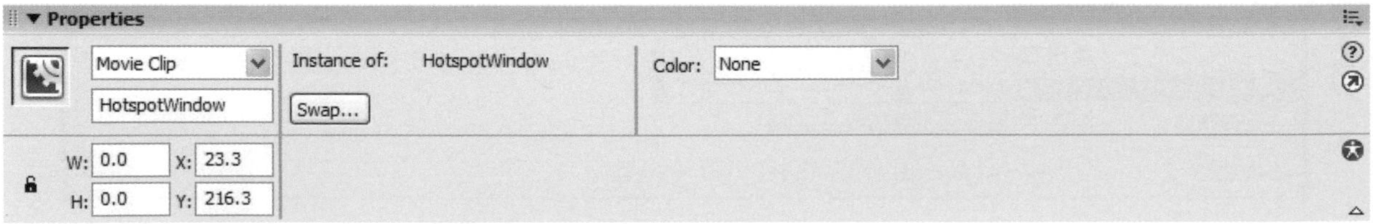

Figure 17.12

Adding code to the hotspots

First we'll add code to the **PianoHotspot** to tell the **HotspotWindow** to go to frame label **PianoHotspot**.

 Select the **PianoHotspot** on the **Stage**.

 Type the following code into the **Actions** panel. Be careful to use capital letters where specified, and to use the right shape of bracket.

Figure 17.13

Without the **on(rollOut)** command, the details would remain in view even after the mouse left the hotspot. The **rollOut** command tells the **HotspotWindow** to return to **Frame 1** (where the initial text is) after leaving the hotspot.

 Press the **Check Syntax** icon; check the code if it shows errors.

 Copy this code. Select the **RoofHotspot** on the **Stage** then paste in the code. Change where it says **PianoHotspot** to **RoofHotspot**.

 Save then preview the movie to test the buttons.

Check Syntax Icon

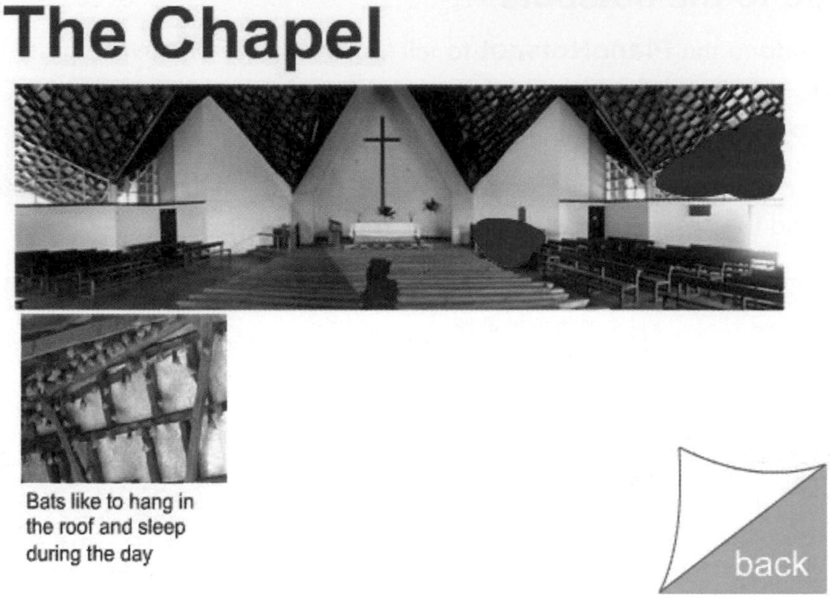

The Chapel

Bats like to hang in
the roof and sleep
during the day

back

Figure 17.14

Hiding the buttons

In the **Timeline** panel, move the **Photo** layer above the **Hotspots** layer.

The buttons will be hidden but will still work.

Tip:

If you need to edit these hotspots, you'll have to either temporarily move the
Hotspots layer above the **Photo** layer, or just hide the **Photo** layer.

– Inserting a Video Clip with Buttons

We will now insert a video clip of a chapel service with play, stop and pause buttons.

 Select **File**, **Import**, **Import to Library** from the main menu bar.

 Locate and select the **ChapelService.wmv** movie then click **Open**.

 Select to **Import the entire video**. Click **Next**.

We'll create a new profile that could be applied to the videos for the other areas of the virtual tour as well as this one (although we won't be creating the other areas in this book).

 Select **Create new profile** from the **Advanced Settings** list.

 Set **Import** to **Movie clip**; this will import the clip as a **Movie clip** symbol in the **Library**. Scale it to **75%**. Click **Next**.

Figure 18.1

 Name the profile **TourVideo** then click **Next**.

 Click **Finish**. Click **Yes** at the prompt about frames.

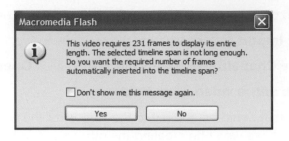

Figure 18.2

🔵 Create a new layer, called **ChapelService**, in the **Chapel** scene.

🔵 With the new layer selected, click and drag an instance of the **ChapelService** movie clip (not the embedded video) from the **Library** onto the **Stage**. Resize it if necessary to look like Figure 18.3.

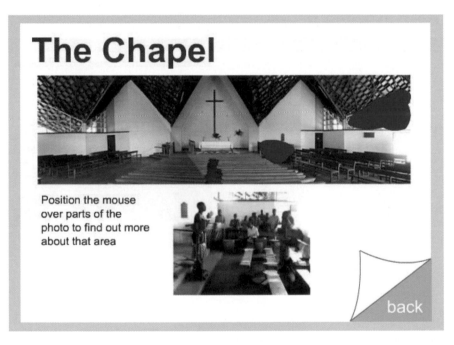

Figure 18.3

Adding buttons in Symbol edit mode

🔵 Double click the movie clip to enter **Symbol edit** mode.

🔵 Open the **DrawingExercises.fla** file and copy across the **Play**, **Pause** and **Stop** buttons to the **VirtualTour** library. Close the **DrawingExercises** file.

🔵 Drag out the buttons to look like Figure 18.4.

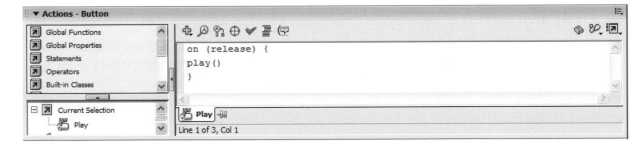

Figure 18.4

Select the **Play** button with the **Selection** tool.

In the **Actions** panel, enter the following code.

Selection Tool

```
on (release) {
play()
}
```

Figure 18.5

For the **Pause** button, type the following into the **Actions** panel:

```
on (release) {
stop()
}
```

Figure 18.6

For the **Stop** button we need it to return to the first frame in the movie; for this we'll use a **gotoAndStop** command. Type this into the **Actions** panel:

```
on (release) {
gotoAndStop(1)
}
```

Figure 18.7

 Save the movie. Press **Ctrl-Enter** to preview it.

The movie plays as soon as you go to the **Chapel** page. We'll add a **Stop** command so that it is paused at the start until someone presses the **Play** button.

 Double-click the **ChapelService** movie to enter **Symbol edit** mode, if you're not still in that mode. Add a new layer called **Actions**. In the first frame of the **Actions** layer, type **stop()** into the **Actions** panel.

 Exit **Symbol edit** mode, save and test the movie. It should work fine now.

This was possible because the movie was in a movie clip symbol with its own timeline. Because the buttons were added in **Symbol edit** mode they are now part of the symbol. If they were added to the **Stage** without being in **Symbol edit** mode, the actions attached to them would be referring to the entire virtual tour not the videoclip; for example the **gotoAndStop(1)** action would return the Flash movie to the first frame of the Main scene in the virtual tour.

Reusing buttons

You can reuse the button shapes in other pages of your virtual tour by clicking and dragging instances from the **Library**. However, you will have to re-enter the **ActionScript** code into the **Actions** panel.

Adding sound effects to buttons

You have already used sounds in the Intro movie. Now we will attach an event sound to the buttons. We'll start by attaching a sound to the play button.

Importing the button sound

You should already have downloaded the sound we will use.

 Select **File**, **Import**, **Import to Library** from the main menu bar.

Locate the **Pop.mp3** file in the **Components/Sounds** folder then click **Open**.

Take a look at the **Library** panel; the **Pop.mp3** file should now be listed.

Figure 18.8

 Double-click the **ChapelService** video then double-click the **Play** button to enter **Button edit** mode. Make sure that it says **PlayButton** above the **Timeline**.

Figure 18.9

Adding the sound to the button

 Make the **Hit** frame a **keyframe**.

 With the **Hit** frame selected, click and drag an instance of the **Pop.mp3** sound onto the **Stage**.

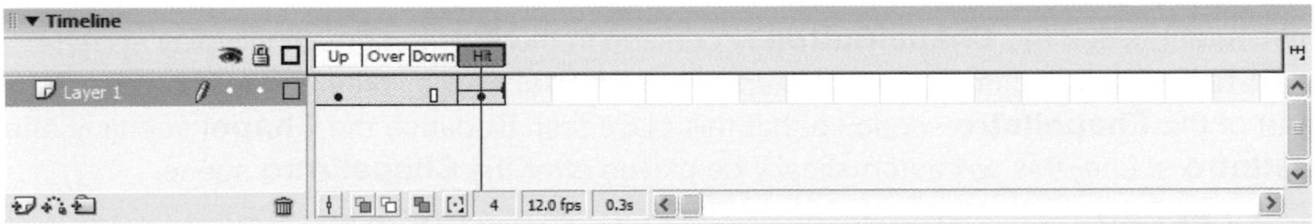

Figure 18.10

 With the **Hit** frame still selected, change the **Sync** option in the **Properties** panel to **Event** (if it isn't already). If this option is set to **Stream**, the sound won't play, because the scene finishes as soon as the button is pressed, and a **Stream** sound will finish with the scene.

175

Click where it says **Chapel** above the **Timeline** to exit **Button edit** and **Symbol edit** modes.

Save the movie and then test it.

Add the button sound to the **BackButton** by double-clicking the button in the **Library** panel. Add a **keyframe** to the **Hit** frame then click and drag the **Pop** sound from the **Library** onto the **Stage**.

By adding the sound to a button in the **Library**, every instance of the **BackButton** taken from the **Library** now will have the **Pop** sound attached to it.

> **Tip:**
>
> You could look for other sounds to attach to buttons on the Internet at a site such as **www.wavcentral.com**.

Adding a tween at the start of the Chapel scene

To make users feel as though they are getting closer to the chapel, we will create a short tween of the **SchoolMap** symbol zooming in on the **Chapel**. We will create all of this in a new scene called **ChapelIntro**, which will be played just before the **Chapel** scene.

Add Scene Icon

Create a new scene by clicking the **Add Scene** icon at the bottom of the **Timeline** panel. Rename the scene **ChapelIntro**.

Click and drag the **ChapelIntro** scene above the **Chapel** scene in the **Scene** panel. This will make it play before the **Chapel** scene.

Rename **Layer 1** of the **ChapelIntro** scene as **MapZoom**.

Moving the ChapelStart frame label

At the moment, when the **ChapelButton** is pressed in the **Main** scene, it will play at frame label **ChapelStart**, which is currently at the start of the **Chapel** scene. We need to move this label to the start of the **ChapelIntro** scene so that this plays first. Because the **Chapel** scene is after the **ChapelIntro** scene, this will automatically be played after the **ChapelIntro** scene.

In the **Chapel** scene, select the first frame of the **FrameLabels** layer. Delete the frame label **ChapelStart** in the **Properties** panel.

In the **ChapelIntro** scene, add a new layer called **FrameLabels**. Name the first frame **ChapelStart**.

Copying the map to the ChapelIntro scene

Go to the **Main** scene by clicking it in the **Scene** panel. First make sure the **SchoolMapLayer** is unlocked. Select the map then press **Ctrl-C** to copy it.

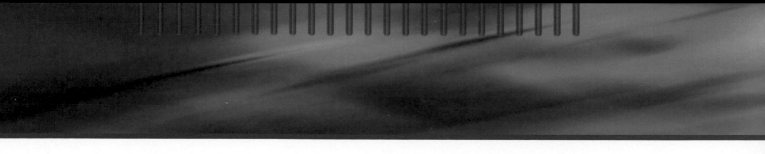

⊙ In the **ChapelIntro** scene, click **Frame 1** of the **MapZoom** layer then select **Edit, Paste in Place** from the main menu bar.

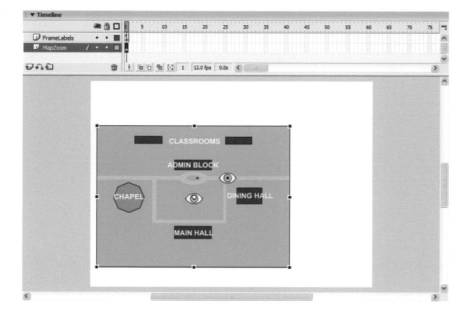

Figure 18.11

⊙ Use **Modify, Convert to Symbol** to make the map a graphic symbol called **MapWithPosts**. We are making this a symbol to make tweening it easier.

⊙ In the **MapZoom** layer convert **Frame 15** to a **keyframe**.

⊙ In **Frame 15**, use the **Free Transform** tool with the **Scale** option to enlarge the map and position the chapel in the centre of the **Stage**. You will find it helpful to view the **MapZoom** layer as outlines so that you can still see the **Stage**. To do this, click the **Outlines** icon next to the layer in the **Timeline** panel.

Free Transform Tool

Outlines Icon

Figure 18.12

177

Add a motion tween by right-clicking between the two **keyframes** in the **Timeline** panel then selecting **Create Motion Tween** from the menu that appears.

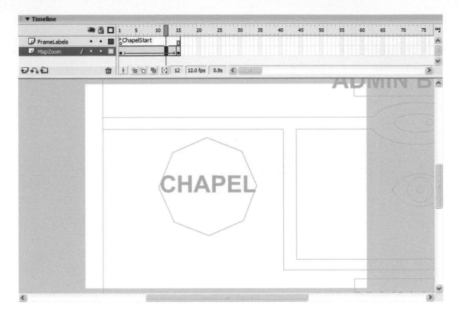

Figure 18.13

Save and test the tour. It should work fine.

Inserting a movie of the chapel entrance

Insert a new layer called **EntranceVideo** in the **ChapelIntro** scene.

Import the video with file name **ChapelEntrance.wmv**. Create a new profile and reduce the video in size so that it is about **600** pixels wide; import it into the current timeline (not as a movie clip symbol) by selecting **Current timeline** under **Track options** at the bottom of the **Advanced Settings** window. Name the profile **EntranceVideo**.

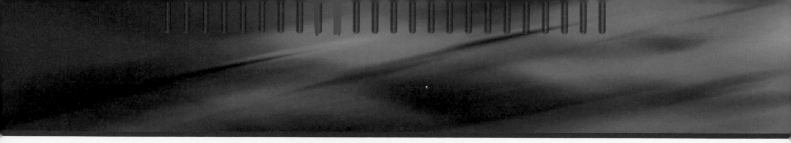

Figure 18.14

 Make **Frame 16** a **keyframe** in the **EntranceVideo** layer. Click and drag the **ChapelEntrance** embedded video from the **Library** on to the **Stage**. Say **Yes** to the prompt about frames.

 Size the movie to fit the **Stage**.

 Save and preview the movie.

 Add some footstep sounds if you like to accompany **Frames 15** to **30**.

Tip:

If you want to save on file space you could use a photo instead of a movie. Start with a photo of the chapel entrance then tween it to zoom in on the entrance to simulate walking towards it.

To finish off the virtual tour you would need to create similar pages for the other buildings on the main page. We won't do that here because you have already learnt the skills you need to do this.

Test, review and amend

It is really important that you test your tour thoroughly yourself, and also get feedback from others.

> **For the SPB:** You will need to include evidence of testing and feedback in your eportfolio. It is a good idea to submit in your eportfolio various screenshots of the Flash workspace during development of the tour, along with the feedback given at each stage.

Good marks... ✓

You will get good marks if you:

- make sure your tour is suitable for the target audience;
- make your tour easy for users to navigate around;
- use different types of multimedia components in the tour;
- test out different designs and seek feedback as you go along;
- make use of the feedback to make positive changes to your tour;
- record the feedback and changes made so they can later be added to the eportfolio;
- test your tour thoroughly.

Bad marks... ✗

You will lose marks if you:

- do not use your structure chart and storyboard when implementing the tour, or if your tour varies significantly from your storyboard;
- do not seek feedback or use the feedback to improve your tour.

> **For the SPB:** You should update your plan as you go along. It is likely you will need to move things around or change some of the timescales. Make sure you keep a copy of the original plan as well as subsequent versions to include in the eportfolio.

Section Four
THE QUIZ

Chapter 19 – Planning the Quiz

The quiz is a fun interactive product that will test users on the information they have gained by looking at your movie and virtual tour, and general knowledge about the country. It will be created in Flash, and will contain a variety of different types of quiz format.

Researching other quizzes

It's important to look at other examples in order to get a good idea of what can be achieved, what works well and to get lots of ideas for your own project before you begin.

Take a look at these sites; each site has a selection of different sorts of quizzes.

http://quizhub.com/quiz/quizhub.cfm

http://www.bbc.co.uk/kent/fun_stuff/quizzes/

Think about which quizzes you like and which you don't. Analyse them in terms of:

- Design – how is it laid out, what colours does it use?
- Graphics
- Animation
- Content – how good are the questions?
- Components – which sorts of components does it use: photos, sounds, videos?
- Combination of techniques – how many different types of question are used?

- Make a list of all the different types of quiz question you can find.

Before implementing the quiz, you have to produce a storyboard that shows exactly how each question will look, and a flow chart to show the paths through the quiz. The storyboard is a set of drawn images with text to explain each question in the quiz. The flow chart shows all the pages in the quiz and which order they go in. It should be a document that could, in theory, be handed to someone else for them to implement with no further explanation from yourself.

For the SPB: You will have to submit your flow chart and storyboard as part of your eportfolio, and will lose marks if you do not submit them or if you do not follow them when implementing your quiz. You can draw them on paper then scan them in, or, if you'd prefer, draw them straight on the computer. You can download blank sheets for the flow chart and storyboard from **www.payne-gallway.co.uk/didaD202**.

You will need to gain feedback on your flow chart and storyboard before you start to implement the quiz in Flash. Marks will be awarded for collecting feedback and altering your work accordingly. In your eportfolio you should include your original flow chart and storyboard, the feedback you collected and the final versions.

This is the flow chart and some storyboard sheets for the sample project:

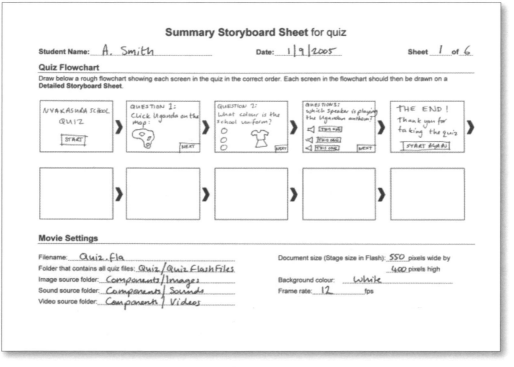

Figure 19.1

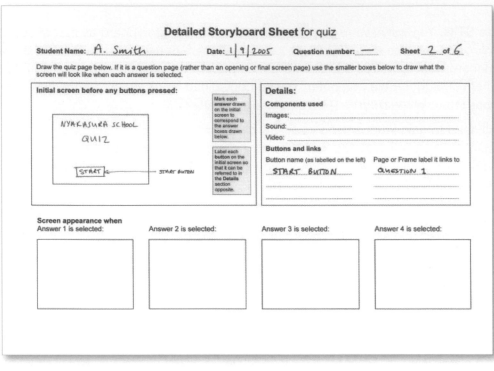

Figure 19.2

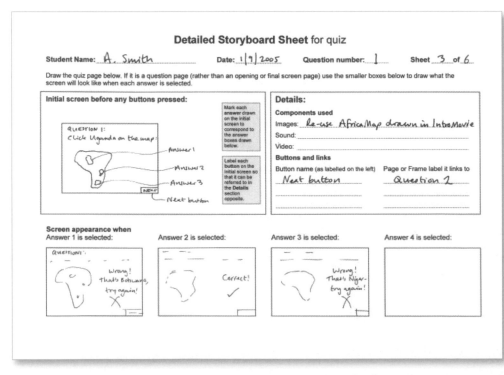

Figure 19.3

Collecting components for your quiz

It is specified in the brief that you must collect all components required for the movie prior to starting work on it. You will have already downloaded the components you need for the sample project.

▶ Make the following entries into your components table (it will be a Word document called **ComponentsTable.doc** in the **Components** folder) under the heading **Quiz components**:

File Name	Primary or Secondary?	Source	Type
British.mp3	S	**www.wavcentral.com**	Sound
French.mp3	S	**www.wavcentral.com**	Sound
Ugandan.mp3	S	**www.wavcentral.com**	Sound

Figure 19.4

For the SPB: Make sure you have collected all the components you need for your quiz before you start. Don't forget to enter all the components into your components table. You will need to include the components table in your eportfolio.

Good marks... ✓

You will get good marks if:

- you produce a flow chart and storyboard for your quiz;
- the flow chart and storyboard are clear enough that they could be handed to someone else for them to create the quiz in Flash;
- it is clear from the storyboard which components are required for the movie;
- you gain feedback for the storyboard and make necessary changes;
- the feedback and changes are recorded so that they can later be included in the eportfolio.

Bad marks... ✗

You will lose marks if:

- the flow chart or storyboard are not detailed enough or are unclear;
- components are not clearly labelled;
- the flow chart or storyboard isn't included in the eportfolio.

Chapter 20 – Implementing the Quiz in Flash

You'll be pleased to hear that you have already learnt most of the Flash skills needed to create the quiz. We'll go through how to create three different types of question. Once you have learnt how to create each type of question you can add more of your own if you like, copying the format of one of the questions covered here.

The quiz will not be scored. To create a scored quiz is quite complicated and requires a lot of ActionScript programming.

The opening screen

It would be nice to create an opening screen for the quiz, rather than going straight to the first question.

- Create a new Flash document.

- Select **File**, **Save As** from the main menu bar. Save the file as **Quiz.fla** in the **QuizFlashFiles** folder (which is in the **Quiz** folder).

- Rename **Scene 1** as **OpeningScreen** by double-clicking the scene name in the **Scene** panel.

- Create an opening screen like the one shown in Figure 20.1 (you can make yours look more interesting if you like!). You need to create the button to enter the quiz, and convert it to a button symbol called **StartButton**. I used the font **Goudy Stout** for the opening screen.

Tip:

Make the button more interesting by swapping the colours when the mouse rolls over it. To do this, double-click the button and then add a **keyframe** in the **Over** frame. Now change the colours in the **Over** frame.

- Click where it says **OpeningScreen** above the **Timeline** panel to exit **Button edit** mode.

Figure 20.1

⦿ In the **Timeline** panel, rename **Layer 1** as **Content**. Add a new layer called **Actions**. In the **Actions** layer, insert a **stop()** command in **Frame 1**.

We'll add the code for the button in a moment.

Question 1

In Question 1, users will have to click the location of Uganda on a map of Africa by selecting from three options. We will use the same map as we used for the **IntroMovie**.

⦿ Create a new scene called **Question1** in the **Scene** panel.

⦿ In the **Question1** scene, insert a new layer called **FrameLabels**. Name the first frame **Q1Start** in the **Properties** panel.

⦿ Insert a layer called **Actions**. Add a **stop()** command in the first frame.

⦿ Go to the **OpeningScreen** by clicking it in the **Scene** panel. Select the button on the **Stage**, then click the small **+** icon at the top of the **Behaviors** panel.

+ Icon

⦿ Select **Movieclip, Goto and Play at frame or label** from the menu that appears.

⦿ Enter **Q1Start** as the frame then click **OK**.

Goto and Play at frame or label

Choose the movie clip that you want to begin playing:

this

🖹 _root

⦿ Relative ○ Absolute

Enter the frame number or frame label at which the movie clip should start playing. To start from the beginning, type '1':

Q1Start

OK   Cancel

Figure 20.2

⦿ Save and preview the quiz. When you click the button you will see a blank screen, because at the moment **Frame 1** of **Question1** is blank.

Copying the Africa symbol from the IntroMovie

- First make sure that you can see the **Library** panel. If you can't, select **Window, Library** from the main menu bar.

- Select **File, Open** from the main menu bar. Find the **IntroMovie.fla** file in the **IntroMovie/IntroMovieFlashFiles** folder.

- If you can't see the **Library** for the **IntroMovie** select **Window, Library** from the main menu bar.

- Click and drag an instance of the **Africa** symbol from the **IntroMovie Library** and drop it on the **Quiz Library**.

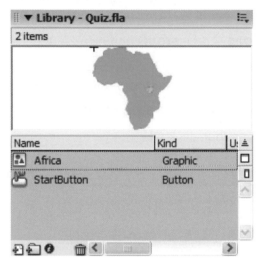

Figure 20.3

- Close the **IntroMovie** by selecting **File, Close** from the main menu bar. You don't need to save changes because you shouldn't have edited the **IntroMovie** anyway.

- Make sure you've got the **Question1** scene selected in the **Scene** panel.

- Click **Layer 1** in the **Timeline** panel to select it.

- Drag out an instance of the **Africa** symbol onto the **Stage**.

- Resize the map and position it on the left to leave room on the right for the response to the user's answer. Add some text as shown in Figure 20.4.

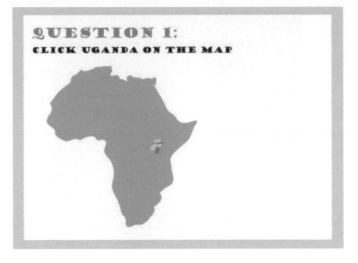

Figure 20.4

 Rename **Layer 1** as **Question**. Create two more layers – **Buttons** and **Answer** – and arrange them as shown in Figure 20.5.

Figure 20.5

Creating the buttons

The buttons will be the outlines of three different countries, one of which will be Uganda. First we will edit the **Africa** symbol to delete where it says Uganda.

 Double-click the map to edit it.

Zoom in on the map, then select and delete all the text.

To edit the dot of Fort Portal you need to enter a couple of layers of grouping. To do this, double-click the dot twice; it should now have a selection mesh over it.

Select the white dot representing Fort Portal then change the colour in the **Properties** panel to match the rest of the country.

Click where it says **Africa** above the **Timeline** panel to exit all the grouping levels but remain in **Symbol edit** mode for the **Africa** symbol.

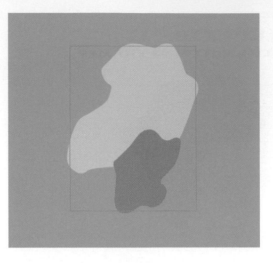

Figure 20.6

 Make sure you are in **Symbol edit** mode but not **Group edit** mode – it should say just **Question1** and **Africa** above the **Timeline** panel.

Figure 20.7

Selection Tool

 With the **Selection** tool, click Uganda once to select it. Select **Edit**, **Copy** from the main menu bar.

 Exit **Symbol edit** mode by clicking where it says **Question1** above the **Timeline** panel.

 Select the **Buttons** layer in the **Timeline** panel.

 Select **Edit**, **Paste in Center** from the main menu bar. A copy of Uganda will be pasted on top of the Uganda map in the **Question** layer.

Outline Icon

 Click the **Outline** icon next to the **Buttons** layer in the **Timeline** panel. This will make it easier to see the Uganda map in the **Answer** layer.

Figure 20.8

Resize and position the outline perfectly over the one on the **Question** layer.

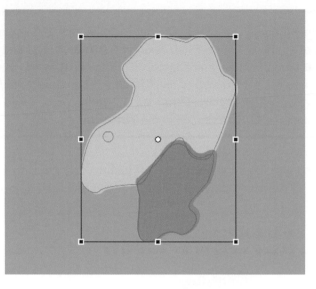

Figure 20.9

Outline Icon

 Click the **Outline** icon again in the **Timeline** panel to turn it off.

 From the map below choose two countries that you will draw on your map. I chose **Niger** and **Botswana**.

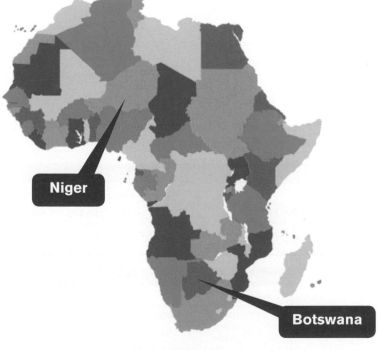

Niger

Botswana

Figure 20.10

Tip:

You can import a map from Google if you like; just right-click the map in Google and select **Copy** from the menu that appears. Now in Flash select the **Answer** layer and select **Edit**, **Paste in Centre** from the menu that appears. Click the **Outlines** icon next to the **Question** layer then resize the pasted map to the **Africa** symbol. Select the **Buttons** layer then draw round two countries with the **Pen** tool. Delete the pasted map when you're finished and deselect the **Outlines** icon in the **Timeline** panel.

Pen Tool

Select the **Buttons** layer. Use the **Pen** tool in Flash to draw the countries onto the map (they don't have to be perfectly drawn). Give them the same fill colour as Uganda.

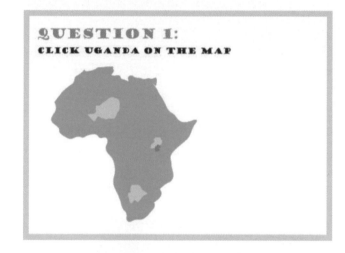

Figure 20.11

Lock the **Question** layer in the **Timeline** panel.

Selection Tool

Use the **Selection** tool to select each outline and fill and make it into a **Button** symbol. Name the buttons after the countries that they represent.

Figure 20.12

Creating the Answer box

The answers will be displayed in a separate **Movie clip** symbol. There will be three frames in the **Answer** symbol, one for the correct answer and two for the wrong answers. Each button will tell the **Answer** symbol to **gotoAndPlay** at a particular frame.

Rectangle Tool

- Select the **Answer** layer in the **Timeline** panel.
- Draw an empty black box on the right of the screen using the **Rectangle** tool.
- Select the rectangle using the **Selection** tool then convert it to a **Movie clip** symbol called **Answer1**.

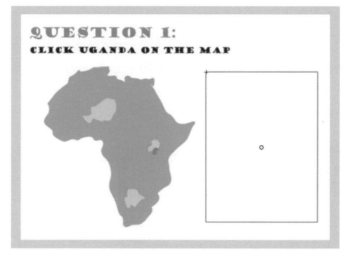

Figure 20.13

- Double-click the border of the **Answer1** symbol on the **Stage** to enter **Symbol edit** mode.

Figure 20.14

- In the **Timeline** panel, create three new layers called **Text**, **Actions** and **FrameLabels**.

Delete Icon

⊙ Delete **Layer1** by selecting it then clicking the **Delete** icon at the bottom of the **Timeline** panel. We don't actually want the black rectangle; it was created as an initial guide.

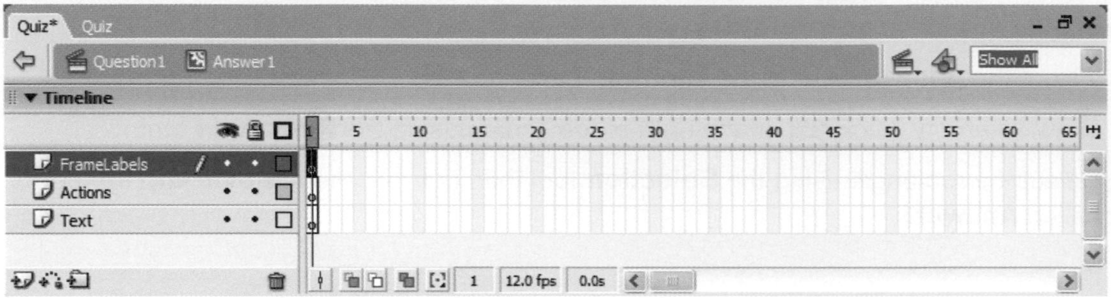

Figure 20.15

⊙ Create a **keyframe** in **Frames 10**, **20**, **30** and **40** in all layers (to do this click in each frame then use the shortcut key **F6**).

⊙ Add the following frame labels.

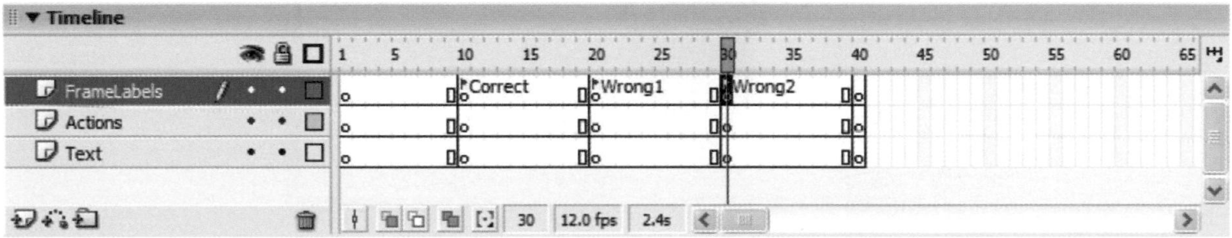

Figure 20.16

⊙ Select **Frame 10** of the **Text** layer. This is where we will add the text that will appear when someone selects the correct answer.

⊙ Enter the following text and tick shape.

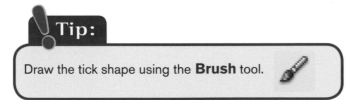

Tip:

Draw the tick shape using the **Brush** tool.

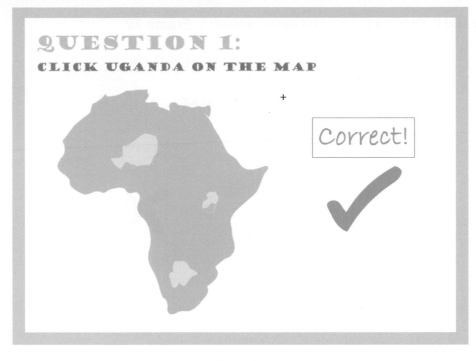

Figure 20.17

Enter the following into **Frame 20** of the **Text** layer.

Figure 20.18

Finally add the text for the second wrong answer in **Frame 30**.

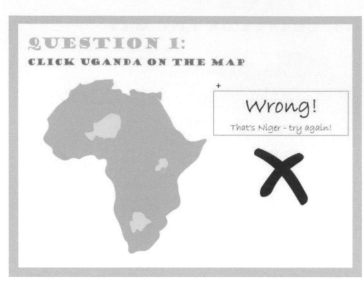

Figure 20.19

Adding Stop commands

We need to add a **stop** command to the first frame (so that the **Answer1** movie clip is paused on the first frame, which is blank) then on each of the frames containing the text we've just added.

 Using the **Actions** panel, add a **stop()** action in the **Actions** layer to **Frames 1**, **10**, **20** and **30**.

Figure 20.20

Exit **Symbol edit** mode by clicking **Question1** above the **Timeline** panel.

Naming a symbol instance

You can no longer see the **Answer1** symbol because it is currently displaying **Frame 1**, which is blank. All you can see is a small cross at the top left of the symbol and a circle in the middle.

 Click the small black circle in the middle of the **Answer1** symbol once to select it (don't double-click it, as we don't want to enter **Symbol edit** mode).

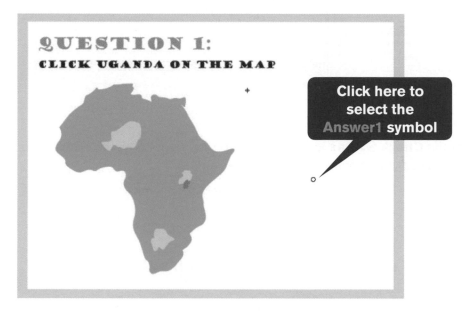

Figure 20.21

 In the **Properties** panel, name the symbol instance **Answer1**.

Figure 20.22

Adding code to the buttons

Now we will add the code to each button (in the shape of a country) that tells the **Answer1** movie clip which frame to display.

 Select the **Uganda** button. In the **Actions** panel, type the following code.

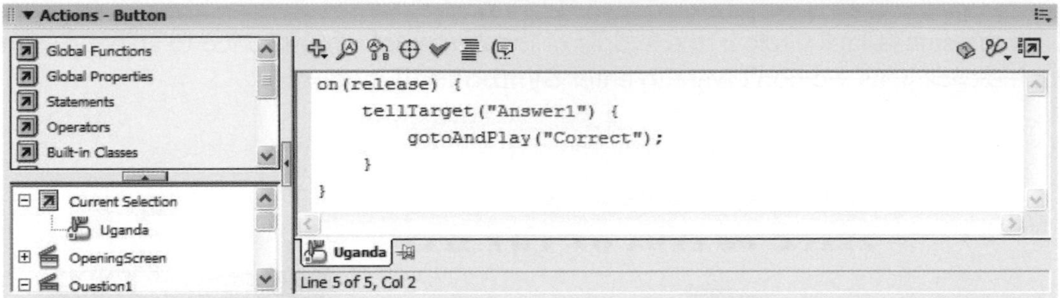

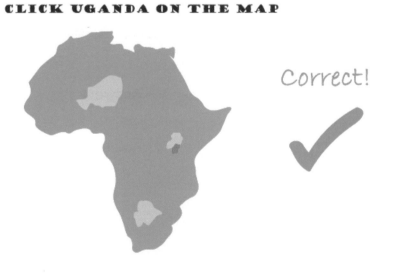

```
on(release) {
    tellTarget("Answer1") {
        gotoAndPlay("Correct");
    }
}
```

Figure 20.23

Check Syntax Icon

 Click the **Check Syntax** icon to check that you have no typing errors in your code (the code won't work if you've missed even one bracket!).

 Save and preview the quiz to check that the button works.

QUESTION 1:

CLICK UGANDA ON THE MAP

Correct!

Figure 20.24

When you click **Uganda** the **Correct** text should be displayed.

Now add code to the other two buttons as shown below. The quickest way is to copy and paste the code from the **Uganda** button then just change the word **Correct** to **Wrong1** or **Wrong2**.

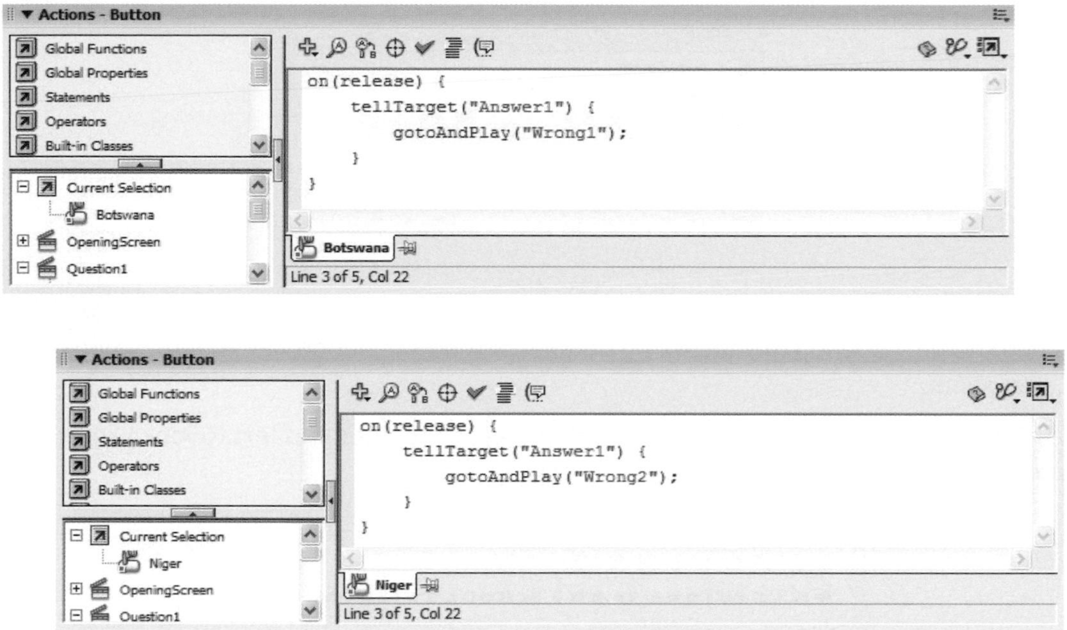

```
on(release) {
    tellTarget("Answer1") {
        gotoAndPlay("Wrong1");
    }
}
```

```
on(release) {
    tellTarget("Answer1") {
        gotoAndPlay("Wrong2");
    }
}
```

Figure 20.25

Save the movie then preview it again to test that all three buttons work.

Creating a scene for Question 2

The quickest thing will be to copy the **Question1** scene then edit it.

Duplicate Scene Icon

🔘 In the **Scene** panel, make sure **Question1** is selected, then click the **Duplicate Scene** icon at the bottom of the panel.

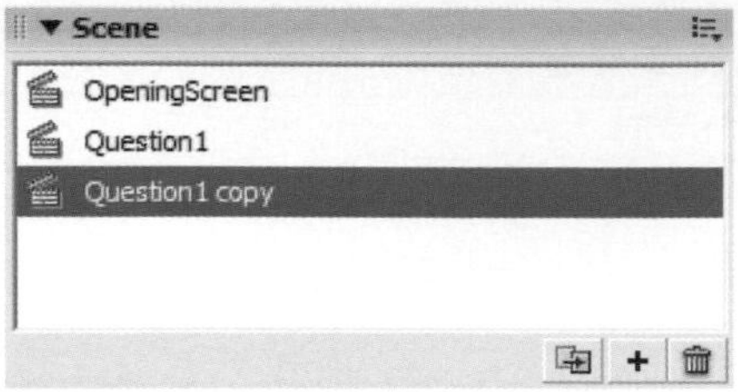

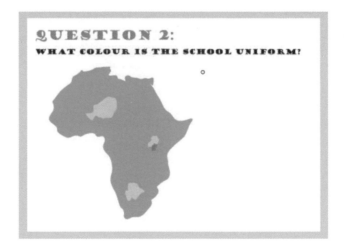

Figure 21.1

🔘 Rename the new scene **Question2** by double-clicking the scene name then typing the new name.

🔘 In the **Question2** scene, unlock the **Question** layer, then edit the text to look like Figure 21.2.

QUESTION 2:
WHAT COLOUR IS THE SCHOOL UNIFORM?

Figure 21.2

🔘 Delete the **Africa** map and the three country buttons.

Oval Tool

🔘 In the **Buttons** layer, use the **Oval** tool to draw some coloured circles (red, green and blue with khaki circles behind) as shown in Figure 21.3.

Tip:

If you draw one circle, you can copy it by holding down the **Ctrl** key then clicking and dragging it. Use the **Properties** panel to edit the colours.

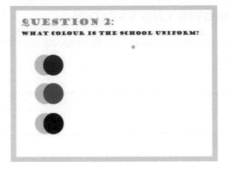

Figure 21.3

● Convert each group of two circles into a **Button** symbol. Name the buttons **Red**, **Green** and **Blue**.

● Change the frame label to **Q2Start** in **Frame 1** of the **FrameLabels** layer.

Duplicating the Answer1 symbol

We'll copy then edit the **Answer1** symbol and use that for the **Answer2** symbol.

● Right-click the **Answer1** symbol on the **Stage** (it will be just a small black circle).

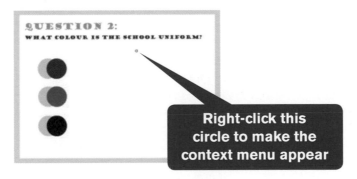

Figure 21.4

● Select **Duplicate Symbol** from the menu that appears.

● Name the symbol **Answer2** then click **OK**.

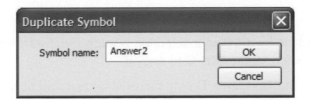

Figure 21.5

● In the **Properties** panel, change the **Instance Name** to **Answer2**.

Editing the Answer2 movie clip symbol

 Double-click the small circle representing the **Answer2** symbol on the **Stage**. You will now be in **Symbol edit** mode.

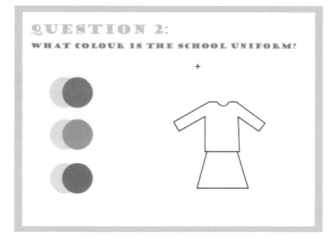

Figure 21.6

Line Tool

 In **Frame 1** of the **Text** layer, draw a uniform outline with no fill using the **Line** tool.

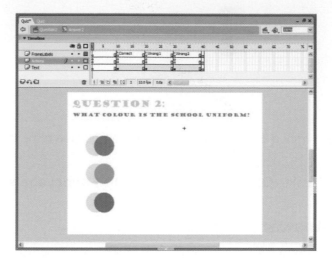

Figure 21.7

Selection Tool

 Select the whole outline by drawing a selection box around it with the **Selection** tool. With the outline selected, press **Ctrl-C** to copy it.

 Select **Frame 10** of the **Text** layer. Delete the existing text and tick.

 Select **Edit, Paste in Place** from the main menu bar.

 Repeat that for **Frames 20** and **30**.

Changing the uniform colour for each answer

- Select **Frame 10** of the **Text** layer (you should still be in **Symbol edit** mode, editing the **Answer2** symbol – it will say **Answer2** above the **Timeline** panel).

- In the **Toolbox**, select the **Paint Bucket** tool. Press **Escape** to deselect everything. If you can't see the tool properties in the **Properties** panel click once on the **Stage**. Now change the colour in the **Properties** panel to match the red of the first dot.

Paint Bucket Tool

> **Tip:**
>
> You can match the colour exactly by clicking the **Red** symbol in the **Library** panel then clicking the dropper on the red colour. If you click the **Red** symbol on the **Stage** you will get a faded red.

- Click the **Paint Bucket** tool in the jumper outline. If it doesn't fill, try changing the option at the bottom of the **Toolbox** to **Close Large Gaps** then try again.

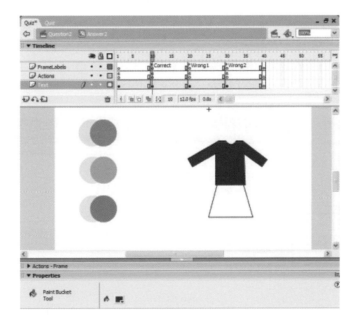

Figure 21.8

- Use the same method to colour the kilt khaki.

- Repeat these steps for **Frames 20** and **30** to turn the jumpers green and blue and the kilts khaki.

Add some text to **Frames 10, 20** and **30** to say **Correct** or **Wrong**. The red jumper is the correct choice.

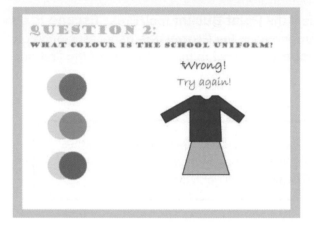

Figure 21.9

 Exit **Symbol edit** mode by clicking **Question2** above the **Timeline** panel.

Adding code to the buttons

 The code is almost identical to that used for the buttons in Question 1. Either copy and paste that code or copy the code below for the red button.

```
on(release) {
    tellTarget("Answer2"){
        gotoAndPlay("Correct");
    }
}
```

Figure 21.10

 If you have copied the text from a button in the **Question1** scene you will need to edit it slightly.

 Copy and paste the code from the **Red** button to the other two buttons (**Green** and **Blue**). Remember to change the text **Correct** to **Wrong1** for the **Green** button and **Wrong2** for the **Blue** button.

 Save the movie. You can't preview it yet because there is no way of getting on to the **Question 2** screen!

Adding a Next Question button

 Go to the **Question1** scene. Select the **Buttons** layer.

 Draw a button in the bottom right corner and write **Next** on it.

 Convert it to a **Button** symbol called **NextButton**.

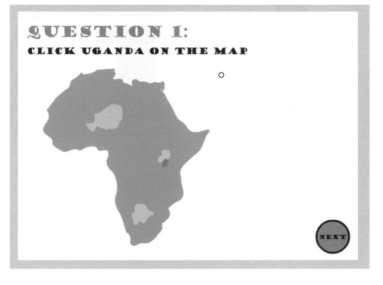

Figure 21.11

 Add a **Goto and Play at frame or label** behaviour to the button using the **Behaviours** panel (select the **+** icon in the **Behaviours** panel then select **Movieclip**, **Goto and Play**). You want it to go to the frame we called **Q2Start**.

+ Icon

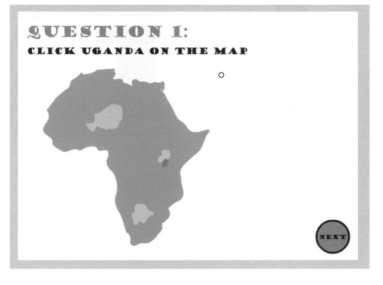

Figure 21.12

205

Save and preview the quiz. It should all work!

QUESTION 2:

WHAT COLOUR IS THE SCHOOL UNIFORM!

Correct!

Figure 21.13

Now we'll add a third question. This will have a slightly different format. The user will have to listen to three national anthems, then decide which one is the Ugandan national anthem.

Duplicating a scene

Duplicate Scene Icon

Select the **Question1** scene in the **Scene** panel. Click the **Duplicate Scene** icon at the bottom of the panel. Rename the new scene **Question3**. Move **Question3** below the other scenes.

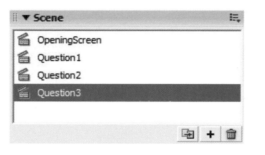

Figure 22.1

Unlock the **Question** layer then delete the **Africa** map.

Delete the three country buttons in the **Buttons** layer.

In the **FrameLabels** layer, edit the frame label to **Q3Start** (it will currently say **Q1Start** because this scene was copied from **Question1**).

Select the **Question2** scene. Click and drag an instance of the **NextButton** from the **Library** panel onto the **Stage**.

Use the **Behaviours** panel to add a **gotoAndPlay** action to the button. You need to make it **gotoAndPlay** at the frame we called **Q3Start**.

Return to the **Question3** scene.

Edit the question text to look like Figure 22.2.

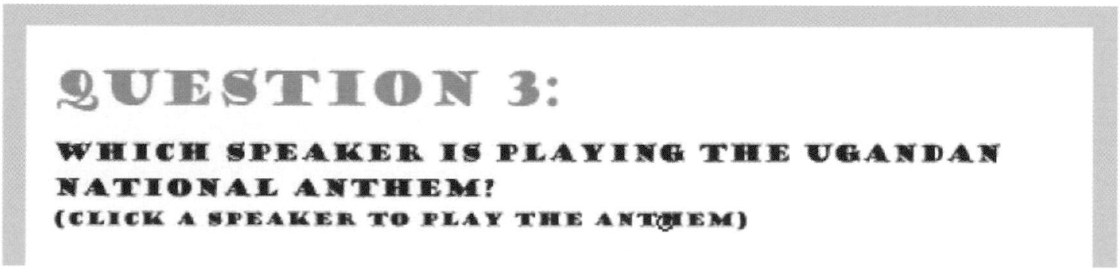

QUESTION 3:

WHICH SPEAKER IS PLAYING THE UGANDAN NATIONAL ANTHEM?
(CLICK A SPEAKER TO PLAY THE ANTHEM)

Figure 22.2

Select **Frame 1** of the **Buttons** layer. Draw a speaker shape, then convert it to a button symbol called **Speaker**. Drag out two more instances of the **Speaker** button.

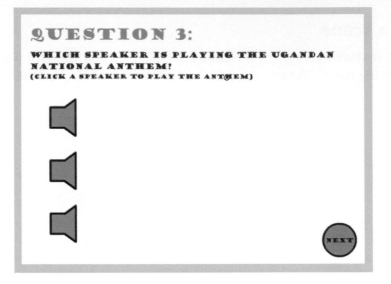

Figure 22.3

Importing sounds

You should already have downloaded the three MP3 files that are the British, French and Ugandan national anthems. They are in the **Components/Sounds** folder.

 Select **File**, **Import**, **Import to Library** from the main menu bar.

 Hold down the **Ctrl** key and select the three MP3 files. Click **Open**.

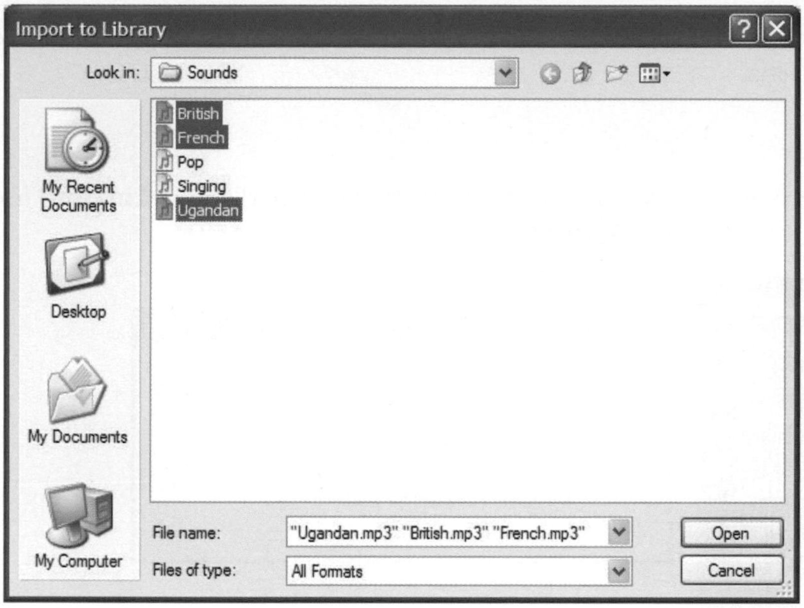

Import to Library [?][X]

Look in: [📁 Sounds] [▾] [◀] [🔼] [📁] [▦▾]

🎵 British
🎵 French
🎵 Pop
🎵 Singing
🎵 Ugandan

My Recent Documents

Desktop

My Documents

My Computer

File name: ["Ugandan.mp3" "British.mp3" "French.mp3"] [▾] [Open]

Files of type: [All Formats] [▾] [Cancel]

Figure 22.4

 The MP3 files appear in the **Library**.

Attaching the Play behaviour to the speakers

 Select the first speaker on the **Stage**.

 In the **Behaviours** panel click the small **+** icon. Select **Sound, Load Sound from Library** from the menu that appears.

 Fill in the window as shown in Figure 22.5 (including capital letters) then click **OK**.

+ Icon

Load Sound from Library

Type the linkage ID of the sound in the library to play:

[British]

Type a name for this sound instance for later reference:

[British]

[✓] Play this sound when loaded

[OK] [Cancel]

Figure 22.5

 Repeat this for the other two speakers, entering **Ugandan** and **French** in the window above.

Save and preview the quiz. The buttons won't work yet – we've got to do one more thing to the MP3 files.

Linkage

Right-click the **British.mp3** file in the **Library** panel, and select **Linkage** from the menu. Click the box **Export for ActionScript** then click **OK**.

> **This must be exactly the same as you entered in Figure 22.5 Even adding the file extension .mp3 will stop it working if there is no file extension in Figure 22.5.**

Linkage Properties

Identifier	British
AS 2.0 Class:	

Linkage: ☑ Export for ActionScript
☐ Export for runtime sharing
☐ Import for runtime sharing
☑ Export in first frame

URL:

OK   Cancel

Figure 22.6

Save and preview the quiz again. You should find that the first button works.

Do the same for the second and third buttons.

Preview again – this time you will find all the anthems play at once if you click each in turn.

Adding a Stop Sounds behaviour

We'll add a behaviour to each button to stop any sounds already playing before starting to play the next sound.

+ Icon

Select the first speaker. Click the **+** icon in the **Behaviours** panel. Select **Sound, Stop All Sounds** from the menu that appears.

Up Arrow

In the **Behaviours** panel, click where it says **Stop all Sounds** (not where it says **On Release**). At the top of the panel click the small up arrow to move this code to the top.

▼ Behaviors

Speaker

Event	Action
On Release	Stop All Sounds...
On Release	Load Sound from Library...

Figure 22.7

● Look at the **Actions** panel. The only code that has been added is one line: **stopAllSounds();**.

```
▼ Actions - Button
  Global Functions         ⊕ ⌕ ⌂ ⊕ ✓ ≣ ⊡                    ⊕ ⌀ ⊡
  Global Properties
  Statements               on (release) {
  Operators
  Built-in Classes
                                //stopAllSounds Behavior
  Current Selection            stopAllSounds();
    Speaker
  OpeningScreen            Speaker
  Question1                Line 23 of 23, Col 2
```

Any line that starts with // is just a comment, not code.

Figure 22.8

● Copy and paste the **stopAllSounds();** line into the **Actions** panel of the other two speakers, just below where it says **on(release) {**.

● Save and preview the quiz. Now only one anthem can be played at a time.

Adding the selection buttons

● Add one button next to the first speaker for the user to press if they are choosing that anthem. Convert it to a **Button** symbol called **ThisOne** then drag out two more instances next to the other two speakers.

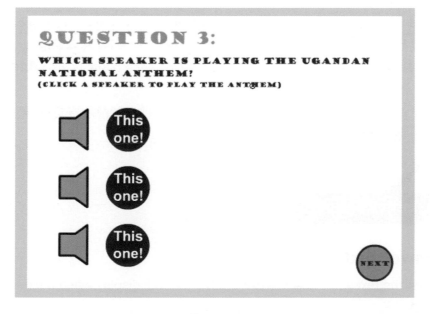

Figure 22.9

Adding the answers

To do this we'll follow the same method used for Question 2.

First we'll duplicate the **Answer1** movie clip symbol then name it **Answer3**.

> Click the **Answer** layer in the **Timeline** panel. Select the **Answer1** movie clip symbol on the **Stage**; it is currently blank so all you can see is a small black dot in the centre of where the symbol is.

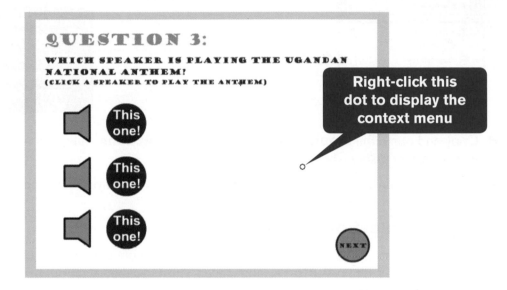

Figure 22.10

> Right-click the dot then select **Duplicate Symbol** from the menu that appears. Name the new symbol **Answer3**.

> Look in the **Properties** panel. Make sure that the instance name is also **Answer3**.

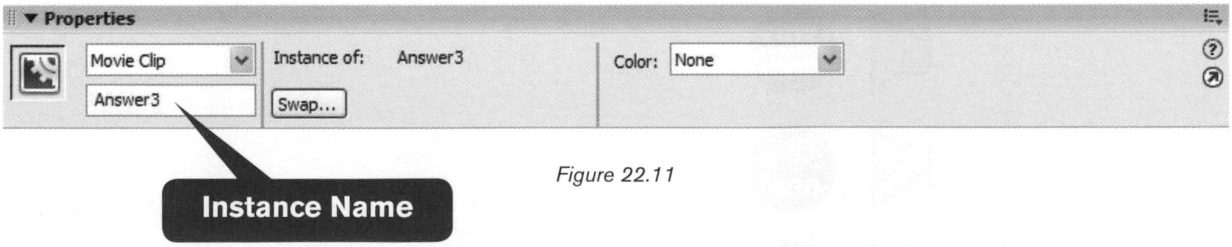

Figure 22.11

Adding answer text

We need to enter the text into the **Answer3** symbol that will display when a user clicks an answer.

Double-click the small dot (representing the **Answer3** movie clip) to enter **Symbol edit** mode.

The text for the **Correct** frame (**Frame 10**) is fine – we'll leave that.

Select **Frame 20** of the **Text** layer. This text does need editing.

Figure 22.12

Change where it says **That's Botswana – try again** to **That's the British national anthem – try again**.

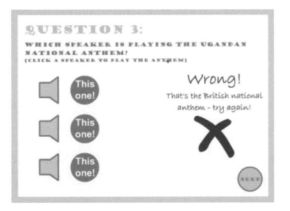

Figure 22.13

Change the text in **Frame 30** to say **That's the French national anthem – try again**.

Exit **Symbol edit** mode by clicking **Question3** above the **Timeline** panel.

Adding code to the buttons

Now we need to add the code to the **ThisOne** buttons to send the **Answer3** movie clip to the relevant frame to display the text **Correct!** or **Wrong!**

Add code to the **ThisOne** buttons next to the speakers to make the **Answer3** movie clip go to the relevant frame, just like you did for questions 1 and 2. The quickest method will be to copy and paste the code in Question 2 then edit it.

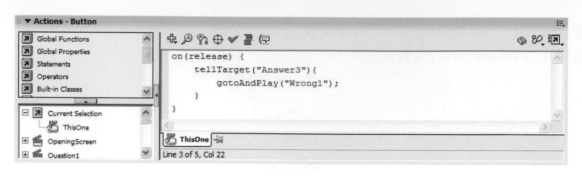

Figure 22.14

 Save and preview the quiz.

Other quiz questions

You can easily add more questions to the quiz. You've already learnt a wide variety of techniques that you can use to create different types of quiz question.

 Think up some other questions – try to make them interesting and fun to answer.

 Implement those questions in Flash.

Final screen

 Create a final screen for the quiz in a new scene called **FinalScreen**.

 Add a **stop()** action in **Frame1** of the **FinalScreen** scene.

 You'll need to make the **Next** button on the **Question3** scene point to the **FinalScreen**.

 Include a button on the final screen that will take users back to the start of the quiz.

Figure 22.15

Test, review and amend

It is really important that you test your quiz thoroughly yourself, and also get feedback from others.

> **For the SPB:** You will need to include evidence of testing and feedback. It is a good idea to submit in your eportfolio various screenshots of the development of the quiz, along with a note of any feedback given and the changes you made as a result.

Good marks... ✓

You will get good marks if you:

- use a variety of multimedia components in the quiz;
- include different types of question in your quiz;
- test out different designs and seek feedback as you go along;
- record the feedback and changes made so they can later be included in the eportfolio;
- make your quiz fun and suitable for the target audience;
- thoroughly test your quiz;
- provide feedback to users when they get questions right and wrong;
- include at least five questions.

Bad marks... ✗

You will lose marks if:

- you do not use your storyboard and flow chart when implementing your quiz;
- you do not seek feedback or do not use the feedback to improve your quiz;
- users find your quiz difficult to use;
- all your questions follow the same format.

> **For the SPB:** You should update your plan as you go along. It is likely you will need to move things around or change some of the timescales. Make sure you keep a copy of the original plan, as well as subsequent versions, to include in the eportfolio.

Section Five
THE EPORTFOLIO

In this section you will create your eportfolio using Dreamweaver. Your eportfolio will basically be a website – a set of linked pages with something about your project on each page. There will be a navigation bar for users to click to get from one page to another, just like in most websites. You can look at the completed eportfolio at **www.payne-gallway.co.uk/didaD202/eportfolio**.

In this chapter you will learn how to create a template that will be the basis of all the other pages in your eportfolio.

Researching other websites

It is important to research other examples before trying to create your own. This will provide you with some good ideas and also give you an idea of what is and isn't possible.

Search for other examples of eportfolios on the Internet. Take a look at the one for the sample project at **www.payne-gallway.co.uk/didaD202/eportfolio**.

Before you start work in Dreamweaver you have to plan out your website. You can do this as paper sketches, or draw straight on the computer if you prefer. If you use paper, scan in your sketches so that you can use them as evidence in your eportfolio.

The paper sketches are known as the **storyboard**. You can download blank forms for your storyboard from the website **www.payne-gallway.co.uk/didaD202**.

Figures 23.1 and 23.2 show two pages of the storyboard for the sample eportfolio that you are going to create.

When you do your storyboards for your eportfolio, you should save them as **EportfolioStoryboard1**, **EportfolioStoryboard2**, and so on, and put them in the **ProjectDocumentation** folder.

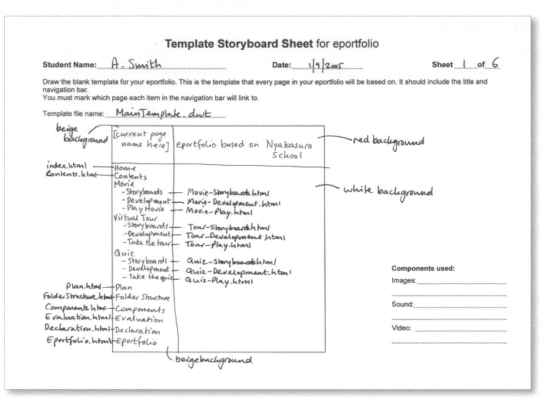

Figure 23.1

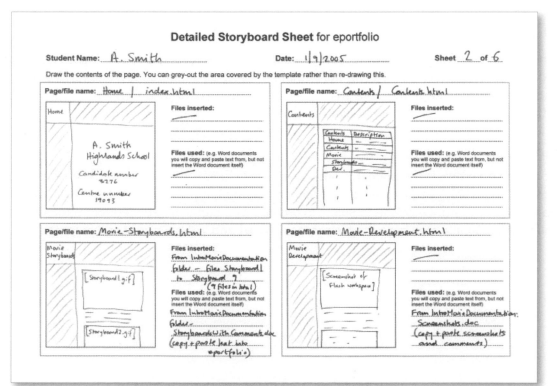

Figure 23.2

Folder structure

When you set up a new site in Dreamweaver, you will be asked where on your computer you want it to be saved. It is therefore a good idea to create a suitable folder structure before creating a new site.

Each page on your site and each image you use will be a separate file. By the time you've created a website with many pages and images there will be a lot of files, so you need to make sure they are well organised from the start.

For any website, the main folders you will want are **HTMLFiles**, **Images**, **Library** and **Templates**. We will also be creating a **FlashFiles** folder.

HTML files

Each page in your website will be an **HTML** file, and will go in this folder.

Images

Any image inserted on a web page is stored separately as an image file. It is common to store all the images used for a website in an **Images** folder in the main website directory. The image files used in the **School website** are all **JPEG** (**.jpg**) and **GIF** (**.gif**) files; another common file type used for images in Dreamweaver is **PNG** (**.png**) – **Portable Network Graphics**.

Library

The library is not actually used in this book but we'll create the folder anyway because it is good practice.

When you are creating your website, you can add various objects, such as images or paragraphs of text, to the library. This is useful for items that are used often, because if a library item is updated, every instance of this library item is also updated (just like in Flash). Each item added to the library is given its own library file, which is stored in this folder.

Templates

As soon as you create a template, Dreamweaver will automatically create the **Templates** folder for you, so you won't need to create that. You can create templates in Dreamweaver in much the same way as in Word. Once the template is created, you can base subsequent pages on that template. All template files have the file extension **.dwt** and will be stored in this folder.

Creating the folders

You can create the folders in Dreamweaver using the **Files** panel. However, if you are completely new to Dreamweaver it may be advisable to use Windows Explorer because you will be more familiar with it. We'll use the **Files** panel later.

Using Windows Explorer

To create the folders in Windows Explorer:

 Open Windows Explorer by right-clicking on the **Start** button and clicking **Explore** from the context menu that appears.

Figure 23.3

 Locate the **Eportfolio** folder you created in Chapter 1.

 Create four more folders in the **Eportfolio** folder, named **HTMLFiles**, **FlashFiles**, **Images** and **Library**. You don't need to create the **Templates** folder yet because Dreamweaver will create it for you when you save your first template.

Your folder structure should now look like Figure 23.4.

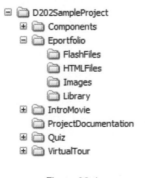

Figure 23.4

 Close Explorer. We're ready to start using Dreamweaver!

Creating a website in Dreamweaver

⊙ Load Dreamweaver. You can do this in one of two ways:

- **Either** double-click the **Dreamweaver** icon on your windows desktop
- **or** click **Start**, **Programs** then find the **Macromedia** folder and select **Macromedia Dreamweaver MX 2004**.

If this is the first time you have opened Dreamweaver, it will ask you about workspace options.

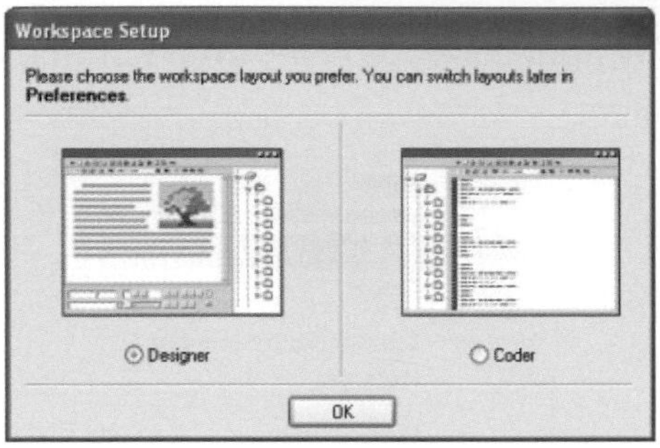

Figure 23.5

⊙ Choose **Designer** by making sure the first option button is selected, then click **OK**.

You will then see this window:

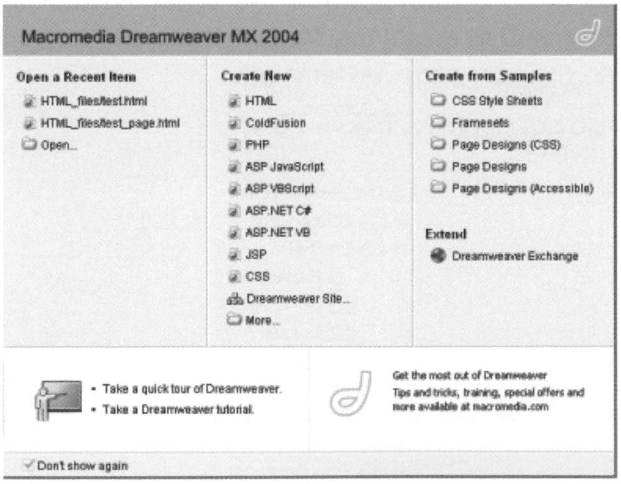

Figure 23.6

You don't want to see this **Start Page** every time you open Dreamweaver, so click the box, in the bottom left of the screen, marked **Don't show again**. Click **OK** in the dialogue box that appears.

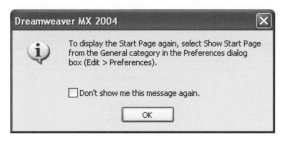

Figure 23.7

The green **Start Page** will stay open until we choose an option from it. Don't choose anything yet – we will do that in a minute.

Changing workspace options

If you selected the wrong workspace option you can correct it using the **Preferences** window as shown below.

 Select **Edit**, **Preferences** from the menu bar at the top of the screen.

 Select **General** from the left-hand list of categories then click the **Change Workspace** button. This will open the window shown in Figure 23.5 on the previous page.

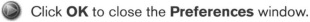

Figure 23.8

 Click **OK** to close the **Preferences** window.

Using the Files panel

🔘 In Dreamweaver, click the **Files** panel in the **Files** panel group on the right of the screen. If you can't see the **Files** panel, select **Window, Files** from the main menu bar.

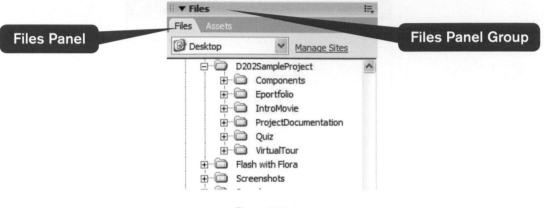

Figure 23.9

Options Icon

🔘 If you have already created your folders, you should be able to navigate to them in just the same way you would in Explorer. If you haven't created them yet, click the **Options** icon at the top right of the **Files** panel, then select **File** from the menu. From here you can create a new folder.

Creating a new site

🔘 The green **Start Page** should still be visible. Select the **Dreamweaver Site** option in the centre column marked **Create New**.

🔘 If the **Start Page** is not visible, select **Site, Manage Sites** from the main menu bar.

Figure 23.10

 In the **Manage Sites** window, click the **New** button, then click **Site** on the small sub-menu that appears. This is equivalent to the **Dreamweaver Site** option on the **Start Page**.

The **Site Definition** window appears. By default the **Basic** tab will be selected. This will take you through the wizard. We will not use the wizard, as it includes a lot of options that we just don't need at this stage.

Click the **Advanced** tab at the top of the window.

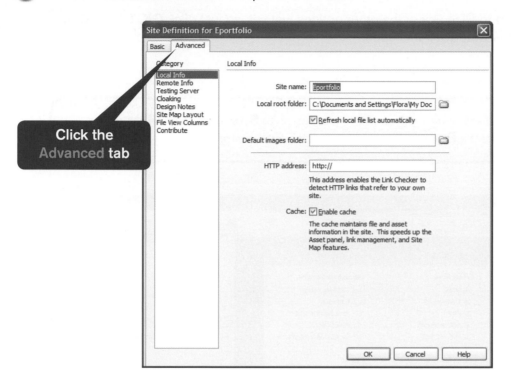

Figure 23.11

Enter **Eportfolio** as the **Site name**.

Click the **Browse** icon next to the **Local root folder** field and locate the **Eportfolio** folder.

Browse Icon

Figure 23.12

● Click **Select**.

● You don't need to fill in any of the other options just yet, so just click **OK**. Click **Done** in the **Manage Sites** window, if it is open.

Tip:

If you want to change any of the options you've just set, go to **Site**, **Manage Sites** on the main menu bar. Select the **Eportfolio** site and click the **Edit** button.

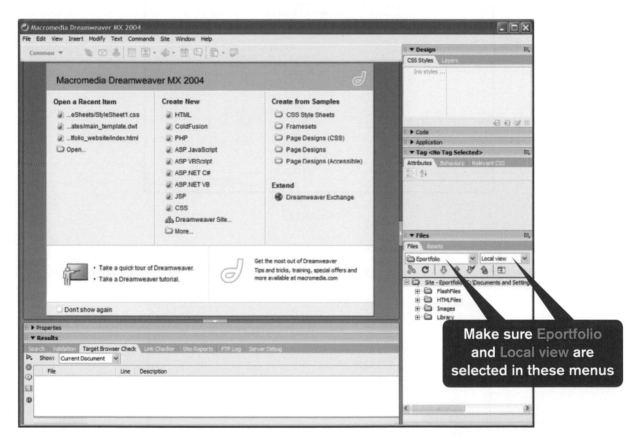

Figure 23.13

Your screen should now look like the one above. Rather than introducing all the different parts of the workspace now, we'll just cover a few basics here and then explain each new part as you need it.

Panels

Many of the useful commands in Dreamweaver are contained in **panels**, just like in Flash.

The panels are located to the right of the workspace – there are five **panel groups** in that list (**Design**, **Code**, **Application**, **Tag Inspector** and **Files**). Don't worry – you don't need to know about most of these right now; in fact, in this book you'll only need to use two of them.

Showing and hiding panels

If you are missing any of the panels shown in Figure 22.13, follow the steps below to add them to your workspace. You don't need to do this now – you can wait until you need to use a particular panel if you like.

Some of the panels are grouped; for example the **Files** panel and the **Assets** panel are both in the **Files** panel group. If you open one of the panels in a group, the whole group will open.

- Select **Window** from the main menu bar.

- Only the names of the **panels** appear in the **Window** menu – not the **panel groups**.
  To open a panel, click the name of the panel in the **Window** menu. It should then appear on the right of the screen with the other panels.

- To close a panel group, click the icon in the top right of the panel group, and select **Close panel group** from the menu.

Options Icon

Window	
✔ Insert	Ctrl+F2
Properties	Ctrl+F3
✔ CSS Styles	Shift+F11
Layers	F2
Behaviors	Shift+F3
Snippets	Shift+F9
Reference	Shift+F1
Databases	Ctrl+Shift+F10
Bindings	Ctrl+F10
Server Behaviors	Ctrl+F9
Components	Ctrl+F7
✔ Files	F8
Assets	F11
Tag Inspector	F9
Results	F7
History	Shift+F10
Frames	Shift+F2
Code Inspector	F10
Arrange Panels	
Hide Panels	F4
Cascade	
Tile Horizontally	
Tile Vertically	
Untitled-1	

Figure 23.14

The Files panel

Notice that all the folders you have set up now appear in the **Files** panel. Dreamweaver has inserted the text **Site - Eportfolio** where the folder name **Eportfolio** was (this is because **Eportfolio** was the name you gave to the site when setting it up); the file path is given in brackets afterwards.

If your folders don't appear in the **Files** panel, make sure you have **Eportfolio** and **Local View** selected, as shown in Figure 23.15.

Figure 23.15

You can easily change folder names, add new folders or delete files using the **Files** panel – you don't need to use Windows Explorer. All folders that are associated with a website are coloured green; because you specified that the site would be stored in the **Eportfolio** folder, all sub-folders within that folder will be associated with that website and will also be coloured green.

Saving a web page

All the pages in the **Eportfolio** website will be based on a template that we will create in the next chapter. Here we'll create and save a web page that is not based on a template, just for practice. We'll then delete the page.

First we need to create a new blank page.

⊙ Select **File**, **New** from the main menu bar.

Leave the options as **Basic page** and **HTML**, and click **Create**.

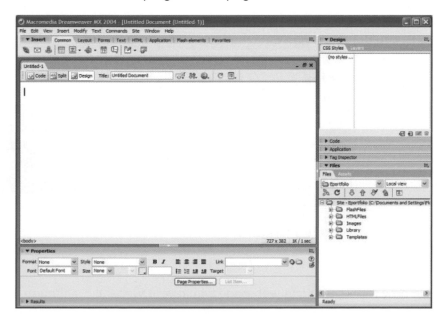

Figure 23.16

If the **Untitled-1** page doesn't take up the whole window as shown in Figure 23.17, click the **Maximize** button at the top right of the page window.

Maximize Button

Figure 23.17

From the main menu bar (not the one in the **Files** panel), select **File**, **Save As**.

The **Save As** dialogue box appears.

We'll save the new page in the **HTMLFiles** folder, so double-click this. Now enter the file name **TestPage.html** in the **File name** box.

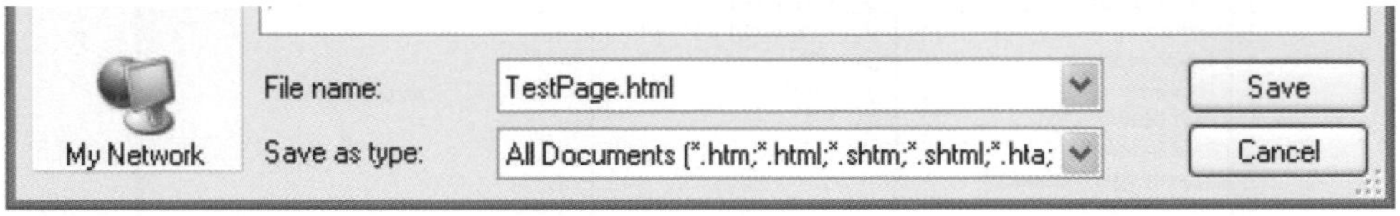

| | File name: | TestPage.html | | Save |
| My Network | Save as type: | All Documents [*.htm;*.html;*.shtm;*.shtml;*.hta; | | Cancel |

Figure 23.18

Tip:

If you don't add the file extension **.html** after the file name, the files will be automatically saved with a **.htm** extension instead. These two file types are exactly the same, but some servers don't like the use of **.htm** files. It is therefore safer to save all files as **.html** files because all servers can work with these.

Notice that in the **Save as type** box it lists many different file extensions next to **All Documents**, not just one; this is fine. Click **Save** when your screen looks like the one above.

In the **Files** panel, click the small plus symbol next to the **HTMLFiles** folder. You should now be able to see the **TestPage** file.

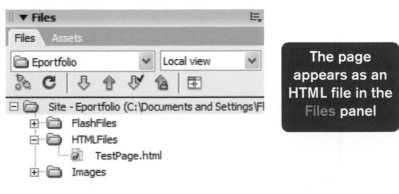

The page appears as an HTML file in the Files panel

Figure 23.19

The **TestPage** file now represents one web page within your website – although it is currently blank.

Deleting a web page

To delete a web page, all you do is delete its file. To avoid confusing error messages, it is best to make sure a file is closed before you try to delete it.

Closing a page

● Close **TestPage** by right-clicking on the page tab and selecting **Close** from the context menu that appears.

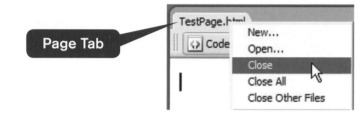

Figure 23.20

The page will disappear.

Tip:

If you wanted to open the page again, you would just double-click it in the **Files** panel.

● In the **Files** panel, click to select the **TestPage** file. Now press the **Delete** key.

Figure 23.21

● Click **Yes** (or **OK** in version MX).

Tip:

If you try to delete a page without closing it first, it will still remain open, and you will see messages saying you should resave it, and asking if you want to. If this happens, don't resave.

Deleting pages that are linked to other pages

If you try to delete a page that has links to it from another page, Dreamweaver will list the links to the site and ask for confirmation that you wish to delete the page.

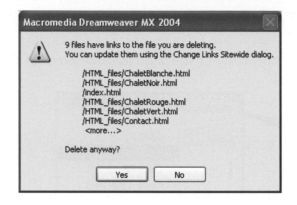

Figure 23.22

> If you just agree to Dreamweaver's warnings it will delete the page. If you get a message about links, this means that when you delete the page, another page will contain a link that doesn't do anything! Open up any pages that Dreamweaver says contain links and delete the links.

> Close Dreamweaver if this is the end of a session, otherwise leave it open for the next chapter.

You'll be pleased to hear that this is where the fun, creative bit starts. The key to a really professional-looking website (or eportfolio) is to use a clean, simple template and to base every page on the same template. The navigation bar is also included on the template, so that whichever page you are on you have access to the same navigation buttons. This not only makes the website look professional and coherent, it also makes it easy for people to browse your website without getting lost!

Creating a new template

You can create a template from scratch, or an existing page can be converted into a template. We'll create a basic page and later save it as a template.

 Select **File**, **New** from the main menu bar.

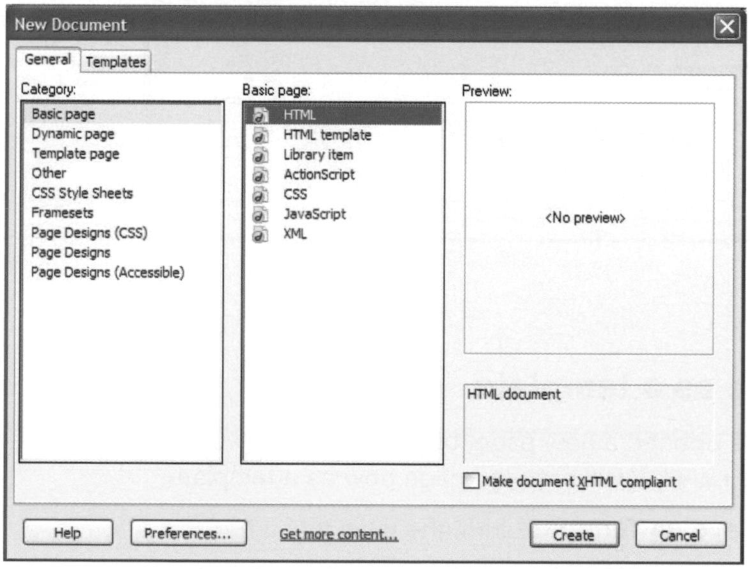

New Document

General | Templates

Category:
- Basic page
- Dynamic page
- Template page
- Other
- CSS Style Sheets
- Framesets
- Page Designs (CSS)
- Page Designs
- Page Designs (Accessible)

Basic page:
- HTML
- HTML template
- Library item
- ActionScript
- CSS
- JavaScript
- XML

Preview:

<No preview>

HTML document

☐ Make document XHTML compliant

Help | Preferences... | Get more content... | Create | Cancel

Figure 24.1

! Tip:

You could create a template page by selecting **HTML template** from the **Basic page** list. This would achieve the same result as saving the basic page as a template.

 Make sure **Basic page** is selected in the **Category** list and **HTML** is selected in the second list. Click **Create**.

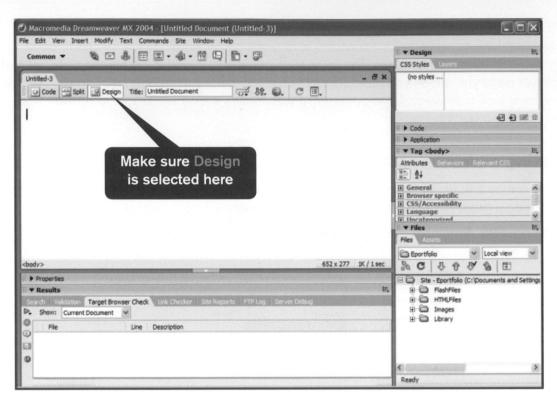

Figure 24.2

Saving a page as a template

Remember – you've opened a new page, but it is not yet saved. When a file is saved it will appear in the **Files** panel. We'll save the page now as a template.

Select **File**, **Save as Template** from the main menu bar.

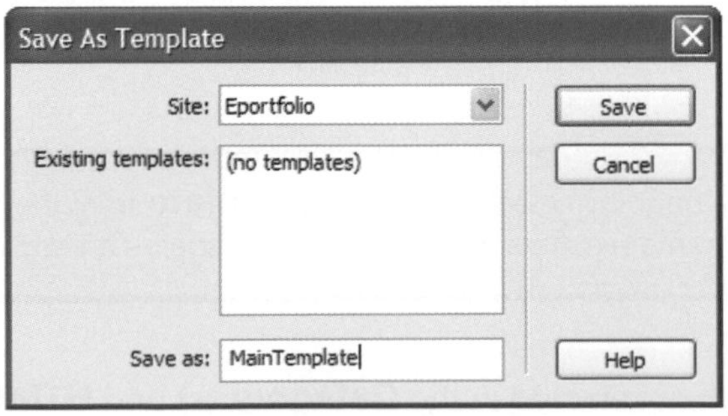

Figure 24.3

Save the template as **MainTemplate** and click **Save**.

The template may not yet be shown in the **Files** panel – you will need to refresh it first.

In the **Files** panel, click the **Refresh** icon.

Figure 24.4

> **Tip:**
>
> Although you didn't specify where Dreamweaver should save the file, it has automatically created a **Templates** folder and put it in there. If you had created the **Templates** folder along with the others, it would have found that and saved it in there.

Tables

You've probably come across tables in Microsoft Word, where they are used to store data in columns and rows. In Dreamweaver, tables can be used to store columns and rows of data, but their main use is actually as a layout tool.

By using a large table, the size of the whole web page, you can adjust the columns and rows to divide up the page into sections.

A large table, the width of the whole page, will be the basis of our template.

The Insert bar

Whenever you want to insert anything, whether it be a table, an image, a navigation bar or some other component, you will use the **Insert** bar. This is located at the top of the screen, just below the main menu bar.

Figure 24.5

There are two different views of the **Insert** bar. The one which appears when you first open Dreamweaver is the one above; we will now change this to show tabs.

 Click where it says **Common** on the **Insert** bar, then select **Show as Tabs** from the menu that appears.

The **Insert** bar now appears as shown below:

Click here to change back to Menu view

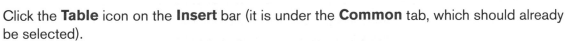

Figure 24.6

Tip:

If you want to know what any of the icons are on the **Insert** bar, just hold the mouse over the icon for a few seconds, and the **Tool tip** will appear with the name of the icon.

Inserting a table

Make sure the cursor is flashing in the top left of the page (it will be unless you've moved it); this is where we want to insert the table.

Table Icon

Click the **Table** icon on the **Insert** bar (it is under the **Common** tab, which should already be selected).

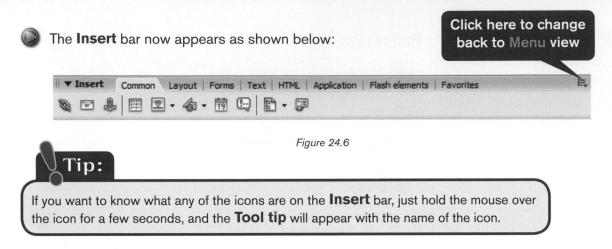

Figure 24.7

Tip:

Most sites use a width of about **800** pixels. At this size, each page of your site will fit onto most screens without users having to scroll across. Some sites are as narrow as **600** pixels – this means that even people with relatively small screens can view a page without scrolling, but you can't fit as much on a page. **www.payne-gallway.co.uk** uses a width of **600** pixels. **www.bbc.co.uk** uses just less than **800**.

Fill out the **Table** dialogue box as shown in Figure 24.7, with **3** rows and **2** columns. Enter the width as **750 pixels**. A value of **0** for the **Border thickness** gives an invisible border.

In Dreamweaver you can choose whether to size an object in **relative** or **absolute** terms. You can size an object **relative** to the size of the browser window by giving the size as a **percentage**. You can give an **absolute** size by specifying the number of **pixels**.

▶ Click **OK**.

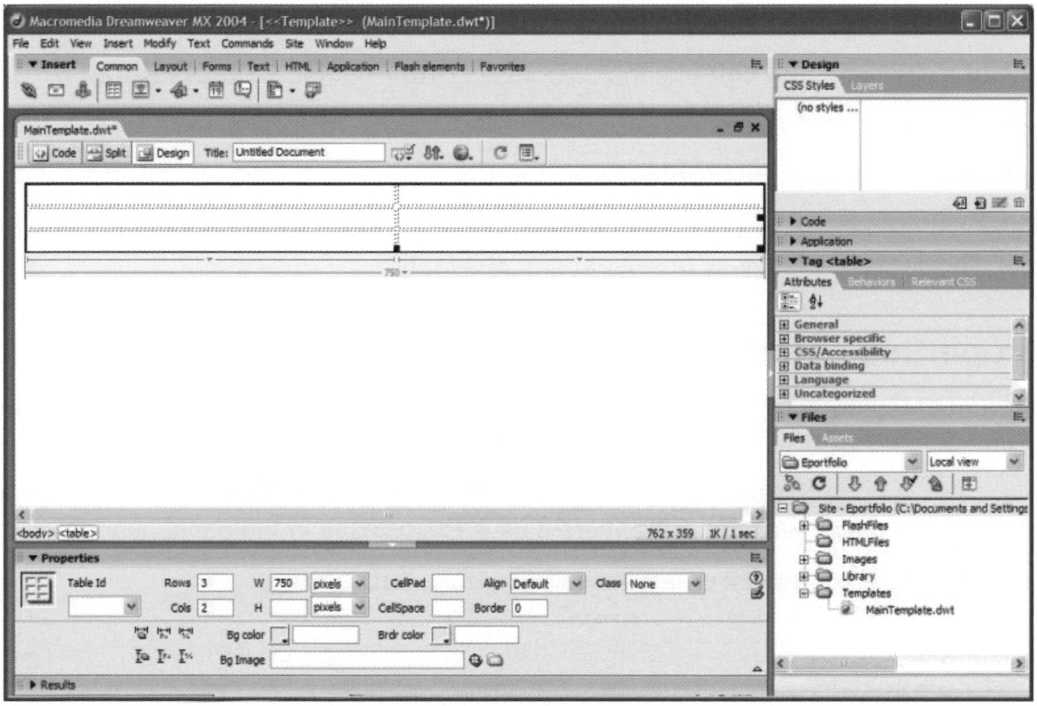

Figure 24.8

The table appears as shown above. It will need resizing but we'll do that in a minute.

Selecting cells, rows and tables

The table in the screenshot above is selected – as yours probably is because you've just created it. You can tell that it is selected because it has a solid black border and small black handles around it. It also has green lines and text indicating the width of the table.

▶ Click away from the table to deselect it. The handles and green lines will disappear.

🔵 Now click in the middle of the table. Look at the text at the bottom left of the page. It should look like Figure 24.9.

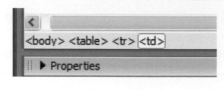

Figure 24.9

These are called tags, and the area they are in is called the **Tag selector**. Clicking on the tags here will select the objects they represent.

Clicking **<td>** will select the **cell** that the cursor is in (**<td>** stands for **table data**).

Clicking **<tr>** will select the **row** the cursor is in (**<tr>** stands for **table row**).

Clicking **<table>** will select the **table** the cursor is in.

🔵 Click each of these tags in turn and watch the black border highlight different parts of the table. This is the easiest way to select parts of a table.

The Properties panel

At the bottom of the screen is the **Properties** panel (sometimes called the **Property inspector**). You can immediately view the properties of any object on the page just by selecting the object.

🔵 If you can't see the **Properties** panel, select **Window**, **Properties** from the main menu bar. If the panel is collapsed, just click where it says **Properties** in the panel header.

🔵 Select the table you've just created by clicking the **<table>** tag.

Figure 24.10

> **! Tip:**
>
> If your **Properties** panel is smaller than the one above you might need to expand yours. To do this, just click the small arrow in the bottom right of the **Properties** panel.

The table properties appear in the **Properties** panel. You'll learn more about these properties in a minute.

🔵 Look at the properties of a **cell** and **row** by selecting them and viewing them in the **Properties** panel.

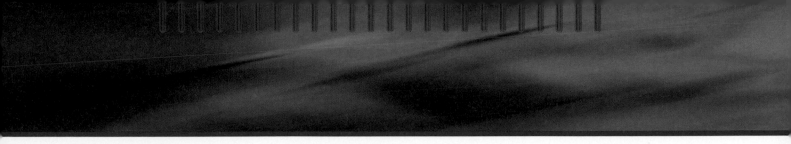

Inserting and deleting rows and columns

Adding or deleting the last row or column

You can add or delete the bottom row or right-hand column simply by changing the number of rows or columns in the table properties (in the **Properties** panel).

Figure 24.11

▶ Make sure the table is selected by clicking the **<table>** tag in the **Tag selector**. Change the number of rows to **4** and columns to **1** using the **Properties** panel. Press **Enter**.

Tip:

When changing properties in the **Properties** panel, you need to either tab out of a cell or press **Enter** for the changes to take effect.

Inserting or deleting a row or column in the middle of a table

▶ Right-click in the top cell in the table.

![Screenshot of Macromedia Dreamweaver MX 2004 showing the Table context menu with options including Select Table, Merge Cells, Split Cell, Insert Row, Insert Column, Insert Rows or Columns, Delete Row, Delete Column, Increase Row Span, Increase Column Span, Decrease Row Span, Decrease Column Span, Table Widths, and Expanded Tables Mode]

Figure 24.12

▶ Select **Table, Insert Column** from the context menu that appears.

The table should now have two columns.

⊙ Use the same menu to delete one of the rows so you are left with three rows.

Merging and splitting cells

You can easily merge and split cells, so that the number of rows and columns varies across the table. The quickest way to merge and split cells is to use the icons in the **Properties** panel.

Merging

Merge Cells Icon

⊙ Select the two cells in the bottom row of the table by clicking and dragging across them. Click the **Merge Cells** icon in the **Properties** panel.

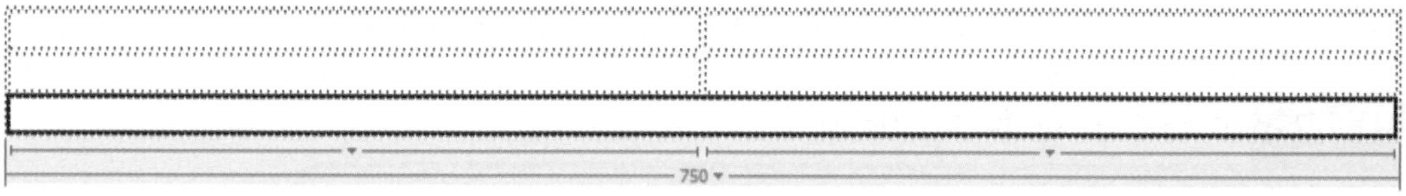

Figure 24.13

The cells are merged, and there's only one column in the last row.

Splitting

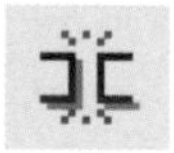

Split Cells Icon

⊙ Select the right-most cell in row **2**.

⊙ Click the **Split Cells** icon in the **Properties** panel.

Split Cell	☒
Split cell into: ○ Rows	OK
⊙ Columns	Cancel
Number of columns: 2 ⇕	Help

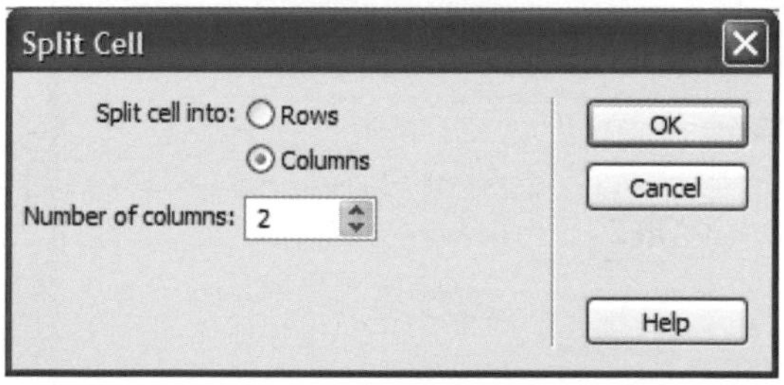

Figure 24.14

The **Split Cell** dialogue box appears. You have the choice of splitting the cell into rows or columns. You can also specify how many rows or columns.

⊙ Enter the settings shown above, and then click **OK**.

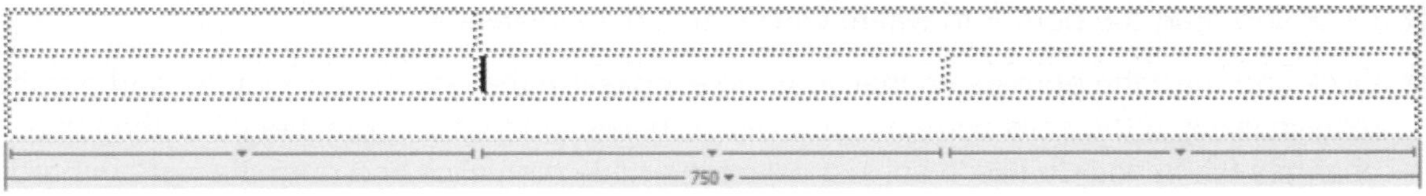

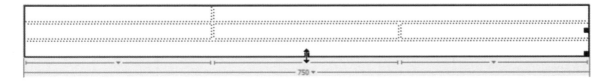

Figure 24.15

The cell is split into two columns.

Resizing cells and tables

Resizing a table

The table should at least fill the visible area on the screen, so we need to make it much longer.

 Select the whole table using the **<table>** tag. Place the mouse over the bottom handle so that it becomes a small double-headed arrow.

Figure 24.16

 Click and drag the handle down so that the table is about **800** pixels (the height will be shown in the **Properties** panel). Release the mouse when you're happy with the size.

> ## ! Tip:
> You don't need to worry that a table cell won't be big enough to fit an object, because the table will always grow to fit whatever you put in.

Resizing cells

To resize cells, just click and drag the table border between the cells.

 Place the mouse over the border you want to resize so that the cursor becomes an arrow. 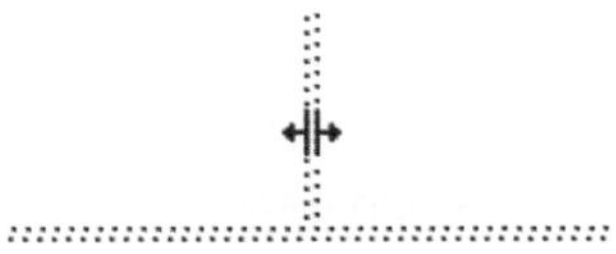

Figure 24.17

Click and drag the border to where you want it, then release it.

 Click and drag the borders so that your table looks like the one below. First try and get the relative sizes of the cells correct – you will probably find that the total height of the table changes when you do this. If so, just select the table then click and drag the bottom border to resize the height to about 800 pixels. I'm afraid resizing tables isn't an exact science in Dreamweaver; it sometimes takes a bit of trial and error – and a lot of patience!

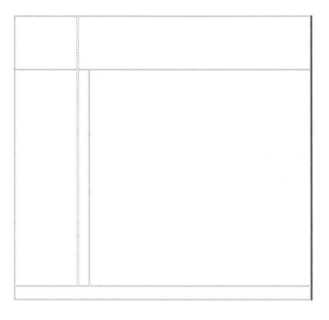

Figure 24.18

Saving the template

It's important to save your work regularly. You save a template in just the same way as you would a normal page.

 Make sure the **MainTemplate.dwt** page tab is selected at the top of the screen (it should be the only page open).

 Select **File**, **Save** from the main menu bar.

 You'll see a message about editable regions – we'll create these later. Just click **OK**.

 Tip:

If the **Save** option is greyed-out on the menu this is because the template is already saved. If this is the case, just go on to the next step.

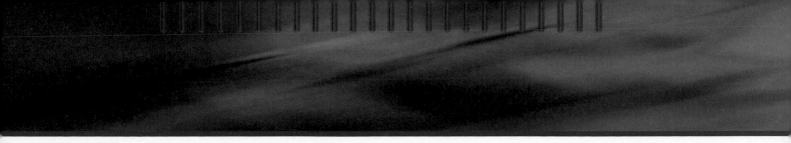

Changing the background colour

We'll change the colour of some of the cells.

 Click in the top right cell.

 In the **Properties** panel at the bottom of the screen, click the small grey square labelled **Bg**.

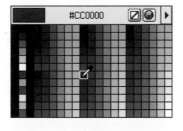

Figure 24.19

 A dropper appears. You can select any colour on your screen with this – you aren't restricted to using one in the colour palette. Choose a red colour.

 Now colour the other cells to look like Figure 24.20.

Tip:

Colours chosen from the palette are **Web Safe**, meaning they will look the same on any browser. The same is not true for a blend of colours, such as from the **Color Picker**.

Figure 24.20

 Save your work.

When you base a web page on a template, all content that is not specifically made into an editable region is locked. As a result, in order to be able to add any content to the page, you need to specify editable regions on the template.

We will define two editable regions in the template so that content can be added in the white area and also in the top left cell.

Templates Icon

Editable Region Icon

⚫ Click in the large white cell in row 2.

⚫ In the **Insert** bar at the top of the screen, make sure the **Common** tab is selected.

⚫ Click the small down-arrow on the **Templates** icon (second icon from the right).

⚫ Click **Editable Region**. You are now asked to enter a name for the editable region.

New Editable Region	✕
Name: `PageContent`	OK
This region will be editable in documents based on this template.	Cancel Help

Figure 25.1

⚫ Enter **PageContent** in the **Name** box. Click **OK**.

Figure 25.2

Repeat this for the top left cell, naming the editable region **PageName**.

> **Tip:**
>
> The **Templates** icon on the **Insert** bar will have changed to the **Editable Region** icon because that was the last option used.

The first editable region will appear quite low down the page because it has been put in the middle of a very long cell. We'll re-align the editable regions to be at the top of each cell.

Editable Region Icon

Aligning cell content

The editable regions appear in the centre of each cell because the properties of the cell specify that the contents should be aligned in the centre. It is not because of the properties of the editable regions.

 Click somewhere in the blank area of the cell containing the first editable region (**PageContent**). Now click the **<td>** tag in the **tag selector**.

 In the **Properties** panel, change the **Vert** property from **Default** to **Top**.

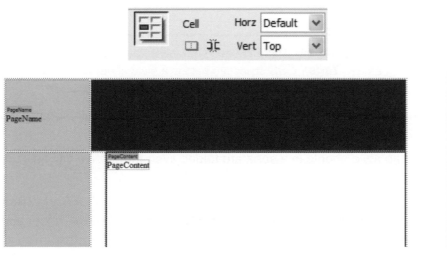

Figure 25.3

CSS styles

CSS stands for **Cascading Style Sheets**. Each style sheet can contain many different styles. For this website we will use just one style sheet, which will contain three text styles. It is possible to export a style sheet so that you can use the styles in other websites you design.

> **Tip:**
>
> Although in this book we will use CSS styles just for text, they are actually used to set the style for all sorts of things including table borders, background colours and more. There's plenty of information about them in the Dreamweaver **Help** – just look up **CSS** in the index.

First we'll create a new style, then we'll apply it to the **PageContent** text.

*New CSS
Style Icon*

- Make sure you can see the **CSS Styles** panel in the **Design** panel group. If not, select **Window**, **CSS Styles** from the main menu bar.

- Click the **New CSS Style** icon at the bottom of the **CSS Styles** panel.

- The **New CSS Style** window appears. Enter the style name as **PageContent** and make sure that the **(New Style Sheet File)** option button is selected next to **Define in**. Click **OK**.

New CSS Style

Name: PageContent

Selector Type: ⊙ Class (can apply to any tag)
○ Tag (redefines the look of a specific tag)
○ Advanced (IDs, contextual selectors, etc)

Define in: ⊙ (New Style Sheet File)
○ This document only

OK   Cancel   Help

Figure 25.4

Note:

Version MX 2004 uses CSS styles only. There are no HTML styles as in previous versions (although you can use **Tags**). CSS styles are held in a style sheet file.

The **PageContent** style we are about to create needs to be put in a style sheet. Since we don't have a style sheet created yet, we need to create one.

It's a good idea to keep style sheets in a separate folder, even though we will only use one style sheet in this site.

- In the **Save Style Sheet File As** window, make a new folder called **StyleSheets** in the **Eportfolio** folder. Save this style sheet as **TextStyles.css** in the new folder and set the **Relative to** box to **Document**, as shown in Figure 25.5.

Tip:

Use the **New Folder** icon to create a folder.

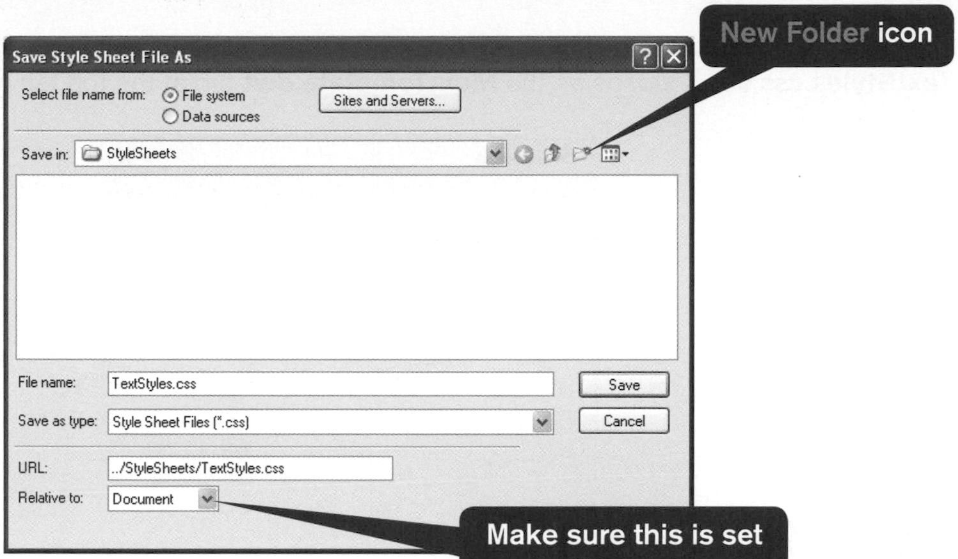

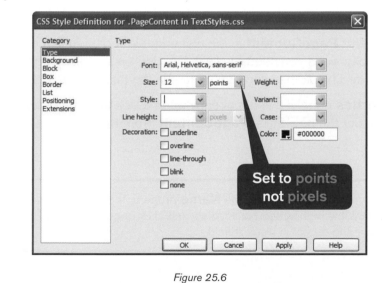

Figure 25.5

🔘 Click **Save**.

The **CSS Style Definition** window appears. We can now set the properties of the **PageContent** style.

Figure 25.6

Note:

Notice in the **Category** list on the left of the **CSS Style Definition** window that you can set properties for all sorts of other objects, not just text (**Type**).

🔘 Change the colour of the text by clicking the small **Color** box on the right. The cursor will change to a small dropper; click the dropper on the black colour in the colour palette.

🔘 Set the other parameters shown in Figure 25.6 and click **OK**.

The style now appears in the **CSS Styles** panel. Notice also that there is a page tab for the **TextStyles.css** sheet alongside the **MainTemplate.dwt** tab at the top left of the page.

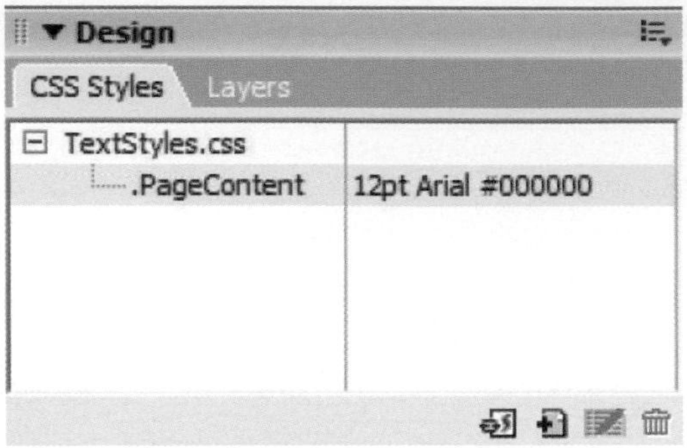

Figure 25.7

Tip:

If you accidentally double-click the style sheet you might find that you are faced with some rather unfriendly looking code! This is because you have selected the **TextStyles.css** page; to escape this simply click the **MainTemplate.dwt** tab at the top of the page.

Now we'll apply that style to the text in the first editable region.

- Click once in the text **PageContent** in the first editable region (it is the text with the white, not the green, background you need to click). We don't want to highlight any of the text; if the text is highlighted black then click once more in the text to deselect it.

- Open the **Properties** panel if it is not already open. Click the small down-arrow next to the **Style** box and select the new style, **PageContent**, from the list.

Tip:

If your **Properties** panel is only displaying the **Name** property then you have probably selected the text (so that it is highlighted black). If so, just click once on the highlighted text to deselect it. Leave the cursor in the text field.

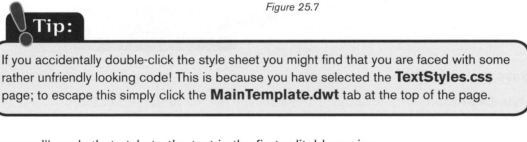

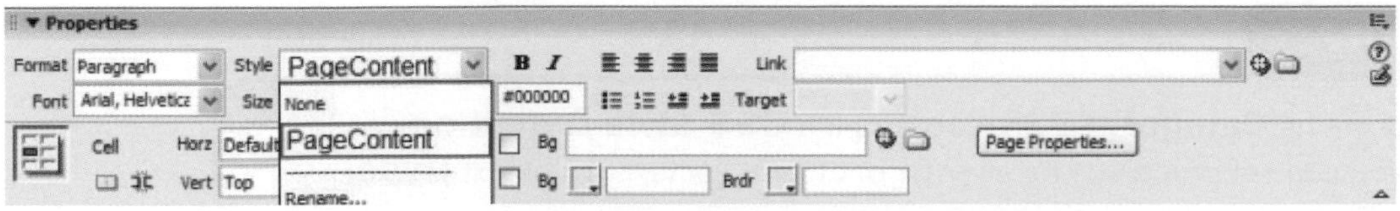

Figure 25.8

The style of the text changes, and takes on the properties of the **PageContent** style.

Now we'll do the same for the **PageName** text.

 Click the **New CSS Style** icon in the **CSS Styles** panel.

New CSS Style Icon

 Enter the name as **PageName**. We want this style to be added to the **TextStyles sheet** that we created, so make sure this is selected in the **Define in** box. Click **OK**.

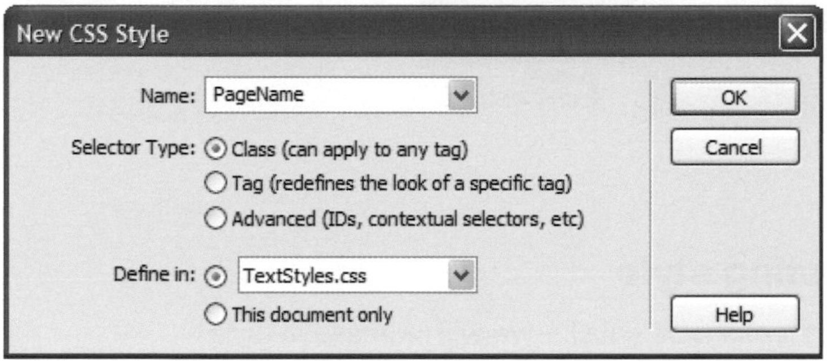

New CSS Style

Name: PageName

Selector Type: ⊙ Class (can apply to any tag)
○ Tag (redefines the look of a specific tag)
○ Advanced (IDs, contextual selectors, etc)

Define in: ⊙ TextStyles.css
○ This document only

[OK] [Cancel] [Help]

Figure 25.9

 Copy the style properties from Figure 25.10. Click **OK**.

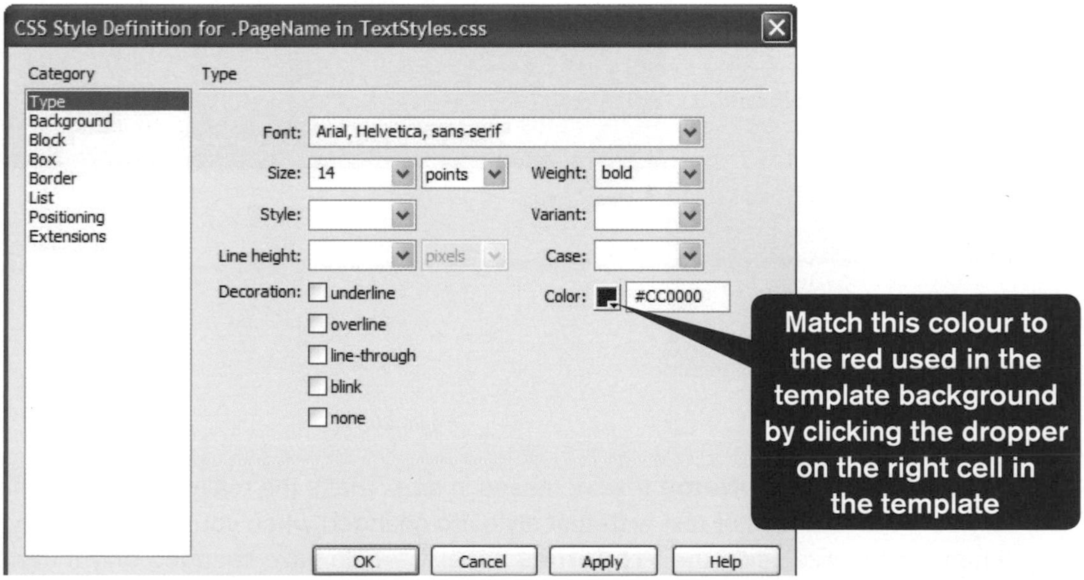

CSS Style Definition for .PageName in TextStyles.css

Category
- Type
- Background
- Block
- Box
- Border
- List
- Positioning
- Extensions

Type

Font: Arial, Helvetica, sans-serif

Size: 14 points   Weight: bold

Style: Variant:

Line height: pixels   Case:

Decoration: ☐ underline   Color: ■ #CC0000
☐ overline
☐ line-through
☐ blink
☐ none

> Match this colour to the red used in the template background by clicking the dropper on the right cell in the template

[OK] [Cancel] [Apply] [Help]

Figure 25.10

! Tip:

You can type in the colour code next to the **Color** box instead of using the dropper.

 Now apply the **PageName** style to the text in the second editable region, just as you did the first.

249

The text and the **CSS Styles** panel should now look like those below:

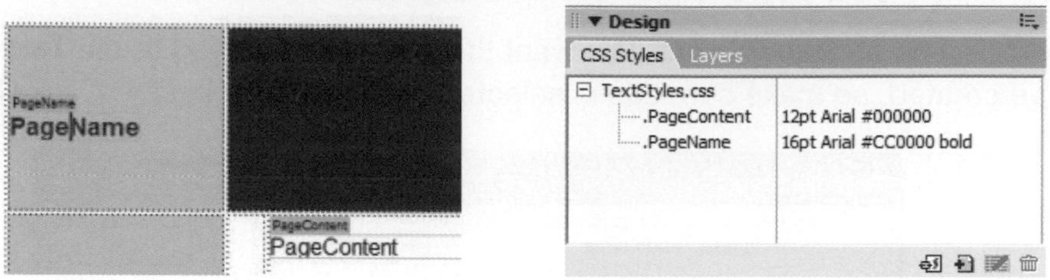

Figure 25.11

Editing an existing style

The **PageName** text looks a bit small – we will increase its size.

Edit Style Icon

Select the **.PageName** style in the **CSS Styles** panel then click the **Edit Style** icon at the bottom of the panel.

Change the size to **16** points then click **OK**.

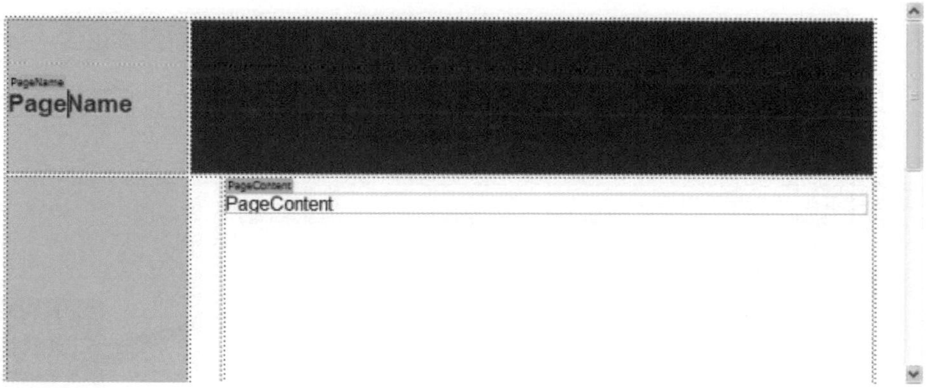

Figure 25.12

Notice that the **PageName** text increases in size. That's the really convenient thing about preset styles – all instances of text with that style are changed when you update the style. If you had changed the size using the **Properties** panel, it would have changed only that particular instance (in our case we only have one instance anyway, but in larger websites you might have hundreds!).

Save the template and its style by selecting **File, Save All** from the menu.

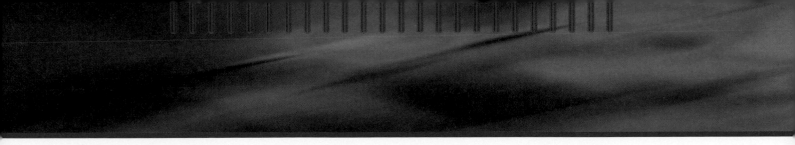

Adding a title to the template

We'll add a simple title to the top of the template so that it will appear on every page of the eportfolio.

- Click in the top right cell of the template. Type **eportfolio based on Nyakasura School**.

- Now highlight the text by clicking and dragging across it with the cursor.

Figure 25.13

We'll create a new CSS style for this title.

- Create a new CSS style called **MainTitle** with the following properties:

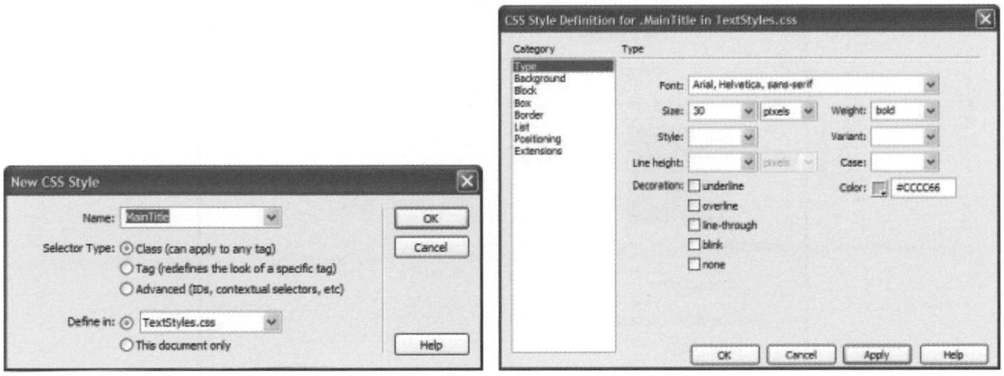

Figure 25.14

- Apply the style to the title text.

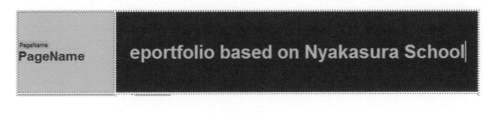

Figure 25.15

- Save and close the file and Dreamweaver if this is the end of a session, otherwise leave it open for the next chapter.

251

Chapter 26 - Creating a Navigation Bar

We will create a simple navigation bar down the left of the template. This navigation bar will then be visible on every page, because every page will be based on the template.

Using Fireworks it is possible to create quite a flashy navigation bar with pop-up menus, but this is quite time-consuming. Here we will create the navigation bar by using text with hyperlinks in Dreamweaver.

We will place the text in a table to make it easy to lay it out.

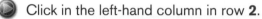

- Click in the left-hand column in row **2**.
- Change the **Vert** property in the **Properties** panel to **Top**. This will ensure that the navigation bar is always at the top of that cell.
- Make sure the **Common** tab is selected in the **Insert** bar. Click the **Table** icon.
- Fill out the **Table** window as shown in Figure 26.1 then click **OK**.

Table Icon

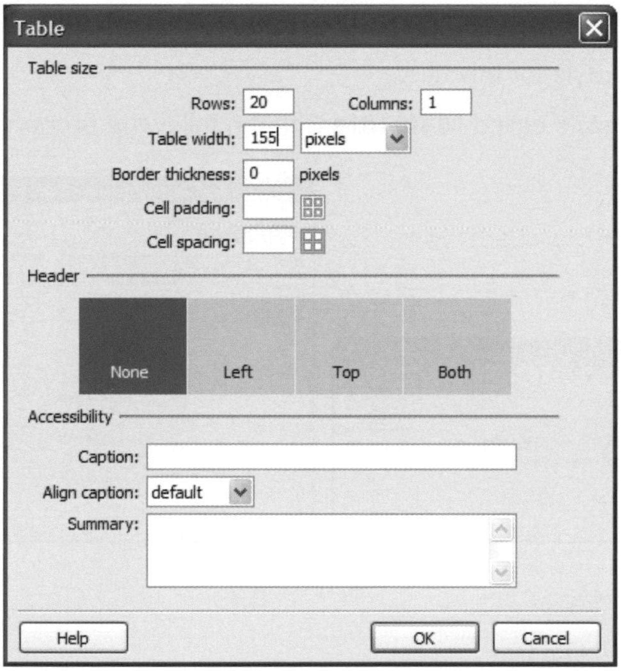

Figure 26.1

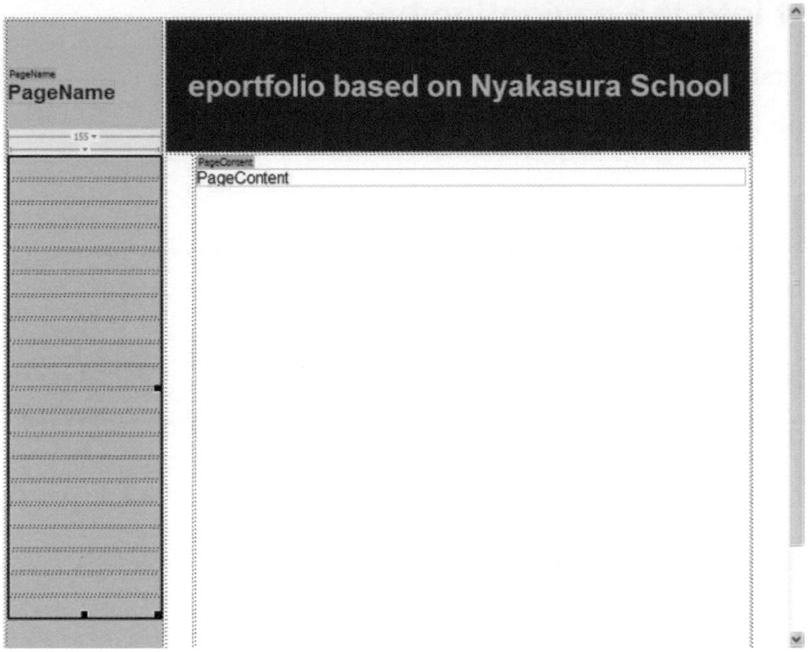

Figure 26.2

Create a new CSS Style called **NavigationBar**. Copy the properties from Figure 26.3.

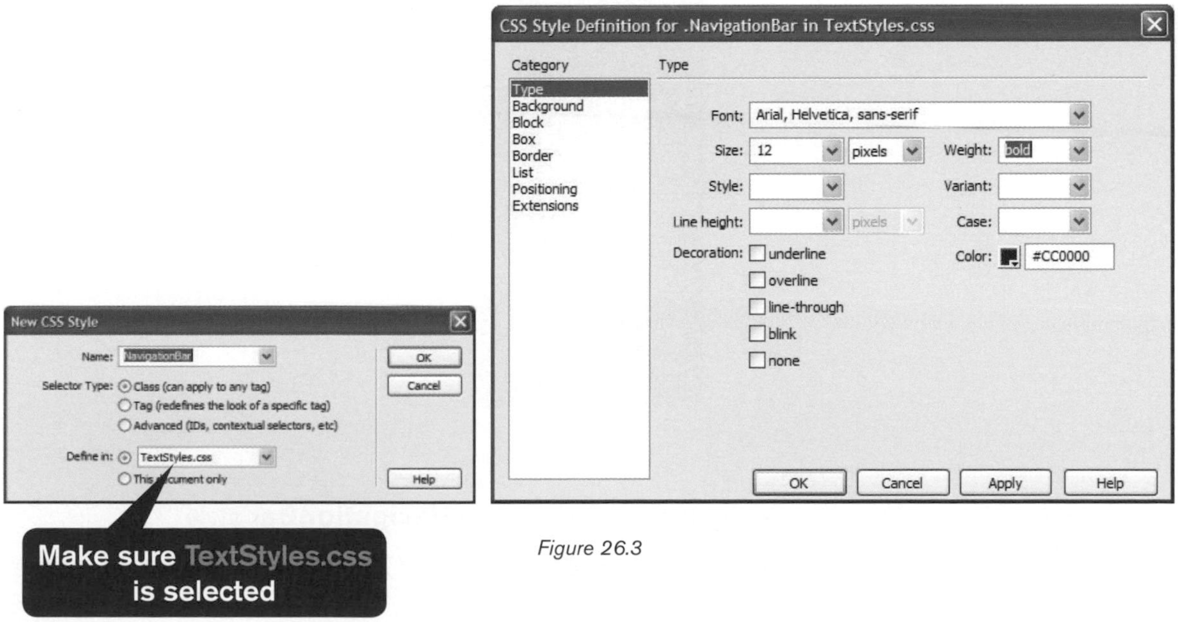

Figure 26.3

Now click in the first cell in the table you have just inserted. Click and hold down to the last cell to select all cells in the table.

In the **Properties** panel, select **NavigationBar** as the **Style**.

Entering text into the navigation bar

⊚ Click in the first cell in the table. Type **Home**.

⊚ Press the **Tab** key to move the cursor to the next cell.

> ❗ **Tip:**
>
> If you press **Enter** instead of **Tab** you will add another line in the existing cell rather then moving to the next cell. If you do this, press **Ctrl-Z** to undo.
>
> You can also press the down arrow key to go to the next cell.

⊚ Type in the other items in the navigation bar as shown in Figure 26.4.

155 ▼
Home
Contents
Movie
Virtual Tour
Quiz
Plan
Folder Structure
Components
Evaluation
Declaration
Eportfolio

Figure 26.4

The text looks a bit small; we'll make it bigger by editing the **NavigationBar** style.

Edit Style Icon

⊚ Select the **NavigationBar** style in the **CSS Styles** panel. Click the **Edit Style** icon at the bottom of the panel.

⊚ Increase the font size to **16 pixels** then click **OK**. The text in the template is updated immediately.

Split Cells Icon

⊚ Select the fourth cell down (it should be blank). Click the **Split Cells** icon in the **Properties** panel. Split the cell into **2 columns**.

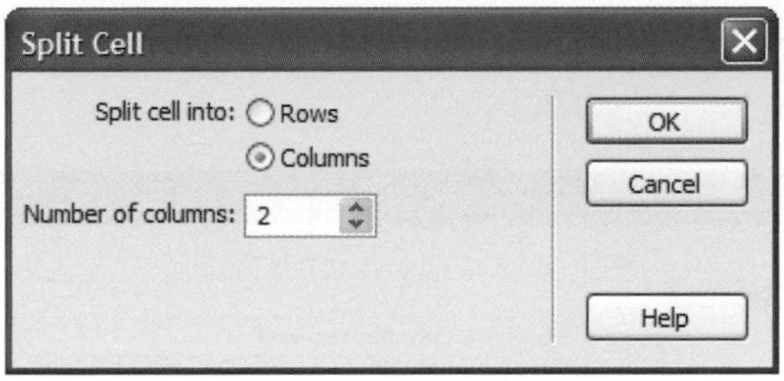

Figure 26.5

 Repeat this for all the blank cells in the navigation bar. (You can simply move to each blank cell in turn and press **Ctrl-Y** to repeat your last action.)

 Click and drag the cell border between the two columns in the first blank cell to the left as shown in Figure 26.6; all the others should move as well.

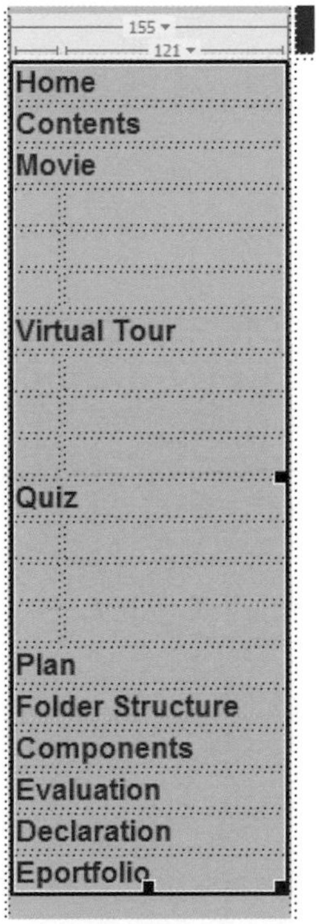

Figure 26.6

Create a new CSS style called **NavigationBarSubItem**. Give it the properties shown in Figure 26.7. Click **OK**.

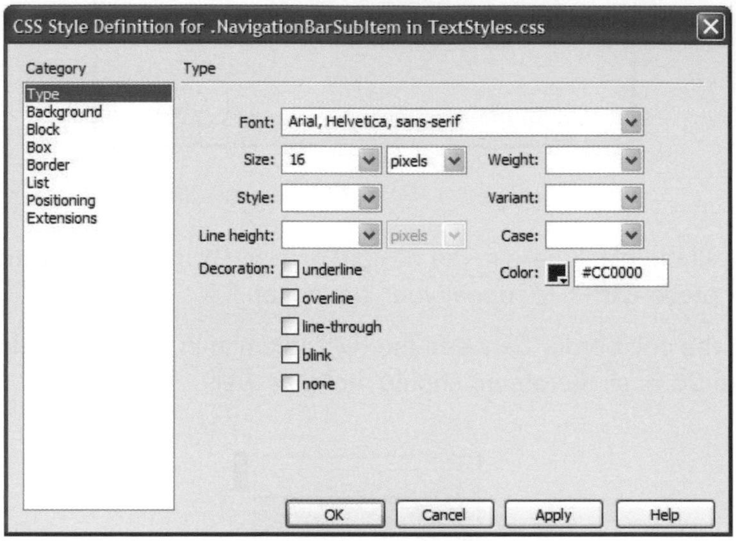

CSS Style Definition for .NavigationBarSubItem in TextStyles.css

Category   Type

Type
Background   Font: Arial, Helvetica, sans-serif
Block
Box   Size: 16   pixels   Weight:
Border
List   Style: Variant:
Positioning
Extensions   Line height: pixels   Case:

                Decoration: ☐ underline   Color: #CC0000
                             ☐ overline
                             ☐ line-through
                             ☐ blink
                             ☐ none

                        OK   Cancel   Apply   Help

Figure 26.7

 Enter the following text into the navigation bar and apply the **NavigationBarSubItem** style to it.

Home
Contents
Movie
    Storyboards
    Development
    Play Movie
Virtual Tour
    Storyboards
    Development
    Take the Tour
Quiz
    Storyboards
    Development
    Take the Quiz
Plan
Folder Structure
Components
Evaluation
Declaration
Eportfolio

Figure 26.8

⊙ Save the template by pressing **Ctrl-S**. Close the page by right-clicking the **MainTemplate. dwt** page tab then selecting **Close** from the menu that appears.

Right-click a page tab to open the context menu

Close the TextStyles.css page if it is open. Say Yes if prompted to save

Figure 26.9

⊙ Close Dreamweaver if this is the end of a session, otherwise leave it open for the next chapter.

Links will be added later on that will take users to the relevant page when a navigation bar item is pressed. You cannot make these links until the pages they will point to have been created.

Chapter 27 - Creating the Home Page

You've created the template that all the pages in your eportfolio will be based on. The first page we'll create will be the **Home** page.

- Load Dreamweaver if it is not already open.

We'll open a new page based on the template.

- Select **File**, **New** from the menu.
- Click the **Templates** tab; the text will change to **New from Template** in the top of the window.
- Choose the same settings as shown below.

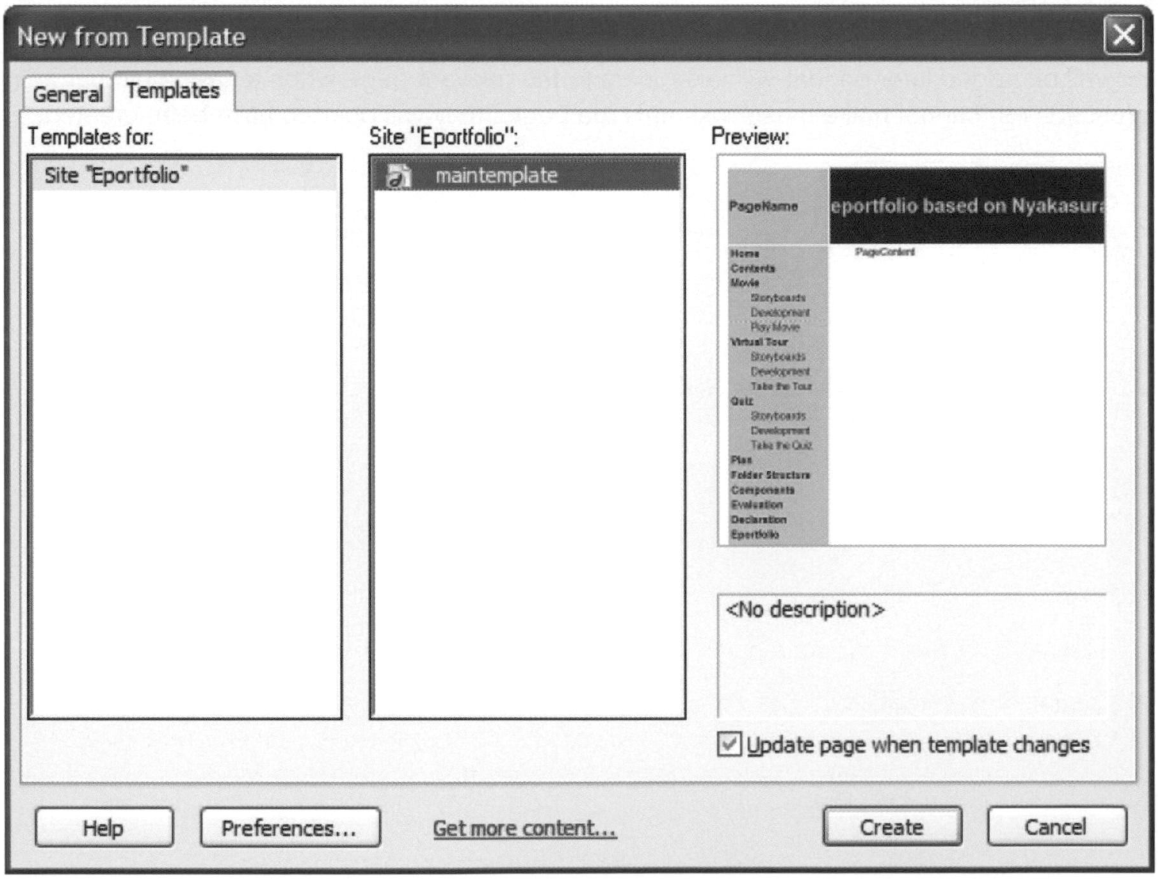

Figure 27.1

- Click **Create**.

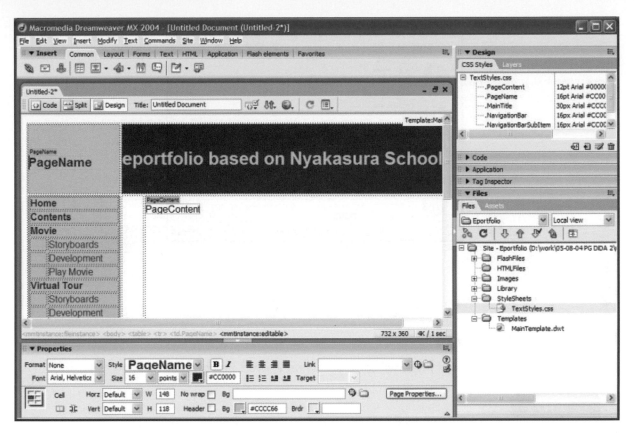

Figure 27.2

 Try changing any part of the template that you didn't specify as **Editable** – it will be locked.

Saving the Home page

 Select **File**, **Save** from the main menu bar. The **Save As** window appears.

All the pages in the website will be saved in the **HTMLFiles** folder except the **Home** page. This is because many servers will look for a file called **index.html** in the root folder of the site to display when the site is opened. We must therefore save the **Home** page as **index.html** and save it in the **Eportfolio** folder.

 Select the **Eportfolio** folder. Enter **index.html** (all lower case) in the **File name** box, as shown in Figure 27.3.

Figure 27.3

 Click **Save**.

Previewing the page

It's very easy to see what the page will look like when viewed in a browser.

 Tip:

Before previewing any page or template you should save it first. If you don't save, the latest changes might not be shown in the browser.

 To preview the template in your default browser (usually Internet Explorer), just press **F12**.

 To preview the template in a different browser, select **File**, **Preview in Browser** from the main menu bar. If the browser you want isn't listed, select **Edit Browser List**.

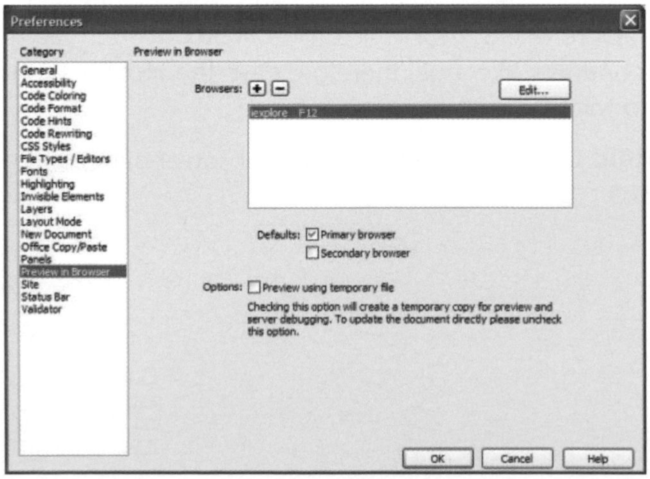

Figure 27.4

Tip:

Other browsers include **Netscape**, **Firefox** and **Opera**.

 The **Preferences** window appears. To add a browser, just click the small **+** button at the top of the window. You'll then be asked to locate the browser software on your computer. You can also select a shortcut key for the new browser (**F12** is the default shortcut for your default browser). Click **OK** when you're done.

When you press the shortcut key, your page will open in a browser, as shown in Figure 27.5.

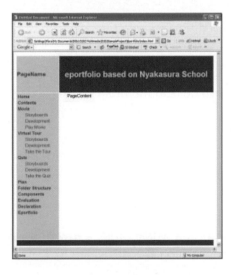

Figure 27.5

This is exactly how you would view any page you create in Dreamweaver.

 You can leave the browser window open while you work on the page in Dreamweaver, but it won't update to reflect any changes you make in Dreamweaver. Each time you make a change, you will need to press the shortcut key, or save the page and refresh the browser window (press **F5**).

Borders

Notice that there is a small gap between the borders in the table. We'll just quickly run through the different options you could choose.

 Return to the Dreamweaver window.

 Open the **MainTemplate.dwt** file by double-clicking it in the **Files** panel (it will be in the **Templates** folder). Select the table (the main table, not the one for the navigation bar) using the **<table>** tag, and look at the table properties.

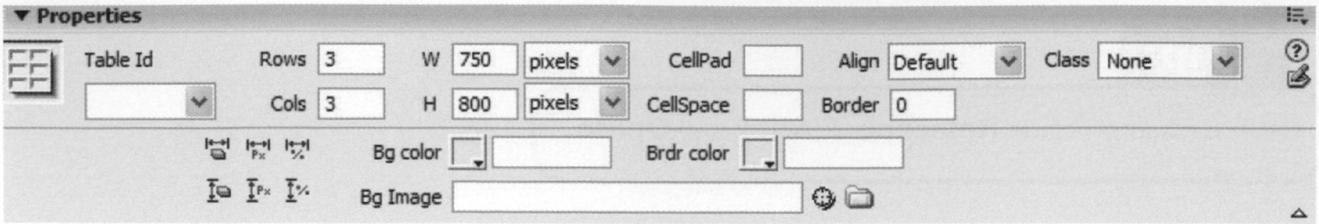

Figure 27.6

The properties that affect the table borders are **CellPad**, **CellSpace**, **Border**, **Brdr color** and **Bg color**.

CellPad

Cell padding is the space around the contents of a cell.

CellSpace

Cell spacing is the space between cells in the table.

Border

You can enter a value for the border. Entering **0** gives an invisible border. The higher the number the thicker the border around the table. The default value is **1**.

Brdr color

You can choose a border colour for the whole table, a row or a cell. Remember that if you want a coloured border you'll have to change the **Border** value to **1**; if it is **0** you won't see it!

Bg color

You can change the background colour in the table, a row or an individual cell.

Changing the border width

We'll change the border width to get rid of the white space between cells.

● With the entire table still selected, enter **0** where it says **CellSpace** in the **Properties** panel, then press **Enter**.

● Select **File**, **Save All** from the main menu bar. This automatically saves all open pages.

You will get the following message which asks if you want the pages based on the **MainTemplate** to be updated to reflect the changes just made.

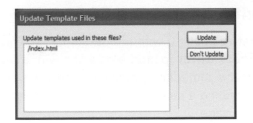

Figure 27.7

- Click **Update**. Click **Close** in the next window.
- Close the **MainTemplate.dwt** file by right-clicking its page tab (under the **Insert** bar) then selecting **Close** from the menu that appears.

Adding text

We're going to insert the page title in the first editable region.

- Click where it says **PageName** (the red text, not black). Delete the text **PageName** and type **Home**.

Figure 27.8

Adding student details

- Now in the **PageContent** editable region, delete the text **PageContent** then type some student details as shown below.

Figure 27.9

Editing text styles without creating CSS styles

You can format the text by first selecting it with the cursor then using the **Properties** panel to change the font properties. Press **Enter** to start a new line with a gap from the previous line, or **Shift-Enter** to start a new line immediately below the previous one. It can be a bit awkward changing text styles without creating a new CSS style – if you find it easier you should create some more CSS styles for this page.

Format the text as shown in Figure 27.10.

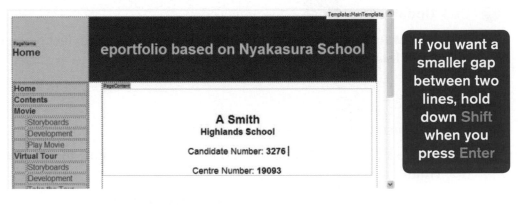

Figure 27.10

Notice that when you change the text properties a new style, called **Style1** or **Style2**, is added in the **CSS Styles** panel. You will sometimes find that when you change the properties of selected text the changes are not reflected in the text selected; in this case re-select **Style1** or **Style2** in the **Style** menu in the **Properties** panel.

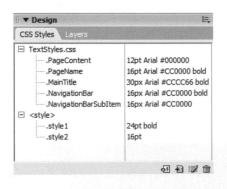

Figure 27.11

Save the **Home** page by pressing **Ctrl-S**. Close it by right-clicking the **index.html** page tab then selecting **Close** from the menu that appears.

Chapter 28 - The Contents Page

- Select **File**, **New** from the main menu bar.
- Select the **Templates** tab then select the **MainTemplate** file. Click **Create**.
- Change the **PageName** text to say **Contents**.
- Select **File**, **Save** from the main menu bar.
- Save the page as **Contents.html** in the **HTMLFiles** folder. Click **Save**.

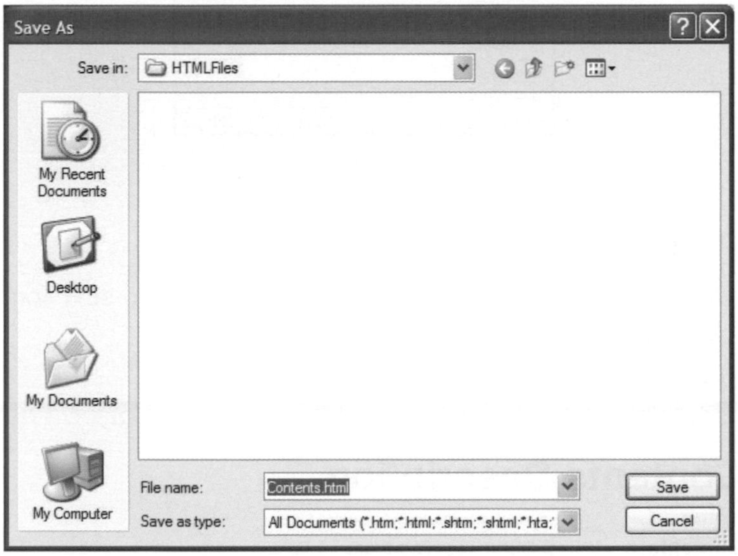

Figure 28.1

The **Contents** page will show a table with the list of eportfolio contents in the left column and a short description in the right. The first step is to insert a table into the **PageContent** editable region.

- Click the cursor in the **PageContent** editable region then delete the text.
- On the **Insert** bar make sure the **Common** tab is selected.
- Click the **Table** icon. Fill out the **Table** window as shown in Figure 28.2.

Table Icon

Table

Table size

Rows: 21   Columns: 2

Table width: 550 pixels

Border thickness: 0 pixels

Cell padding:

Cell spacing:

Header

None   Left   Top   Both

Accessibility

Caption:

Align caption: default

Summary:

Help   OK   Cancel

Figure 28.2

 Click **OK**. The table is inserted into the editable region.

 Enter the following titles and text into the table. You will need to split some of the cells, just as you did for the navigation bar table.

550
111 (100)   388 (408)

Contents	Description
Home	Student details with outline of project
Contents	Contents page (this page)
Movie	
Storyboards	Storyboards for IntroMovie
Development	Evidence of development: screenshots of Flash workspace plus feedback
Play Movie	IntroMovie.swf file of tour (embedded into web page)
Virtual Tour	
Storyboards	Storyboards for the virtual tour
Development	Evidence of development: screenshots of Flash workspace plus feedback
Take the Tour	VirtualTour.swf file (embedded into web page)
Quiz	
Storyboards	Storyboards for the quiz
Development	Evidence of development: screenshots of Flash workspace plus feedback
Take the Quiz	Quiz.swf file (embedded into web page)
Plan	Initial and final project plan
Folder Structure	Folder structure used for the development of products and eportfolio
Components	Components table, evidence of preparation of original components, evidence of preparation of ready-made components inc. screenshots of Fireworks workspace
Evaluation	Review and evaluation of the project with feedback
Declaration	Student and teacher declaration of own work
Eportfolio	Storyboards for eportfolio

Figure 28.3

- Save the page by pressing **Ctrl-S** (this is the same as selecting **File, Save** from the main menu bar, or right-clicking the page tab and selecting **Save**).

- Preview the page in Internet Explorer by pressing **F12**.

Tip:

If you want to be able to see the table borders, change the **Border** value in the **Properties** panel to **1**, and the border colour to black.

- Close the **Contents** page by right-clicking the page tab, then selecting **Close** from the menu that appears.

Creating the Movie Storyboards page

We will now create the page that will open when the user clicks the **Storyboards** sub-menu item under **Movie**.

The storyboards have already been drawn and scanned so that they are a series of GIF or JPEG files that can be inserted into a website.

- Create a new page based on the **MainTemplate**. Save the page as **Movie-Storyboards.html** in the **HTMLFiles** folder.

- Change the **PageName** text to say **Movie Storyboard**.

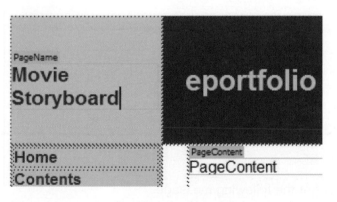

Figure 28.4

Inserting an image

- Click the mouse in the **PageContent** editable region and delete the **PageContent** text that's there. Press **Enter** to insert a blank line.

- In the **Insert** panel, make sure the **Common** tab is selected, then click the small down-arrow on the **Images** icon (the fifth icon from the left).

Images Icon

Select **Image** from the menu that appears.

Figure 28.5

 Navigate to the **IntroMovieDocumentation** folder, which is in the **IntroMovie** folder. Select the **MovieStoryboard1** file.

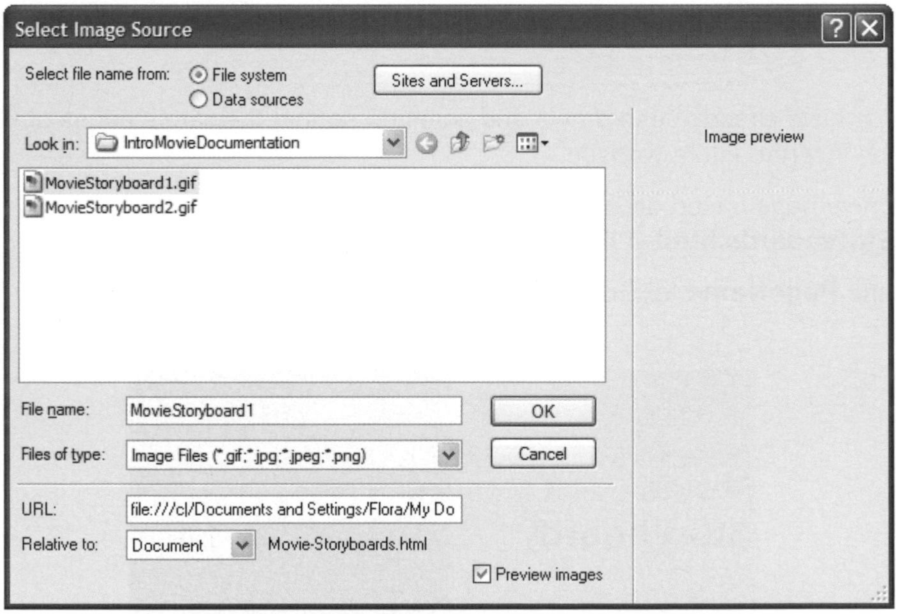

Figure 28.6

 Click **OK**. You will get the following message.

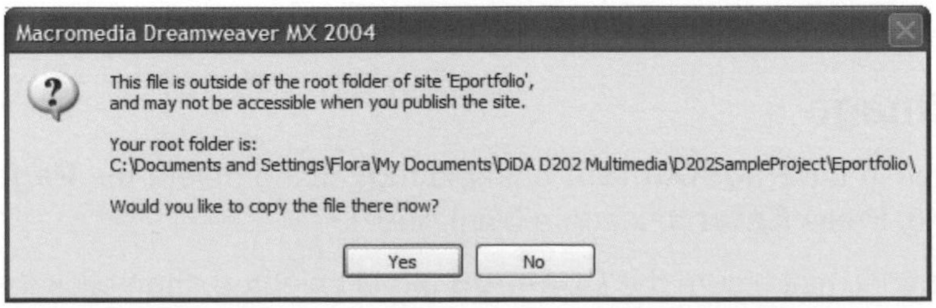

Figure 28.7

This is because all images inserted into your eportfolio must be saved somewhere in the site root folder, which is the **Eportfolio** folder. It is giving you the option here of creating a copy of the image, which will be saved in the root directory **Eportfolio** (or another folder within the root directory).

 Click **Yes** to save a copy. Select the **Images** folder; leave the **File name** as **MovieStoryboard1**.

Copy File As	? X

Save in: ⌒ Images ▾ ◉ ⬀ ⬈ ▦▾

File name:	MovieStoryboard1	Save
Save as type:	All Files (*.*) ▾	Cancel

Figure 28.8

 Click **Save**.

 The **MovieStoryboard1** image has been inserted onto the page; it should be about the right size because it is sized to 700 pixels wide (this will make the page a bit wider than others in the eportfolio, but it really needs to be this wide so that people can read it).

 To resize the storyboard, scroll down to the bottom right corner, then hold down **Shift** while you click and drag the corner node of the storyboard. It will need to be selected first.

 You can add some text before or after it if you like.

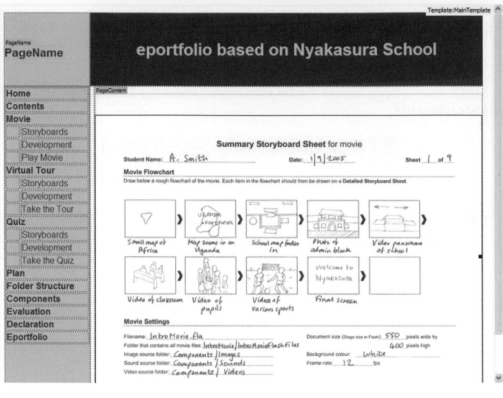

Figure 28.9

 Add the **MovieStoryboard2** image below the first, following the same method.

Adding borders to the storyboards

 To add a border, first select a storyboard then in the **Properties** panel type **1** where it says **Border**.

Inserting a Back to Top link

Since some of the pages in your eportfolio will be quite long, it makes sense to add a **Back to Top** link in the template that will appear on every page. To do this we'll use **named anchors**.

Named anchors

 Open the **MainTemplate** page by double-clicking it in the **Files** panel.

 Write **Back to Top** right at the bottom of the page. Use the **Properties** panel to change the font size and colour. If the changes don't seem to take effect, pick a style from the **Style** menu.

Figure 28.10

 Select the whole table that the template is in using the left-most **<table>** tag in the **Tag Selector**. Now press the left arrow key.

 Click the **Named Anchor** icon on the **Insert** bar.

Named Anchor Icon

 Enter **Top** as the **Anchor name**, then press **OK**.

Named Anchor	[X]
Anchor name: Top|	OK
	Cancel
	Help

Figure 28.11

A small anchor symbol will appear where the cursor was. This won't appear in a browser – it will be invisible.

Inserting the link

 Highlight the text **Back to Top** at the bottom of the page.

 Scroll up so that you can see the anchor.

 Now look in the **Properties** panel; there is a small target icon next to the **Link** field. Click and drag this target icon and drop it on the **Top** anchor at the top of the page.

Target Icon

#Top will now be written in the **Link** field. Once the link is made, it may turn blue. If so, re-select the style in the **Properties** panel.

▼ Properties	
Format Paragraph ∨ Style None ∨ **B** *I* ≣ ≣ ≣ ≣ Link #Top ∨ ⊕ ☐	⑦
Font Arial, Helvetica ∨ Size 12 ∨ points ∨ ■ #000000 ≔ ≔ ≛ ≛ Target ∨	
▦ Cell Horz Default ∨ W 556 No wrap ☐ Bg ⊕ ☐ Page Properties...	
☐ ◟ Vert Top ∨ H Header ☐ Bg ☐ Brdr ☐	▵

Figure 28.12

Drag this

271

The Flash file is inserted into the web page.

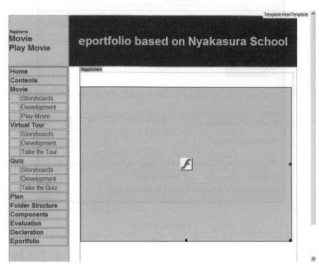

Figure 28.17

Save the page then preview it in a browser. You might need to click at the top of the page to **Allow Blocked Content**.

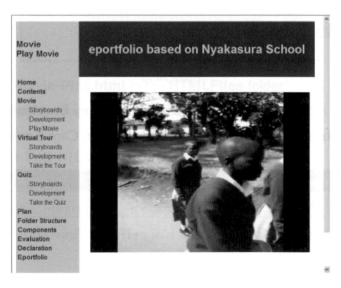

Figure 28.18

Close the browser window then the **Movie-Play.html** page in Dreamweaver.

Now we'll add the links to the **Home**, **Contents**, and **Movie-Storyboard** and **Movie-PlayMovie** pages.

- Open the **MainTemplate.dwt** page by double-clicking it in the **Files** panel.

- Select the text **Home** in the navigation bar by double-clicking it.

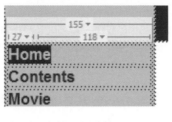

Figure 29.1

- Look in the **Properties** panel. Notice that there is a small target icon next to the **Link** field.

Target Icon

Figure 29.2

- Make sure that you can see the **index.html** file in the **Files** panel; it will be in the **Eportfolio** folder not the **HTMLFiles** folder.

- Click and drag the target icon from the **Properties** panel and drop it on the **index.html** file in the **Files** panel.

Target Icon

- The link has been added to the **Link** field in the **Properties** panel.

Notice that the **Home** text has now turned blue and is underlined. We will turn it back to red, but leave the underline to signify that it is a hyperlink.

- With the **Home** text highlighted re-select **NavigationBar** from the **Style** menu in the **Properties** panel. The text should now be red and underlined.

- Repeat this for **Contents**, this time dragging the target onto the **Contents.html** file in the **HTMLFiles** folder in the **Files** panel.

- Now select where it says **Storyboards** under **Movie** in the navigation bar.

- Click and drag the target to the **Movie-Storyboards.html** file in the **Files** panel.

- With the text still selected choose the **NavigationBarSubItem** style in the **Properties** panel.

- Repeat this for the **Play Movie** text in the navigation bar, linking it to the **Movie-Play.html** file.

- Save the **MainTemplate** by pressing **Ctrl-S**. Click **Update** to update all pages based on the template. Click **Close** in the next window.

- Close the **MainTemplate**.

- Open the **index.html** page in Dreamweaver then press **F12** to preview it in a browser.

- Test the links on the navigation bar to make sure they work.

Accessibility

There are things you can add to your eportfolio website to make it much easier to use for someone who is blind or partially-sighted. There is software available that will read text on a screen, and any other text you might have hidden on the page for this purpose. For example, you can attach text to an image so that it can be read out to someone browsing your site. In fact, you can attach text to a variety of objects in Dreamweaver.

Tip:

It is a requirement in the DiDA mark scheme that you include accessibility features in your eportfolio.

- Select **Edit**, **Preferences** from the main menu bar. Click **Accessibility** in the left-hand list.

- Check the boxes next to the objects that you want to add alternative text to. Just select **Images** to begin with, as shown in Figure 29.3. Click **OK**.

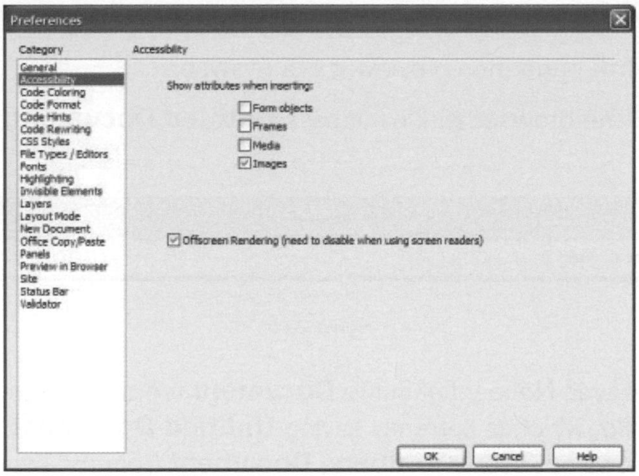

Figure 29.3

To add a long description to an image, you must create the description in a file of its own. Let's do this for the first of the movie storyboard images.

- Create a new folder called **Descriptions** under **Images**.

- Create a new blank HTML file and type the text **Summary storyboard for the IntroMovie** into it.

Tip:

It would be helpful to go into much more detail than this. Think about what information might be useful to someone who was interested in your storyboard but had difficulty seeing it.

- Save the file as **MovieStoryboard1.html** in the new **Descriptions** folder.

- Open up the **Movie-Storyboards.html** page. Delete the first storyboard then re-insert it by dragging it from the **Images** folder in the **Files** pane.

- The **Image Tag Accessibility Attributes** window appears. Type **Storyboard 1** in the **Alternative Text** field. Click the folder icon and navigate to **MovieStoryboard1.html** for the **Long description**. Click **OK**.

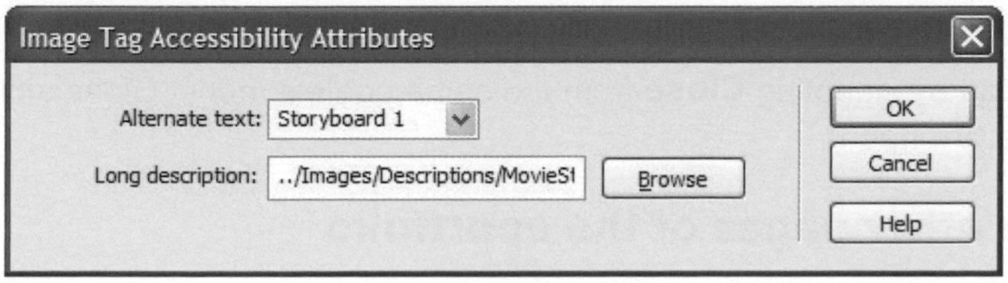

Figure 29.4

- Save and close the page.

- Save and close any other pages that are open.

Chapter 29 - Adding Links to the Navigation Bar

Adding a Page Title

- Open the **index.html** page then preview it in a browser.

Notice that in the top of the browser window it says **Untitled Document**. If you enter a page title it will appear here.

Untitled Document - Microsoft Internet Explorer
File Edit View Favorites Tools Help

Figure 29.5

- Return to Dreamweaver. Notice that in the **Document** toolbar (at the top of the page) there is a field named **Title**, which is currently saying **Untitled Document**. (If you cannot see the **Document** toolbar, select **View**, **Toolbars**, **Document** from the main menu bar.)

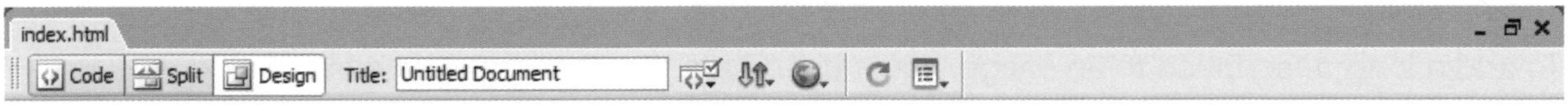
index.html
Code
Split
Design
Title: Untitled Document

Figure 29.6

Tip:

When using a search engine, have you ever seen entries listed under a title starting with **Untitled**? This is because whoever created that page did not add a page title!

- Change the **Title** to **eportfolio - Home**. Now save the page and preview it again to see the effect.

Eportfolio - Home - Microsoft Internet Explorer
File Edit View Favorites Tools Help

Figure 29.7

Tip:

If you already have a browser window open that is showing your home page try clicking the **Refresh** icon in your browser window instead of pressing **F12** again.

- Close the page by selecting **Close** from the same context menu. Close any browser windows that are open.

Creating the other pages of the eportfolio

We won't go into detail on how to create the remaining pages. Having created the initial pages you will already have picked up the technical skills to be able to implement these in Dreamweaver. Many of the remaining pages will be very similar in content to the eportfolio you created for DiDA D201.

Development pages

You need to provide evidence of development for each of the **movie**, **virtual tour** and **quiz**. These will go on pages named **Movie-Development**, **Tour-Development** and **Quiz-Development**, and you will need to add the links on the navigation bar to go to each of these pages.

You will have had experience providing evidence of development in D201. You will need to provide screenshots of the Flash workspace at various stages throughout the development of your project. You should have saved some versions of each Flash file in various stages of development; you can include screenshots of these development versions and also embed an SWF file of a half-finished file if appropriate.

For each screenshot you should clearly label the date it was taken along with the feedback received on the project at that point. List the changes you made as a result of the feedback. All these details should be written in a **Screenshots.doc** file (in a suitable **Documentation** folder) during development.

Plan

This needs to include a screenshot of both your initial and final project plan. You should also explain any big differences between them.

Folder structure

You should include a screenshot of Windows Explorer showing all the folders used for your project.

Components

This should include a screenshot of your completed Components Table. It also specifies in the DiDA SPB that you need to include as supporting evidence:

- Preparation of at least 3 different ready-made components

  This might include:

  - Screenshots of a downloaded photo in image-editing software (such as Fireworks) used to edit the component to make it suitable for use

  - Screenshots of a scanned image before and after editing (the image may need to be cropped, the image tidied or file size reduced)

- Development of at least 2 different types of original component

  This might include:

  - Screenshots of the creation of a graphic in a graphics package (such as Fireworks)

- Details of how you took video or photos, including any hardware and software used to edit them (and screenshots of the editing software)
- Details of how you recorded sounds using a sound recorder
- Screenshots of sound editing software used to edit a recorded sound.

Eportfolio

This should include your eportfolio storyboard sheets, the feedback you received and any changes you made as a result of the feedback. There should be a short review of the eportiolio.

Declaration

This should be a short statement from you and your teacher verifying that the eportfolio and its contents are all your own work.

Evaluation

The **Evaluation** page should contain the review and evaluation of the whole project, including the eportfolio. You will have completed a similar process for D201.

Some of the feedback and changes you made to your products (the movie, virtual tour and quiz) will already be included in the **Development** pages. The **Evaluation** page should contain a summary of the feedback and changes of these products but should also contain the feedback you received about the eportfolio itself, and the changes you made as a result of that feedback. This might include screenshots of the Dreamweaver workspace in various stages of development of the eportfolio.

Checking the file size of the eportfolio

To check how much file space your eportfolio takes up:

Open Windows Explorer and find the **Eportfolio** folder. Right-click it then select **Properties** from the menu that appears. The file size is listed here.

Figure 29.8

If your eportfolio exceeds **15MB**, try optimising the images more using Fireworks. Select them in Dreamweaver then in the **Properties** panel click the **Fireworks** icon to edit an image directly from Dreamweaver.

Fireworks Icon

Uploading your eportfolio

For further instructions on uploading your eportfolio to a remote site using Dreamweaver, go to **www.payne-gallway.co.uk/didaD202**.

Good marks... ✓

You will get good marks if:

- you use a storyboard to plan your eportfolio and include the storyboard in the eportfolio;
- all three products are included in the eportfolio and are clearly labelled;
- you include screenshots as evidence of development of the three products and the eportfolio itself;
- screenshots are clearly labelled with a date and an explanation of content;
- feedback that has been collected at various stages of the project is included, along with an explanation of changes made as a result of the feedback.

Bad marks... ✗

You will lose marks if:

- the file size of the whole eportfolio exceeds 15MB;
- you include files that are not in one of the approved file formats listed in the SPB;
- you do not include accessibility features in your eportfolio.

Index